Christina Latham-Koenig
Clive Oxenden

ENGLISH FILE

Intermediate Student's Book A

Paul Seligson and Clive Oxenden are the original co-authors of *English File 1* and *English File 2*

Contents

Do you drink a lot of coffee?

Yes, but I'm trying to cut down at the moment.

1A Mood food

1 VOCABULARY food and cooking

a Do the quiz in pairs.

FOOD QUIZ

Can you think of...?

ONE red fruit, **ONE** yellow fruit, **ONE** green fruit
TWO kinds of food that some people are allergic to
THREE kinds of food that come from milk
FOUR vegetables that you can put in a salad
FIVE containers that you can buy food in
SIX things that people sometimes have for breakfast

b ➤ **p.152 Vocabulary Bank** *Food and cooking.*

c **1 4**))) Listen to these common adjectives to describe food. Do you know what they mean? Then say one kind of food which we often use with each adjective.

fresh frozen low-fat raw spicy takeaway tinned

2 PRONUNCIATION short and long vowel sounds

a Look at the eight sound pictures. What are the words and sounds? What part of the symbol tells you that a sound is long?

1	squid chicken ~~spicy~~ grilled	5	sausages roast chocolate box
2	beef steamed beans breakfast	6	raw fork boiled salt
3	prawns salmon lamb cabbage	7	cook sugar mushrooms food
4	margarine carton jar warm	8	cucumber beetroot fruit duck

b Look at the words in each list. Cross out the word which *doesn't* have the sound in the sound picture.

c **1 5**))) Listen and check.

d ➤ **p.166 Sound Bank.** Look at the typical spellings of the sounds in **a**.

3 LISTENING & SPEAKING

FOOD & EATING

1 **Is there any food or drink that you couldn't live without? How often do you eat / drink it?**

2 **Do you ever have**
  a ready-made food?
  b takeaway food? What kind?

3 **What's your favourite**
  a fruit?
  b vegetable?
  Are there any that you really don't like?

4 **When you eat out do you normally order meat, fish, or vegetarian?**

5 **What food do you usually eat**
  a when you're feeling a bit down?
  b before doing sport or exercise?
  c before you have an exam or some important work to do?

a **1 6**))) Listen to five people talking. Each person is answering one of the questions in *Food & Eating* above. Match each speaker with a question.

[4] Speaker A
[ ] Speaker B
[ ] Speaker C
[ ] Speaker D
[ ] Speaker E

b Listen again and make notes about their answers. Compare with a partner.

c Ask and answer the questions with a partner. What do you have in common?

4 READING

a Are the foods in the list **carbohydrates** or **proteins**? With a partner, think of four more kinds of food for each category.

cake chicken pasta salmon

b With a partner, answer the questions below with either **carbohydrates** or **proteins**.

What kind of food do you think it is better to eat...?

- for lunch if you have an important exam or meeting
- for breakfast
- for your evening meal
- if you are feeling stressed

c Look at the title of the article. What do you think it means? Read the article once to find out, and to check your answers to **b**.

d Read the article again. Then with a partner, say in your own words why the following people are mentioned. Give as much information as you can.

1 Dr Paul Clayton
2 people on diets
3 schoolchildren
4 Paul and Terry
5 nightclub owners in Bournemouth

e Find adjectives in the article for the verbs and nouns in the list. What's the difference between the two adjectives made from *stress*?

stress (*noun*) (x2) relax (*verb*) wake (*verb*) sleep (*verb*) power (*noun*) violence (*noun*) oil (*noun*)

f Ask and answer the questions with a partner.

1 What time of day do you normally eat protein and carbohydrates? How do they make you feel?
2 How often do you eat chocolate? Does it make you feel happier?
3 After reading the article, is there anything you would change about your eating habits?

Mood food

We live in a stressful world, and daily life can sometimes make us feel tired, stressed, or depressed. Some people go to the doctor's for help, others try alternative therapies, but the place to find a cure could be somewhere completely different: in the kitchen.

Dr Paul Clayton, a food expert from Middlesex University, says 'The brain is affected by what you eat and drink, just like every other part of your body. Certain types of food contain substances which affect how you think and feel.'

For example, food which is high in carbohydrates can make us feel more relaxed. It also makes us feel happy. Research has shown that people on diets often begin to feel a little depressed after two weeks because they are eating fewer carbohydrates.

On the other hand, food which is rich in protein makes us feel awake and focused. Research has shown that schoolchildren who eat a high-protein breakfast often do better at school than children whose breakfast is lower in protein. Also, eating the right kind of meal at lunchtime can make a difference if you have an exam in the afternoon or a business meeting where you need to make some quick decisions. In an experiment for a BBC TV programme two chess players, both former British champions, had different meals before playing each other. Paul had a plate of prosciutto and salad (full of protein from the red meat), and his opponent Terry had pasta with a creamy sauce (full of carbohydrate). In the chess match Terry felt sleepy, and took much longer than Paul to make decisions about what moves to make. The experiment was repeated several times with the same result.

Another powerful mood food could become a secret weapon in the fight against crime. In Bournemouth in the south of England, where late-night violence can be a problem, some nightclub owners have come up with a solution. They give their clients free chocolate at the end of the night. The results have been dramatic, with a 60% reduction in violent incidents.

Why does chocolate make people less aggressive? First, it causes the brain to release feel-good chemicals called endorphins. It also contains a lot of sugar, which gives you energy, and can help stop late-night tiredness turning into aggression. These two things, together with a delicious taste, make chocolate a powerful mood changer.

Mood food – what the experts say

- Blueberries and cocoa can raise concentration levels for up to five hours.
- Food that is high in protein helps your brain to work more efficiently.
- For relaxation and to sleep better, eat carbohydrates.
- Dark green vegetables (e.g. cabbage and spinach) and oily fish (e.g. salmon) eaten regularly can help to fight depression.

Adapted from a British newspaper

5 LISTENING & SPEAKING

a Ask and answer the questions with a partner.

RESTAURANTS

1 How often do you eat out?
2 What's your favourite...?
  a kind of food (French, Italian, etc.)
  b restaurant dish
3 How important are these things to you in a restaurant? Number them 1–4 (1 = the most important).
  ☐ the food
  ☐ the service
  ☐ the atmosphere
  ☐ the price
4 Have you ever tried English food? What did you think of it?

b 1 7)) Read the text about Steve Anderson. Then listen to **Part 1** of an interview with him, and number the photos in the order he mentions them.

c Listen again. Why does he mention each thing?

d 1 8)) Now listen to **Part 2** and answer the questions.

1 What does he say is the best and worst thing about running a restaurant?
2 What's the main difference between British and Spanish customers?
3 What kind of customers does he find difficult?
4 How does he think eating habits in Spain are changing?

e What about you? Answer the questions with a partner.

1 What was your favourite food when you were a child?
2 Is there anything that you like / don't like cooking?
3 In your country, when people eat out would they normally tell the chef what they really think about the food?
4 Do you know anyone who is a 'difficult customer' in restaurants?

A

STEVE ANDERSON has always had a passion for food. He was first taught to cook by his mother, who is half Burmese. After studying physics at university, he got a holiday job helping on a cookery course in Italy, where he met several famous chefs. One of them, Alastair Little, later employed him as a trainee chef. Two years later he moved to Valencia in Spain and opened a restaurant, *Seu Xerea*, now one of the most popular restaurants in town.

B

C

D

E

F

6 GRAMMAR

present simple and continuous, action and non-action verbs

a 1 9 Listen again to some of the things Steve said. Circle the form of the verb he uses.

1 This week for example *I cook | I'm cooking* nearly every day. We *usually close | are usually closing* on Sundays and Mondays, but this Monday is a public holiday.
2 The British always *say | are saying* that everything is lovely.
3 Actually, I think *I prefer | I am preferring* that honesty, because it helps us to know what people like.
4 Unfortunately, I think *they get | they're getting* worse. People *eat | are eating* more unhealthily.

b With a partner, say why you think he has chosen each form.

c **p.132 Grammar Bank 1A.** Learn more about the present simple and the present continuous, and practise them.

d Make questions to ask your partner with the present simple or continuous. Ask for more information.

On a typical day
- What / usually have for breakfast?
- / drink Coke or fizzy drinks? How many glasses / drink a day?
- Where / usually have lunch?
- What / usually have for lunch during the week?
- / ever cook? What / make?
- / prefer eating at home or eating out?

At the moment / nowadays
- / need to buy any food today?
- / want anything to eat right now? What?
- / take vitamins or food supplements at the moment?
- / try to cut down on anything at the moment?
- / the diet in your country / get better or worse?

7 SPEAKING

WHAT DO YOU THINK?

1 Men are better cooks than women.
2 Both boys and girls should learn to cook at school.
3 Cheap restaurants usually serve bad food.
4 On a night out with friends, where and what you eat isn't important.
5 Not all fast food is unhealthy.
6 Every country thinks that their cuisine is the best in the world.

a 1 13 Listen to two people discussing sentence 1. Who do you agree with more, the man or the woman? Why?

b 1 14 Listen to the phrases in the **Useful language** box. Copy the intonation.

Useful language: Giving your opinion (1)

I agree.	I'm not sure.	For example...
I don't agree.	(I think) it depends.	In my opinion...

c In small groups, say what you think about sentences 2–6. Try to use the **Useful language** phrases.

G future forms: present continuous, *going to*, *will / won't*
V family, adjectives of personality
P sentence stress, word stress, adjective endings

Are you seeing your grandparents this weekend?

No, I'm going to stay at home. I'll probably see them next weekend.

1B Family life

1 VOCABULARY & SPEAKING
family

a Look at some photos showing family members. What's happening in each one? What do you think the relationship is between the people?

b With a partner, explain the difference between each pair.

1 a father and a parent
2 a mother and a stepmother
3 a brother and a brother-in-law
4 a grandfather and a great-grandfather
5 a nephew and a niece
6 a child and an only child
7 your immediate family and your extended family

c The BBC recently did a survey of 21st-century families in the UK. Read *Changing – for the better?* and try to guess what the missing percentages are. Choose from the list.

17% 26% 60% 75% 85%

d 1 15 Listen and check. Do any of the statistics surprise you? Which ones do you think would be very different if the survey was carried out in your country?

e Work in small groups. Say what you think and give reasons.

Do you think that…?
- families should have a meal together every day
- children should leave home as soon as they can afford to
- parents should charge their children rent if they live at home and have a job
- parents should be 'friends' with their children on social networking sites, e.g. *Facebook*
- elderly parents should live with their children when they are too old to live alone

Useful language:
Giving your opinion (2)
We often use *should* + verb to say what we think is the right thing or a good thing (to do), e.g.
*I think families **should have** dinner together every day because...*
*I don't think parents **should be** friends with their children on* Facebook *because...*

Changing – for the better?

Family life is changing in the UK – but not in the way we might think. When the BBC did a survey of families in Britain, they expected to find that family relationships were suffering because of the decline in traditional family structures.

However, some of the results were quite surprising...

58% of men and 39% of women aged 20–24 still live at home with their parents.

1 ______ think that it is right for parents to charge rent to children over 25 who have a job and are living at home.

30% use the internet at least once a week to contact their families.

On average, adults live 130 kilometres from their parents.

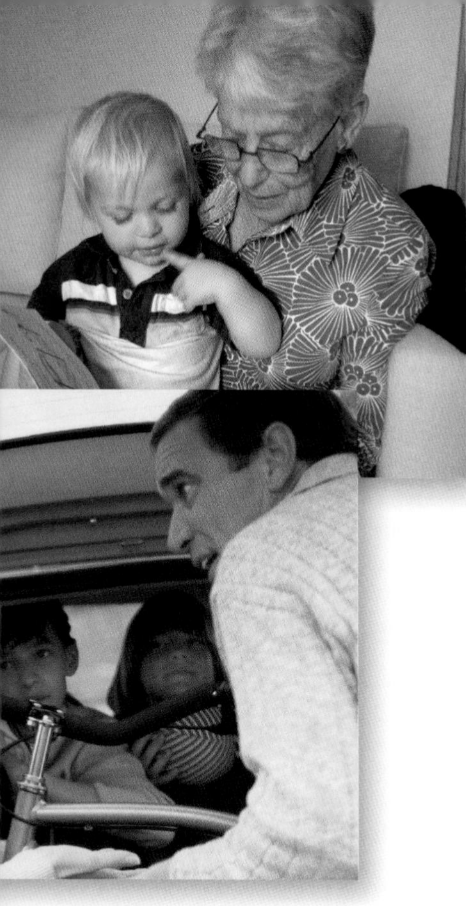

95% of people say that they have a close family.

2 ______ of people have a meal with their immediate family every day.

3 ______ say that their families never argue.

4 ______ have family members who they don't speak to any more.

5 ______ think that families should look after grandparents.

75% of people are happiest with their families.

17% are happiest with friends.

2 GRAMMAR future forms

a 1 16 Listen to three dialogues between different family members. Who is talking to who (e.g. brother to sister)? What are they talking about?

b Listen again and match two sentences with each dialogue (1–3).

A ☐ Shall I make you a cup of tea?
B ☐ You'll drive too fast.
C ☐ I'm not going to go to university yet.
D ☐ I'm staying the night there.
E ☐ I'll drive really slowly.
F ☐ It's going to be cold tonight.

c With a partner, decide which sentence (A–F) is…

☐ a plan or intention
☐ an arrangement
☐☐ a prediction
☐ a promise
☐ an offer

d ➤ **p.133 Grammar Bank 1B.** Learn more about future forms and practise them.

3 PRONUNCIATION sentence stress

Sentence stress
An important aspect of speaking English is stressing the words in a sentence which carry the information, and not stressing the other ones. This will help you to communicate better and to speak with good rhythm.

a 1 21 Listen to the rhythm in these three dialogues.

1 A Are you **coming home** for **dinner tonight**?
B **No**. I'm **going out** with my **friends**.
2 A **What** are you **going** to **do** in the **summer**?
B We're **going** to **rent** a **house** with my **sister** and her **husband**.
3 A Do you **think** they'll **have children soon**?
B I **don't think** so. **Not** for a **few years anyway**.

b Practise them with a partner. Copy the rhythm.

c Ask and answer the questions below. Give as much information as possible.

ARE YOU…?
- having dinner with your family tonight
- or is anyone in your family getting married soon
- doing something with a family member this week
- visiting a relative this weekend

ARE YOU GOING TO…?
- have a new nephew or niece soon
- have a big family get-together soon
- go on holiday with your family this year
- buy a present for a member of your family this month

DO YOU THINK…?
- the number of people getting divorced will go up or down in the future
- the birth rate will go up or down in your country
- anyone in your family will live to be 90 or more
- you will move away from (or back to) the area where your family live

4 1 22 SONG *Our House* ♫

5 READING

a Which do you think has more advantages, being an only child, or having brothers and sisters? Why?

b Work in pairs. **A** read *The younger brother*, **B** read *The only child*.

c Tell your partner about 1 and 2 below. Whose childhood sounds happier?

1 other family members who are mentioned
2 how the writer's experience as a child affects him / her now

d Look at the highlighted words in the two texts. Try to work out their meaning from the context. Then match them with definitions 1–12.

1 ____________ *adj* ill
2 ____________ it's no surprise that
3 ____________ *noun* competition between two people
4 ____________ *noun* the time when you were a child
5 ____________ *noun* a meeting of people, e.g. family
6 ____________ *noun* people who are fully grown
7 ____________ *adj* knowing about or being conscious of sth
8 ____________ *noun* a school where children can live during the year
9 ____________ *verb* think that sb or sth is important
10 ____________ *verb* divided sth between two or more people
11 ____________ *verb* try to hurt sb else
12 ____________ *noun* a group of friends

> ***each other***
> *When brothers and sisters get older they value **each other** more.*
> Use *each other* to talk about an action between two people or groups of people, e.g. *I don't get on very well with my dad – we don't understand **each other**.*

e Talk to a partner. Do you have brothers and sisters, or are you an only child? Do you feel positive or negative about it?

Younger brother or only child?

HOW WAS IT FOR YOU?

THE YOUNGER BROTHER
NOVELIST TIM LOTT

Rivalry between brothers is normal, but there was a special reason for the tension between us. I was very ill when I was born, and spent three months in hospital with my mother. My brother did not see her at all during that time, as he went to stay with an aunt. When our mother returned home, it was with a sick newborn baby who took all the attention. No wonder he hated me (although if you ask Jeff, he will say that he didn't – we remember things differently).

My brother and I were completely different. We shared the same bedroom, but he was tidy, and I was really untidy. He was responsible, I was rebellious. He was sensible, I was emotional. I haven't got any positive memories of our childhood together, though there must have been good moments. Jeff says we used to play Cowboys and Indians but I only remember him trying to suffocate me under the bedcovers.

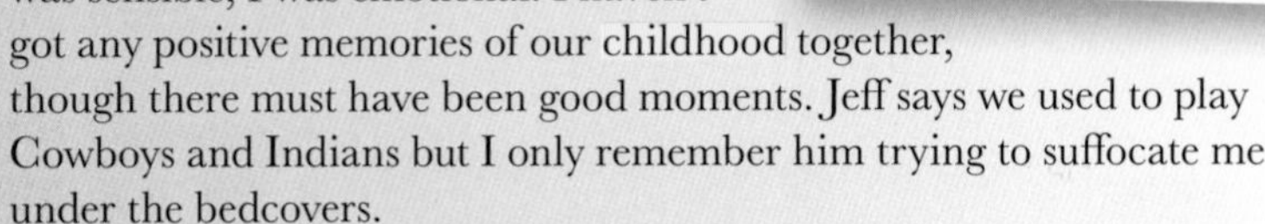

My relationship with Jeff has influenced my attitude towards my own four daughters. If the girls fight, I always think that the younger child is innocent. But the good news about brothers and sisters is that when they get older, they value each other more. Jeff is now one of my best friends, and I like and admire him greatly. For better or for worse, we share a whole history. It is the longest relationship in my life.

THE ONLY CHILD
JOURNALIST SARAH LEE

I went to boarding school when I was seven, and the hardest thing I found was making friends. Because I was an only child, I just didn't know how to do it. The thing is that when you're an only child you spend a lot of your time with adults and you're often the only child in a gathering of adults. Your parents go on living more or less the way they have always lived, only now you are there too.

I found being an only child interesting because it gave me a view of the world of adults that children in a big family might not get. And I know it has, at least partly, made me the kind of person I am – I never like being one of a group, for example. If I have to be in a group, I will always try to go off and do something on my own, or be with just one other person – I'm not comfortable with being one of a gang.

My parents are divorced now and my mother lives in the US and my father in the UK. I feel very responsible for them – I feel responsible for their happiness. I'm the closest relative in the world to each of them, and I am very aware of that.

Adapted from a British newspaper

6 VOCABULARY adjectives of personality

a Without looking back at *The younger brother* text, can you remember who was *tidy, responsible, and sensible* and who was *untidy, rebellious, and emotional*? Do you know what the adjectives mean? Would you use any of them to describe yourself?

b ➤ **p.153 Vocabulary Bank** *Personality.*

c Write down the first three adjectives of personality that come into your head. Don't show them to your partner. Now go to ➤ **Communication** *Personality p.108.*

7 PRONUNCIATION word stress, adjective endings

a **1 26** Underline the stressed syllable in these multi-syllable adjectives. Listen and check.

1 jea|lous an|xious am|bi|tious ge|ne|rous re|be|llious
2 so|cia|ble re|li|a|ble
3 re|spon|si|ble sen|si|ble
4 com|pe|ti|tive tal|ka|tive a|ggre|ssive sen|si|tive
5 un|friend|ly in|se|cure im|pa|tient i|mma|ture

b Listen again and answer the questions.

1 Is ***-ous*** pronounced /aʊs/ or /əs/?
2 Is ***-able*** pronounced /əbl/ or /eɪbl/?
3 Is ***-ible*** pronounced /əbl/ or /ɪbl/?
4 Is ***-ive*** pronounced /əv/ or /ɪv/?
5 Are ***-ous*** | ***-able*** | ***-ible*** | ***-ive*** stressed?
6 Are ***un-*** | ***in-*** | ***im-*** stressed?

8 LISTENING & SPEAKING

a What's your position in the family? Are you the oldest child, a middle child, the youngest child, or an only child?

b **1 27** Look at the cover of Linda Blair's book. Now listen to a journalist talking about it on a radio programme. Complete the chart by writing four more adjectives of personality in each column.

Oldest children	Middle children	Youngest children	Only children
sensible	relaxed	outgoing	self-confident

c Compare with a partner. Then listen to the four sections one by one. Check your answers. What reasons or examples does the journalist give?

d Look at the completed chart above. In pairs, say…

...if you think it is true for **you** – and if not, why not?

...if you think it is true for **other people** you know (your brothers and sisters, friends, etc.)

9 WRITING

➤ **p.113 Writing** *A description of a person.* Write a description of a friend you know well.

Practical English Meeting the parents EPISODE 1

1 VIDEO INTRODUCTION

a Look at the photos. Describe Jenny and Rob.

b 1 28 Watch or listen to Jenny and Rob talking. Complete the gaps.

Jenny Zielinski and Rob Walker work for a [1]__________ called *New York24seven*. She's American and he's [2]__________. Rob came to New York a few [3]__________ ago. He had met Jenny when she went to [4]__________ on a work trip. They got on very well, and he was offered a job for a month in [5]__________. Later he was offered a [6]__________ job. Jenny helped Rob [7]__________ an apartment, and they are enjoying life in the USA, although Rob misses his friends and [8]__________.

> **British and American English**
> *apartment* = American English
> *flat* = British English

2 VIDEO REACTING TO WHAT PEOPLE SAY

a 1 29 Watch or listen to Jenny introducing Rob to her parents. What bad news does Rob have for Jenny? What good news does Jenny have for her parents?

> **British and American English**
> *mom* = American English
> *mum* = British English

b Watch or listen again and mark the sentences **T** (true) or **F** (false). Correct the **F** sentences.

1 Rob left the chocolates at the office.
2 Rob's desk is usually very tidy.
3 It's the second time that Rob has met Jenny's parents.
4 Sally has prepared a big dinner.
5 Jenny's new job is Managing Director.
6 Jenny is going to be Rob's manager.

c (1 30)) Look at some extracts from the conversation. Can you remember any of the missing words? Watch or listen and check.

1
Jenny Don't forget the chocolates.
Rob OK. Oh ________!
Jenny I don't ________ it. Don't tell me you forgot them?
Rob I think they're still on my desk.
Jenny ________ kidding.

2
Jenny Mom, I'm really sorry – we bought you some chocolates, but we left them at the office.
Sally What a ________. ________ mind.

3
Jenny But I also have some good news.
Sally ________? What's that?

4
Sally So you've got a promotion? ________ fantastic!
Harry That's great ________!

5
Sally Let's go and have dinner.
Jenny What a ________ idea!

d (1 31)) Watch or listen and repeat the phrases in the chart below. Copy the rhythm and intonation.

REACTING TO WHAT PEOPLE SAY

What you say when you hear...	
something surprising	You're kidding. I don't believe it.
something interesting	Really?
some good news	How fantastic! That's great news! What a great idea!
some bad news	Oh no! What a pity. Never mind.

***How* + adjective, *What* + noun**
We often use *How* + adjective or *What* + noun to respond to what people say.
How interesting! How awful! How amazing!
What a pity! What a good idea! What terrible news!

e Practise the dialogues in **c** with a partner.

f ➤ **Communication** *How awful! How fantastic!* **A** *p.104* **B** *p.109.*

3 VIDEO HARRY FINDS OUT MORE ABOUT ROB

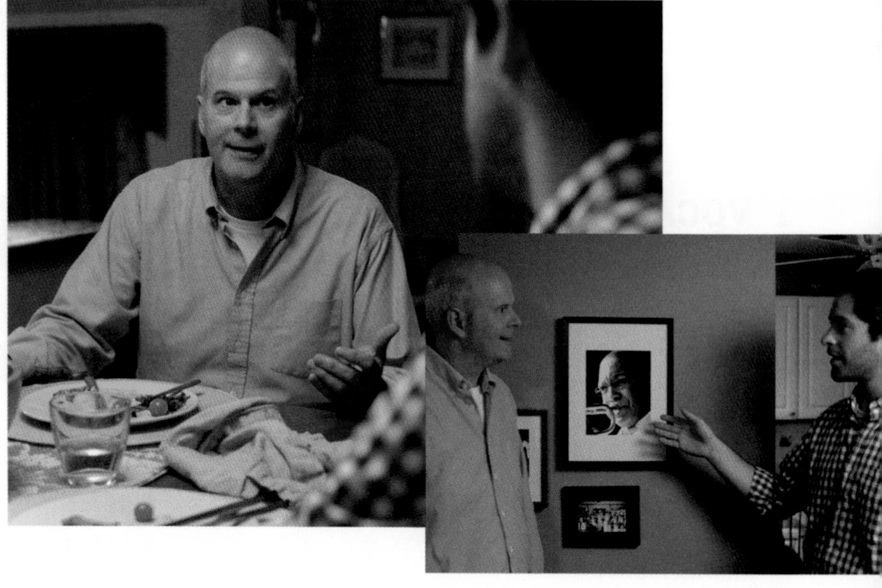

a (1 32)) Watch or listen to the after dinner conversation. Does the evening end well or badly?

b Watch or listen again and answer the questions.

1 What university did Jenny go to?
2 Is Harry impressed by Rob's job? Why (not)?
3 What does Harry like doing in his free time?
4 Who are most of the photos in the dining room of?
5 Who are Miles Davis, John Coltrane, and Wynton Marsalis?
6 What surprises Harry about Rob?

c Look at the **Social English phrases**. Can you remember any of the missing words?

Social English phrases

Harry How do you ________ your career?
Rob Not ________. I'm more of a writer.
Rob Oh, you know, interviews, reviews, ________ like that...
Rob I ________, I like photography.
Harry That's ________ most of them are of Jenny.
Harry How ________!
Rob Well, he's a really nice ________.
Harry Go ________, son!

d (1 33)) Watch or listen and complete the phrases.

e Watch or listen again and repeat the phrases. How do you say them in your language?

Can you...?
- [ ] react to good news, bad news, unexpected news, and interesting news
- [ ] introduce yourself and other people
- [ ] use phrases which give you time to think, e.g. *you know, I mean*, etc.

G present perfect and past simple
V money
P the letter *o*

Have you paid the phone bill yet?

Yes, I paid it yesterday.

2A Spend or save?

1 VOCABULARY money

a 1 34 Listen to a song about money. Complete the gaps with phrases A–G.

A a material world
B comes with a fee
C foot the bill
D for free
E paper or plastic
F shopping sprees
G with money

b Listen again and read the lyrics. Which phrase (A–G) means...?

1 __________ rich
2 __________ cash or credit cards
3 __________ you have to pay for it
4 __________ pay the bill
5 __________ that you don't have to pay for
6 __________ buying a lot of things at one time
7 __________ a consumer society

c What do you think the song is saying? Do you think it is...?

- very cynical
- sad, but sometimes true
- offensive to women (and men)

d ➤ **p.154 Vocabulary Bank** *Money*.

Educated, [1]____
He's well-dressed
Not funny
And not much to say in
Most conversations
But he'll [2]____ in
All situations
'Cause he pays for everything

Girls don't like boys, girls like cars and money
Boys will laugh at girls when they're not funny

[3]____
Don't matter
She'll have it
Vacations
And [4]____
These are a few
Of her favourite things
She'll get what she wants
If she's willing to please
His type of girl
Always [5]____
Hey, now, there's nothing [6]____

Girls don't like boys, girls like cars and money
Boys will laugh at girls when they're not funny
And these girls like these boys like these boys like these girls
The girls with the bodies like boys with Ferraris
Girls don't like boys, girls like cars and money

All of these boys, yeah get all of these girls
Losing their souls in [7]____

2 PRONUNCIATION the letter *o*

a Can you remember which word rhymes with *money* in the song *Girls & Boys*?

b Look at some more words with the letter *o*. Put them in the correct column.

clothes cost dollar done honest loan money note nothing owe shopping some sold won worry

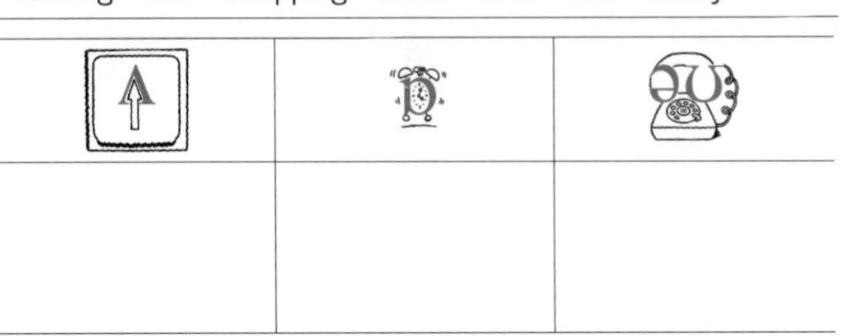

c 1 38 Listen and check.

d Look at some words with the letters *or*. How is *or* normally pronounced when it's stressed? Which two are different?

afford order worth organized mortgage store work

e 1 39 Listen and check.

f Practise saying these sentences.

Let's go shopping for clothes.
Can I borrow some money?
He won a million dollars.
They can't afford to pay the mortgage.
I work in a store.
I've done nothing wrong.

3 READING & SPEAKING

a Read the questionnaire and choose your answers.

b Compare your answers with a partner. Say why.

c ➤ **Communication** *Spender or saver? p.108.* Find out if you are a spender or a saver.

4 LISTENING

a 1 40 Listen to six people answering the question *Are you a spender or a saver?* How many are savers?

b Listen again and match speakers 1–6 with A–F. Who…?

A ☐ always has money in the bank
B ☐ often ends up with no money
C ☐ thinks he / she is careful with money, but not mean
D ☐ enjoys spending money on his / her hobby
E ☐ can save money if he / she needs to
F ☐ prefers to live now than worry about the future

ARE YOU A **SPENDER** OR A **SAVER**?

1 You go shopping and you see something very expensive that you really want, but can't afford. You…

a buy it with your credit card. You can worry about the bill next month.
b already have some money in the bank and plan to save for a couple of weeks and then buy the thing you want.
c borrow the money and agree to pay back a small amount every week.

2 You get £100 for your birthday. You…

a spend some of it and save some.
b go straight to a shopping centre and spend it all.
c put all of it in your bank account until you know what you want to spend it on.

3 Do you always know how much money you have, how much money you have spent, and on what?

a Yes. I'm very organized and know exactly what I have and what I've spent.
b No. I haven't got a clue. When I have money I usually just spend it.
c I usually have a rough idea about what I spend my money on.

4 You've borrowed some money from a friend, but you don't think that you'll be able to pay it back by the time you promised to. You…

a don't worry about it. Hopefully your friend will forget about it too!
b work out how much money you have and how much you owe. You speak to your friend and explain the situation and offer to pay the money back in small instalments.
c speak to your friend and promise that you'll pay him / her back, but it might take a bit longer than you first thought.

5 You have a friend who often borrows money from you and never pays it back. He / she wants to borrow £50. You…

a lend him / her the money. You can afford it and it doesn't matter if you don't get it back.
b say no; he / she owes you too much already.
c lend the money, but explain that it is the last time, until he / she has paid back this loan.

5 GRAMMAR present perfect and past simple

a Read the conversation. What are they arguing about?

b 1 41 Read the conversation again and put the verbs in the present perfect or the past simple. Then listen and check.

David I [1] *haven't seen* (see) those shoes before. Are they new?
Kate Yes. I [2] __________ (just buy) them. Do you like them?
D They're OK. How much [3] __________ they __________ (cost)?
K Oh, not much. They [4] __________ (be) a bargain. Under £100.
D You mean £99.99. That isn't cheap for a pair of shoes. Anyway, we can't afford to buy new clothes at the moment.
K Why not?
D [5] __________ you __________ (see) this?
K No. What is it?
D The phone bill. It [6] __________ (arrive) this morning. And we [7] __________ (not pay) the electricity bill yet.
K Well, what about the iPad you [8] __________ (buy) last week?
D What about it?
K You [9] __________ (not need) a new one. The old one [10] __________ (work) perfectly well.
D But I [11] __________ (need) the new model.
K Well, I [12] __________ (need) some new shoes.

c Do we use the present perfect (**PP**) or past simple (**PS**)...?

1 for a completed action in the past ______
2 for recent actions when we don't ask / say exactly when ______
3 in sentences with *just*, *yet*, and *already* ______

d ➤ **p.134 Grammar Bank 2A.** Learn more about the present perfect and past simple, and practise them.

e In pairs, interview each other with the questions. Ask for more information.

HAVE YOU EVER...?

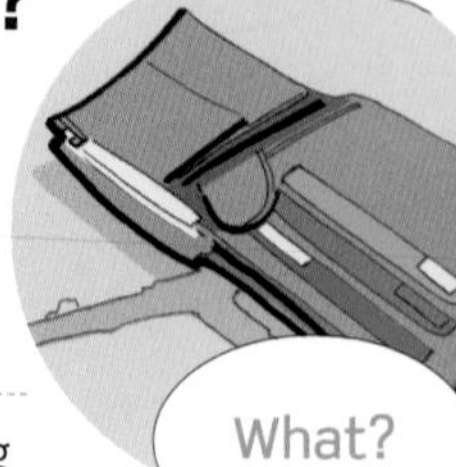

- bought or sold something on eBay or a similar site
- lost a credit card or your wallet
- saved for something for a long time
- wasted money on something you've never used

- won any money (e.g. in a lottery)
- lent money to someone who didn't pay you back
- bought something online and then discovered that it was a scam
- been charged too much in a restaurant

When?

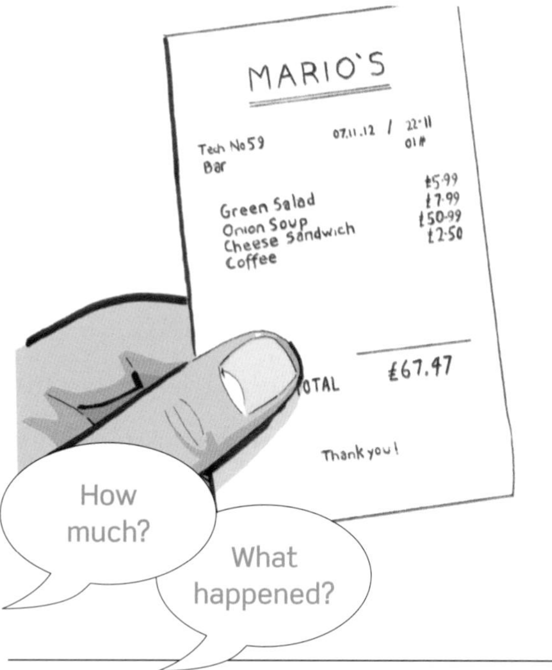

Have you ever bought or sold something on eBay?

Yes, I sold my old computer.

Who did you sell it to? How much did you sell it for?

6 READING & SPEAKING

a In pairs, answer the questions. Give as much information as you can.

1 Think of two people you know personally or have heard of who are very rich. Did they…?
  a earn their money (how?)
  b inherit their money (who from?)
  c win it (how?)
2 If they earned their money, was it because…?
  a they were very lucky
  b they worked very hard
  c they had a special talent

b Now read an article about a millionaire. How did he become so rich? Why is his success surprising? How did he make his daughter proud of him?

c Now read the article again and number the events in the order in which they happened.

A ☐ He became a millionaire again.
B ☐ He learnt to read and write.
C ☐ He lost all his money.
D *1* He sold old clothes in the market.
E ☐ He opened a department store.
F ☐ He won an important prize.
G ☐ He opened a small clothes shop.
H ☐ He became a millionaire.
I ☐ He sold clothes in the market again.
J ☐ He wrote his autobiography.
K ☐ His shop was on the front page of a newspaper.

d What do you think you can learn from Jeff's story?

e Look at the highlighted words and phrases related to money and business. With a partner, try to work out the meaning from the context.

f Complete the questions with one of the highlighted words and phrases. Then ask and answer the questions with a partner.

1 When was the last *recession* in your country? How long did it last (has it lasted)?
2 Do you know anybody who works as a ________? What does he (she) sell? Does he (she) enjoy his (her) job?
3 If you were completely ________, who would you ask to lend you some money?
4 Have you ever bought something the first day it ________? What?
5 Do you know anybody who has ________ on their own? Is it successful?

THE MILLIONAIRE WITH A SECRET

Jeff Pearce was a successful businessman – but he had a secret: he couldn't read or write.

His name is not really Jeff. His mother changed it because he could never spell his real name, James, and she thought Jeff was easier.

Pearce was born in Liverpool in the 1950s, in a very poor family. At school, all the teachers thought he was stupid because he couldn't learn to read or write – at that time, not many people knew about dyslexia. But there was something that he was good at: selling things. Pearce's first experience as a salesman was when he was a boy, and he and his mother used to go door-to-door asking for old clothes that they could sell in the market. He instinctively knew what people wanted, and it soon seemed that he could make money from anything. His mother always believed in him and told him that one day he would be successful and famous.

In 1983, when he already owned a small boutique, he decided to invest £750 in leather trousers, and to sell them very cheaply in his shop. 'It was a bit of a gamble, to tell you the truth,' he says. But Liverpool loved it, and there were photos of shoppers sleeping in the street outside his boutique on the front page of the local newspaper. The first day the trousers went on sale, the shop took £25,000. Jeff became a millionaire, but later he lost most of his money in the recession of the Nineties. He was almost 40, and he was broke again. He even had to go back to selling clothes in the market. But he never gave up, and soon he set up a new business, a department store, called *Jeff's*, which again made him a millionaire.

However, success didn't mean anything to Jeff because he still couldn't read or write. Even his two daughters did not realize that their father couldn't read. When one of them asked him to read her a bedtime story he went downstairs and cried because he felt so ashamed. At work he calculated figures in his head, while his wife Gina wrote all the cheques and read contracts.

In 1992 Pearce was awarded a Businessman of the Year prize for the best clothes store in Liverpool. It was at this moment that he told his friends and colleagues the truth, and decided to write a book about his experience. But first he had to learn to read and write. He went to evening classes, and employed a private teacher, but he found it very difficult because of his dyslexia. Finally, with the help of a ghost-writer*, his autobiography, *A Pocketful of Holes and Dreams*, was published, and became a best-seller. Recently, he was woken in the middle of the night by someone knocking on his front door. It was his daughter to whom he hadn't been able to read a bedtime story all those years earlier. She had come to tell him that she had just read his book. 'Dad, I'm so proud of you,' she said – and burst into tears in his arms.

*A **ghost-writer** is somebody who writes a book for another person

Adapted from The Times

G present perfect + *for* / *since*, present perfect continuous
V strong adjectives: *exhausted*, *amazed*, etc.
P sentence stress, stress on strong adjectives

How long have you been working here?

For a long time! Since 2001.

2B Changing lives

1 LISTENING

a Look at the photos. Where do you think they were taken? What can you see in each photo?

b 1 45 You are going to listen to an interview with Jane, talking about a trip she made in 2008. Listen to **Part 1**. Where did she go? What did she decide to do after the trip?

c Listen again. What does Jane say about:

1. her normal job
2. the holiday to Uganda
3. what happened when the lorry broke down
4. the condition of the school
5. the children
6. what the headmaster asked her for

d 1 46 Now listen to **Part 2**. Correct the wrong information in these sentences.

1. Jane's son chose the name *Adelante África*, which means 'Go forward, Africa' in Spanish.
2. The new school opened in 2012.
3. Today the school has 75 children.
4. *Adelante África* has also been trying to improve the children's English.
5. They are building a home for the teachers.
6. Two of Jane's children have been helping in Uganda.
7. Jane says the school has changed children's lives because it has given them an education.
8. Jane thinks that she gives more than she gets.
9. The website has a video Jane's daughter took of her teaching the children.

e Compare your answers with a partner. Then listen again to check.

f Do you know anybody like Jane who does a lot of work for a charity? What do they do?

2 GRAMMAR present perfect + *for / since*, present perfect continuous

a Match the questions and answers.

1 How long has Jane been a writer? ____
2 How long has *Adelante África* had a website? ____
3 How long has she been working for *Adelante África*? ____

A Since 2008.
B For about 22 years.
C For four years.

b Answer with a partner.

1 Are the three questions and answers in **a** about…?
 a a period of time in the past
 b a period of time from the past until now
 c a period of time in the present
2 What's the difference in form between the first two questions and question 3?

c ➤ **p.135 Grammar Bank 2B.** Learn more about the present perfect with *for / since* and the present perfect continuous, and practise them.

3 PRONUNCIATION sentence stress

a 1 49 Listen once and try to write down the stressed words in the large pink rectangles.

1 *How* *long* ___ ___ ___ *learning* *French* ?
2 ___ ___ ___ ___ ___ ___ ___ .
3 ___ ___ ___ ___ ___ ___ ?
4 ___ ___ ___ ___ ___ .
5 ___ ___ ___ ___ ___ ___ ?
6 ___ ___ ___ ___ ___ ___ ___ .

b Look at the stressed words and try to remember what the unstressed words are. Then listen again to check and write them in.

c Listen again and repeat the sentences. Copy the rhythm.

d 1 50 Listen and make questions.

It's snowing. *How long has it been snowing?*

4 SPEAKING

a Look at the circles, and write something in as many as you can.

A social networking site you use regularly

A friend you know very well

A sport you play regularly (or a kind of exercise you do regularly)

The car / motorbike / bike you have

The place where you live

A bar or restaurant you often go to

A gadget you have which is very important for you

An organization, club, gym, etc. you are a member of

Something you are learning (to do)

b Compare circles with a partner. Ask your partner at least three questions about the things they've written. One question must be *How long have you…?*

How long have you been using Twitter?
For about a year.
Do you write things on it or do you just read other people's tweets?
Why did you buy a Nissan Juke?
Because it's small, and it's quite 'green'.
How long have you had it?

5 READING & LISTENING

a In your country, are there charity events to raise money for a good cause? Have you ever taken part in one? What did you do? How much money did you raise?

b You're going to read an article about Helen Skelton, who agreed to kayak down the Amazon for charity. Read the introduction and answer the questions.

1 What did Helen do last year for charity?
2 What is she hoping to do this year?
3 What is dangerous about the trip?
4 What experience does she have?

c Before you read the texts of Helen's first three phone calls, imagine what kind of problems you think she had on her journey. Then read and check. Were you right?

d 1 51 Read **Phone calls 1–3** again and complete the gaps with the correct word. Then listen and check.

1	a in front	b behind	c back
2	a freezing	b hot	c boiling
3	a exhausted	b angry	c lost
4	a down	b up	c over
5	a long	b wide	c short
6	a ice cream	b coffee	c chocolate
7	a sleep	b paddle	c rest
8	a boring	b interesting	c worrying
9	a being	b feel	c feeling
10	a sick	b well	c hard

e 1 52 Now listen to the rest of Helen's journey down the Amazon. Did she manage to finish?

f Listen again. Then answer the questions.

Phone call 4
1 Why hasn't she had any music for three days?
2 What does she do to pass the time?
3 Why didn't she celebrate reaching the halfway point?

Phone call 5
4 What have been driving her mad this week?
5 What wildlife has she seen?
6 Why is she starting to feel a bit sad?

The 6.00 news
7 How many kilometres did she do altogether?
8 How long did the journey take?
9 What did Helen miss?
10 What is the first thing she is going to do when she gets home?

g Tell your partner about an adventure sport you've done, or an exciting experience you've had. Was it a positive experience? Why (not)? How did you feel?

TV presenter's Amazon

Helen Skelton hopes to become the first woman to kayak down the Amazon River.

Helen Skelton is a 26-year-old TV presenter of *Blue Peter*, a BBC programme for young people. She has never been afraid of a challenge. Last year she became the second woman to complete the 78-mile Ultra Marathon in Namibia, running the three consecutive marathons in 23 hours and 50 minutes. But when *Blue Peter* decided to do something to raise money for the charity Sports Relief (which sponsors projects in the UK and abroad) Skelton said that she wanted an even bigger challenge. So they suggested that she kayak 3,200 kilometres down the Amazon from Nauta in Peru to Almeirim in Brazil.

This is a very risky trip. There are no roads, no towns, only rainforest and the river (which is sometimes more than 40 kilometres wide and infested with crocodiles). If she falls ill, it will take around 11 hours to fly her to a hospital.

Adapted from The Telegraph website

Phone call 1

"Everything went wrong. I only managed half a day on Wednesday, the first day, and on Thursday we started late, so I'm already [1]_____. I've been suffering from the heat. It's absolutely [2]_____, and the humidity is 100% at lunchtime. I went the wrong way and I had to paddle against the current. I was [3]_____! They asked me, 'Do you want to give [4]_____?' but I said, 'No!' Because I've also been having a wonderful time! There are pink dolphins – pink, not grey – that come close to the boat. I think that if I can do 100 kilometres a day, then I can make it."

hallenge

Helen has only been kayaking once before in her life, so she has been training four hours a day. Last week she arrived at the Amazon in Peru. After two days kayaking she made the first of her phone calls to the BBC.

Phone call 2

"I've been on the Amazon for a week now, and I've been paddling for six out of the seven days. The river is incredibly [5]_____, and it's very hard to paddle in a straight line. The water is so brown that I can't see my paddle once it goes under the surface. It looks like melted [6]_____. I start at 5.30 in the morning, and I [7]_____ for at least ten hours, from 5.30 a.m. until dark, with only a short break for lunch. My hands have been giving me problems – I have big blisters. I now have them bandaged in white tape.

I'm usually on the water for at least ten hours; it's [8]____ at times, exciting at others. I listen to music on my iPod. I've been listening to *Don't Stop Me Now* by Queen to inspire me!"

Phone call 3

"I haven't been [9]_____ very well this week. The problem is heat exhaustion. They say it's because I haven't been drinking enough water. I've been travelling 100 kilometres a day, which is my target. But yesterday after 84 kilometres I was feeling [10]_____, and my head was aching and I had to stop and rest."

6 VOCABULARY & PRONUNCIATION
strong adjectives

Strong adjectives
Some adjectives have a strong meaning, e.g.
I had to paddle against the current. I was ***exhausted****!* (= very tired)
I've had a ***fantastic*** *time!* (= very good)
With strong adjectives you can use *absolutely* or *really*, but NOT ~~*very*~~.
I've been suffering from the heat. It's ***absolutely boiling****.* NOT ~~*very boiling*~~.

a Complete the sentences with a normal adjective.

1 **A** Was Lisa's father *angry* about the car?
B Yes, he was **furious**!
2 **A** Is Oliver's flat _____?
B Yes, it's really **tiny** – just a bedroom and a sitting room.
3 **A** Are you _____ of flying?
B Yes, I'm **terrified**! I never fly anywhere.
4 **A** Was the food _____?
B Yes, it was **delicious**.
5 **A** Are you very _____?
B I'm **starving**! I haven't eaten all day.
6 **A** Is your parents' house _____?
B It's **enormous**. It has seven bedrooms.
7 **A** Was it _____ in Moscow?
B It was **freezing**! Minus 20 degrees.
8 **A** Was Jack's kitchen _____?
B It was **filthy**. It took us three hours to clean it.
9 **A** Are your parents _____ about the wedding?
B They're **delighted**. In fact, they want to pay for everything!
10 **A** Was the film _____?
B It was **hilarious**. We laughed the whole way through.
11 **A** Are you _____ you locked the door?
B I'm **positive**. I remember turning the key.
12 **A** Were you _____ to hear that Ted is getting married?
B I was absolutely **amazed**! I never thought it would happen.

b **1 53** Listen and check. How are the strong adjectives pronounced? Practise the dialogues in pairs.

c ➤ **Communication** *Are you hungry?* **A** *p.104* **B** *p.109.*

d Ask and answer with a partner. Ask for more information.

1 Have you ever been swimming in a place where the water was absolutely freezing?
2 Is there anything that makes you furious about car drivers or cyclists in your country?
3 Are there any animals or insects that you're terrified of?
4 What's the most delicious meal you've had recently?
5 Is there a comedian or a comedy series on TV in your country that you think is absolutely hilarious?

7 WRITING

➤ **p.114 Writing** *An informal email.* Write an informal email to thank somebody you have been staying with and to tell them what you have been doing recently.

1&2 Revise and Check

GRAMMAR

Circle a, b, or c.

1 My sister ______ fish or seafood.
a doesn't like b don't like c doesn't likes

2 I have a quick breakfast because ______ in a hurry.
a I usually b I usually am c I'm usually

3 I ______ TV when I'm having a meal.
a never watch b don't never watch
c am never watching

4 I usually drink a lot of diet Coke, but at the moment ______ to cut down.
a I try b I'm trying c I'm triing

5 ______ any brothers or sisters?
a Are you having b Are you have c Do you have

6 What ______ when you leave school?
a you are going to do b are you going do
c are you going to do

7 I can't see you this evening because ______ some friends.
a I'm meeting b I meet c I'll meet

8 **A** Would you like something to drink?
B Yes, ______ an orange juice, please.
a I have b I'm having c I'll have

9 **A** I can't open this jar.
B ______ help you?
a Shall I b Will I c Do I

10 That's a lovely dress. Where ______ it?
a have you bought b did you buy
c did you bought

11 ______ good at saving money.
a I've never been b I haven't never been
c I've never

12 I got $50 for my birthday, but I ______.
a didn't spend it yet b haven't spent it yet
c yet I haven't spent it

13 I've had this computer ______.
a for about three years b since about three years
c for about three years ago

14 **A** How long ______ in Paris?
B Since last March.
a is he living b has he living c has he been living

15 ______ the same gym for five years.
a I'm going to b I've been going to c I go to

VOCABULARY

a Circle the word that is different.

1	prawns	mussels	duck	squid
2	lamb	crab	beef	pork
3	cherry	pear	peach	beetroot
4	raspberry	cucumber	pepper	cabbage
5	fried	baked	chicken	roast

b Write the opposite adjective.

1 honest ______
2 mean ______
3 selfish ______
4 hard-working ______
5 quiet ______

c Write verbs for the definitions.

1 to spend money on sth that is not necessary ______
2 to receive money from sb who has died ______
3 to get money by working ______
4 to get money from sb that you will pay back ______
5 to keep money so that you can use it later ______

d Write the strong adjectives.

1 tired ______
2 hungry ______
3 cold ______
4 dirty ______
5 angry ______

e Complete the phrasal verbs.

1 Shall we eat ______ tonight? I don't feel like cooking.
2 I'm allergic to milk, so I have to cut ______ dairy products from my diet.
3 We live ______ my salary. My wife is unemployed.
4 I'll lend you the money if you promise to pay me ______.
5 I took €200 ______ of my bank account.

PRONUNCIATION

a Circle the word with a different sound.

1	peach	steak	beef	steamed
2	money	bossy	positive	cost
3	roast	sociable	owe	account
4	filthy	bill	tiny	chicken
5	afford	pork	worth	organized

b Underline the stressed syllable.

1 sal|mon
2 in|vest
3 i|mma|ture
4 de|li|cious
5 sen|si|ble

CAN YOU UNDERSTAND THIS TEXT?

a Read the newspaper article once. How much did winning the lottery change Tony Bryan's life?

Life-changing, or is it...?

You win the lottery. Do you buy a 10-bedroomed mansion, a gold-plated yacht and a Picasso? Or do you just live a bit more comfortably?

In January 2006, Tony Bryan was working in a factory that produces the flavourings they put on fried chicken. He got a message telling him to call his wife, Rachel, urgently. He called his wife, but the line was engaged. Expecting the worst, he jumped into his car and raced home. His seven-year-old daughter opened the door with a smile and said, 'We've won the lottery, Daddy.' He found Rachel in the living room holding a lottery ticket worth £2.6m. Their lives had changed for ever.

Today, he and his family live in a nice house with a lot of land. They have two goats, and ducks and chickens. It seems that they have adapted brilliantly. They are enjoying their money, but they have not stopped working. They run a caravan park in the field next to the house, and they sell their own vegetables. They haven't exactly been relaxing.

'All your life you get up and go to work to earn money to buy a car, or a holiday, or a better house,' says Tony. 'If you take that away, what is the point of getting up? So you quit your job, you start to get up late, you watch morning TV, then you go shopping, then wait for school pick-up time. After a couple of weeks, you begin to wonder what the point of it is. We had six months going on nice holidays, but then we had to sit down and decide what to do in the long-term.'

So they didn't buy an Aston Martin or even a Mercedes. 'I couldn't justify spending £30,000 on a car,' he says. 'It's a ridiculous amount, no matter how much money you have.' They are very careful with their money. 'You don't stop worrying when you win the lottery. You just worry about different things. I felt guilty that we had lots of money. We were just lucky...'

As I leave, the telephone rings. 'It's £8 per night for a caravan...' says their daughter. I set off home, past their vegetable stall at the end of the drive. Tomatoes are 50p a kilo. A cucumber is 50p.

Adapted from The Sunday Times

b Read the article again. Mark the sentences **T** (true), **F** (false), or **DS** (doesn't say).

1 Tony was very worried when he got his wife's message.
2 Tony continued working in a factory for a few months after the lottery win.
3 He and his family now live in the city.
4 They lived very differently for the first six months after the lottery win.
5 Tony thinks that if you don't work, it's hard to know what to do with your life.
6 Their daughter now goes to a private school.

c Choose five new words or phrases from the article. Check their meaning and pronunciation, and try to learn them.

VIDEO CAN YOU UNDERSTAND THESE PEOPLE?

1 54)) **In the street** Watch or listen to five people and answer the questions.

Emma

Andrew

Ben

Zenobia

Simone

1 Emma says she ______.
 a has liked ice cream since she was a little girl
 b often feels ill after eating chocolate ice cream
 c prefers ice cream to chocolate

2 Andrew likes Asian restaurants because ______.
 a he doesn't like cooking
 b it's cheaper than eating at home
 c he can't cook that type of food at home

3 Ben and his brother went ______ together.
 a running b to university c on holiday

4 Zenobia buys a bag ______.
 a if it's cheaper than usual b every three months
 c if she needs a new one

5 Simone took part in a charity bike ride ______.
 a when she was nine b for a television programme
 c around a track

CAN YOU SAY THIS IN ENGLISH?

Do the tasks with a partner. Tick (✓) the box if you can do them.

Can you...?

1 ☐ describe your diet and the typical diet in your country, and say how it is changing
2 ☐ agree or disagree with the following statement, and say why: *Our favourite food is usually something we liked when we were children.*
3 ☐ describe members of your family, saying what they look like and what they are like
4 ☐ describe some of your plans and predictions for the future (e.g. your studies, your family life)
5 ☐ ask and answer the following questions:
- Have you ever won any money? How much did you win? What did you do with it?
- How long have you been learning English? Where did you first start learning?

VIDEO **Short films** Oxfam
Watch and enjoy this film
www.oup.com/elt/englishfile

G comparatives and superlatives
V transport
P /ʃ/, /dʒ/, and /tʃ/, linking

What's the best way to get around London?

Probably the Tube, although buses are cheaper.

3A Race across London

1 VOCABULARY & SPEAKING
transport

a In pairs, can you think of four different forms of public transport in towns and cities in your country?

b ➤ **p.155 Vocabulary Bank** *Transport*.

2 PRONUNCIATION /ʃ/, /dʒ/, and /tʃ/

a 2 4 Look at the pictures. What are the words and sounds? Listen and repeat.

ʃ	dʒ	tʃ

b Write three words from the list in each column.

adventure bridge catch coach crash journey rush station traffic jam

c 2 5 Listen and check. Practise saying the words.

d Look at the words in the columns. What are the typical spellings for these sounds? Go to the **Sound Bank p.167** and check.

e 2 6 Listen to the pairs of words. Can you hear the difference? Practise saying them.

/tʃ/ and /dʒ/

1 a cheap b jeep
2 a chain b Jane
3 a choke b joke

/ʃ/ and /tʃ/

4 a ship b chip
5 a shoes b choose
6 a wash b watch

f 2 7 Listen and circle the word you hear.

g 2 8 Listen and write five sentences.

3 READING & LISTENING

a You are going to read about a race which the BBC car programme *Top Gear* organized across London. Read the introduction and answer the questions.

1 Where do they have to go from? Where to?
2 What are the four methods of transport?
3 Which one do you think will be the fastest? Why?
4 In what order do you think the other three will arrive? Why?

TopGear Challenge

What's the fastest way to get across London?

On *Top Gear*, a very popular BBC TV series about cars and driving, they decided to organize a race across London, to find the quickest way to cross a busy city. The idea was to start from Kew Bridge, in the south-west of London, and to finish the race at the check-in desk at London City Airport, in the east, a journey of approximately 15 miles. Four possible forms of transport were chosen, a bike, a car, a motorboat, and public transport. The show's presenter, **Jeremy Clarkson**, took the **boat** and his colleague **James May** went by **car** (a large Mercedes). **Richard Hammond** went by **bike**, and **The Stig** took **public transport**. He had an Oyster card. His journey involved getting a bus, then the Tube, and then the Docklands Light Railway, an overground train which connects east and west London.

They set off on a Monday morning in the rush hour…

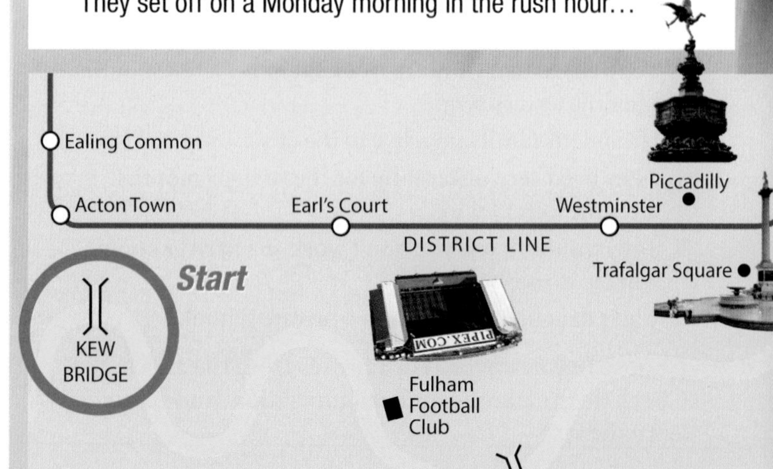

His journey was along the River Thames. For the first few miles there was a speed limit of nine miles an hour, because there are so many ducks and other birds in that part of the river. The river was confusing, and at one point he realized that he was going in the wrong direction. But he turned round and got back onto the right route. Soon he was going past Fulham football ground. He phoned Richard and asked him where he was – just past Trafalgar Square. This was good news for Jeremy. He was ahead of the bike! He reached Wandsworth Bridge. The speed limit finished there, and he could now go as fast as he liked. Jeremy felt like the fastest moving man in all of London. He was flying, coming close to 50 miles an hour! How could he lose now? He could see Tower Bridge ahead. His journey was seven miles longer than the others', but he was now going at 70 miles an hour. Not far to the airport now!

Richard could use bus lanes, which was great, but of course he had to be careful not to crash into the buses! He hated buses! Horrible things! When the traffic lights turned red he thought of cycling through them, but then he remembered that he was on TV, so he had to stop! When he got to Piccadilly he was delighted to see that there was a terrible traffic jam – he could go through the traffic, but James, in his Mercedes, would get stuck. He got to Trafalgar Square, and then went into a cycle lane. From now on it was going to be easier...

He started off OK. He wasn't going fast but at a steady speed – until he was stopped by the police! They only wanted to check the permit for the cameraman in the back of the car, but it meant that he lost three or four valuable minutes! The traffic was getting worse. Now he was going really slowly. 25 miles an hour, 23, 20... 18... It was so frustrating!

b Now read about the journeys by boat, bike, and car. Do you still think your predictions in **a** 3 and 4 are right?

c Read the three journeys again and answer the questions with **Je** (Jeremy), **R** (Richard), or **Ja** (James).

Who...?

1 ☐ was asked to show a piece of paper
2 ☐ went much faster in the later part of his journey
3 ☐ nearly did something illegal
4 ☐ went more slowly in the later part of his journey
5 ☐ was happy to see that there was a lot of traffic
6 ☐ got slightly lost
7 ☐ had the most exciting journey

d Look at the highlighted verbs and verb phrases. With a partner, work out their meaning from context.

e 2 9 Now listen to what happened to The Stig. Follow his route on the map.

f Listen again. What information or warning do you hear when you are travelling on the Tube?

g 2 10 With a partner, write down the order in which you now think the four people arrived. Then listen to what happened. What order did they arrive in? Why do you think that Jeremy Clarkson was annoyed?

h Think of your nearest big city. What kind of public transport is there? If a race was organized there between a bike, a car, and public transport, what order do you think they would arrive in?

i ➤ **Communication** *I'm a tourist – can you help me?* **A** *p.104* **B** *p.109.*

Glossary
1 mile the unit of distance used in the UK and the USA (=1.6 kilometres); 15 miles = approx 25 km
The Stig nickname given to one of the members of the *Top Gear* team
Oyster card a kind of travel card which you use to travel on public transport in London
the Tube nickname for the London Underground

4 GRAMMAR comparatives and superlatives

a Read the sentences. Are the highlighted phrases right or wrong? Tick (✓) or cross (✗) them and correct the wrong sentences.

1 ☐ What's the quicker way to get across London?
2 ☐ Driving is more boring than going by train.
3 ☐ The boat was nearly as fast than the bike.
4 ☐ Oxford is the same distance from London as Brighton.
5 ☐ There aren't as much trains as there were before on this line.
6 ☐ It was the more exciting journey I've ever had.
7 ☐ The worst time of day to travel in London is between 7.30 a.m. and 9.30 a.m.
8 ☐ Women drive more careful than men.

b ➤ **p.136 Grammar Bank 3A.** Learn more about comparatives and superlatives, and practise them.

5 PRONUNCIATION linking

Linking

We often link words together in English, especially when we speak fast. We link words:

1 when a word ends in a consonant sound and the next word begins with a vowel sound, e.g. *more‿exciting*
2 when a word ends in a consonant sound and the next word begins with the same consonant sound, e.g. *a dangerous‿cyclist*
3 when a word ends in /t/ or /d/ and the next word begins with /t/ or /d/, e.g. *the biggest‿dog*

a **2 14** Listen and repeat the sentences. Try to link the marked words and copy the rhythm.

1 **Riding**‿a **motorbike**‿is **more**‿**exciting** than **driving**.
2 The **fastest**‿**train**‿**only takes**‿an‿**hour**‿and‿a **half**.
3 It's **more difficult**‿to **drive**‿at **night** than **during** the **day**.
4 My **father's worse**‿at‿**driving** than my **mother**.
5 The **most**‿**dangerous road**‿in my **town**‿is the **ring road**.

b Talk to a partner. For each group of three things compare them using the **bold** adjective, i.e. for **1** decide which is the most dangerous, and then compare the other two. Say why.

1 **dangerous:** cycling; riding a motorbike; driving
2 **easy:** learning to drive; learning to ride a bike; learning to ride a horse
3 **relaxing:** flying; travelling by train; driving
4 **difficult:** sleeping on a train; sleeping in a plane; sleeping on a bus
5 **boring:** being stuck in a traffic jam; waiting at an airport; waiting for a bus

I think cycling is the most dangerous because sometimes drivers don't notice cyclists. Riding a motorbike is more dangerous than driving.

6 LISTENING

a Read the text and then talk to a partner.

1 Which of these things do you (or people you know) do when they are driving?
2 Which do you think are the most dangerous? Number them 1–3 (1 = the most dangerous).
3 Which one do you think is the least dangerous?

b **2 15** Now listen to a safety expert. Number the activities 1–7. Were your top three right?

c Listen again for more information about each activity and why it is dangerous.

Which of these things are the most (and least) dangerous when you're driving a car?

A British car magazine tested drivers in a driving simulator. The drivers had to drive in the simulator and do the things in the list below.

⚠	Eating or drinking	☐
⚠	Talking on a mobile (not 'hands free')	☐
⚠	Setting or adjusting a satnav	☐
⚠	Listening to your favourite music	☐
⚠	Listening to music you don't know	☐
⚠	Sending or receiving text messages	☐
⚠	Doing your hair or putting on make-up	☐

7 SPEAKING

a Look at the statements below and decide whether you agree or disagree. Tick (✓) the ones you agree with and put a cross (✗) next to the ones you disagree with. Think about your reasons.

- Slow drivers cause more accidents than fast drivers.
- People who drink and drive should lose their driving licence for life.
- Speed cameras do not stop accidents.
- Drivers who are over 70 are as dangerous as young drivers.
- Cyclists should have to wear helmets.
- The minimum age for riding a motorbike should be 25.
- The speed limit on motorways should be lower.

b In groups, give your opinions on each statement. Try to use expressions from the box. Do you agree?

Agreeing and disagreeing

I agree / don't agree	with this. with Juan.
I think / don't think	you're right. that's
I completely / totally	agree. disagree.

8 WRITING

➤ **p.115 Writing** *An article for a magazine.* Write a magazine article about transport in your town or city.

9 2 16 **SONG** *500 Miles* ♫

G articles: *a / an, the*, no article
V collocation: verbs / adjectives + prepositions
P /ə/, sentence stress, /ðə/ or /ðiː/?

Do you think women talk more than men?

Yes, in general I think they probably do.

3B Stereotypes – or are they?

1 READING & SPEAKING

a In pairs, answer the questions.

1 Are you a talkative or a quiet person?
2 Who is...?
  a the most talkative person in your family
  b the most talkative person you know
3 Do you think that, generally speaking, women are more talkative than men?
4 What topics do a) men talk about more than women? b) women talk about more than men?

b Look at the definition of *stereotype*. Then **A** read the article *Men talk just as much as women* and **B** read the article *A gossip with the girls?* Find answers to questions 1–4.

stereotype /ˈsteriətaɪp/ ***noun*** a fixed idea about a particular type of person or thing, which is often not true in reality. ➤ **stereotype** ***verb*** *In advertisements, women are often stereotyped as housewives.*

1 What was the stereotype that the researchers wanted to investigate?
2 Where was the research done?
3 How was the research done?
4 What did the research show?

c In pairs, tell each other about your article, using questions 1–4 to help you.

d Now read both articles again and look at the highlighted words and phrases, which are commonly used in articles about research. Match them with definitions 1–10.

1 *In fact* *adverb* really
2 ________ *verb* make less
3 ________ usually do it
4 ________ *adverb* a little bit
5 ________ linking word used to connect or contrast two facts
6 ________ *verb* say that sth is true
7 ________ as said or shown by sb
8 ________ *verb* include several different things in addition to the ones mentioned
9 ________ *adverb* nearly
10 ________ not completely believed, doubted

e Which of the two pieces of research do you think is...?

1 more credible
2 more important
3 more surprising

Men talk just as much as women – can it really be true?

Research by psychologists at the University of Arizona has shown that the stereotype that women talk more than men may not be true. In the study, hundreds of university students were fitted with recorders and the total number of words they used during the day was then counted.

The results, published in the New Scientist, showed that women speak about 16,000 words a day and men speak only slightly fewer. In fact, the four most talkative people in the study were all men.

Professor Matthias Mehl, who was in charge of the research, said that he and his colleagues had expected to find that women were more talkative.

A GOSSIP WITH THE GIRLS? JUST PICK ANY ONE OF FORTY SUBJECTS

Women are experts at gossiping – and they often talk about trivial things, or at least that's what men have always thought. However according to research carried out by Professor Petra Boynton, a psychologist at University College London, when women talk to women their conversations are not trivial at all, and cover many more topics (up to 40) than when men talk to other men.

Women's conversations range from health to their houses, from politics to fashion, from films to family, from education to relationship problems. Almost everything, in fact, except football. Men tend to talk about fewer subjects, the most popular being work, sport, jokes, cars, and women.

However, they had been sceptical of the common belief that women use three times as many words as men. This idea became popular after the publication of a book called *The Female Brain* (2006) whose author, Louann Brizendine, claimed that 'a woman uses about 20,000 words per day, whereas a man uses about 7,000.'

Professor Mehl accepts that many people will find the results difficult to believe. However, he thinks that this research is important because the stereotype, that women talk too much and men keep quiet, is bad not only for women but also for men. 'It says that to be a good male, it's better not to talk – that silence is golden.'

Professor Boynton interviewed over 1,000 women for her study. She also found that women move quickly from one subject to another in conversation, whereas men usually stick to one subject for longer periods of time.

Professor Boynton also says that men and women chat for different reasons. In social situations women use conversation to solve problems and reduce stress, while men chat with each other to have a laugh or to swap opinions.

2 GRAMMAR articles: *a / an, the*, no article

a Complete 1–4 with *a / an, the*, or – (no article).

1 'Have you heard this joke? ____ man with ____ dog walks into ____ bar. ____ man says to ____ barman, "Can I have ____ beer and ____ whisky for my dog…?"'

2 'I've just read ____ article on ____ internet about how eating ____ strawberries makes you look younger…'

3 'I'm sure there's something wrong between us because we never go out to ____ dinner or to ____ cinema any more.

4 'Did you watch ____ match ____ last night? I can't believe that ____ referee didn't see that it was ____ penalty…'

b According to the article *A gossip with the girls?*, who do you think would probably say 1–4, a man or a woman?

c ➤ **p.137 Grammar Bank 3B.** Learn more about articles and practise them.

3 PRONUNCIATION
/ə/, sentence stress, /ðə/ or /ðiː/?

a **2 20** Listen and repeat the sound and words.

a about anniversary cinema problem relationship spider usually woman

b **2 21** Listen and repeat the sentences. Then practise saying them with the /ə/ sound.

1 **What** are we **going** to **have** for **lunch today**?
2 I'd **like** to **see** a **good film tonight**.
3 We **need** to **go** in the **other direction**.
4 Could you **ask** the **woman over there**?
5 There's a **cinema** and there are **lots** of **shops**.

c **2 22** Listen and underline five phrases where *the* is pronounced /ðiː/ (not /ðə/). Why does the pronunciation change?

the cinema the end the other day the world the sun the internet the kitchen the answer the Earth

4 SPEAKING

Prove that the research in *A gossip with the girls?* is wrong! Work in pairs or small groups.

If you're a **woman**, try to talk for two minutes about:

football cars computers

If you're a **man**, try to talk for two minutes about:

fashion shopping your family

5 READING & LISTENING

a Do you think it is a stereotype that women are better than men at looking after small children? Do you know any men who stay at home and look after their children? How do they manage?

b Look at an illustration from a new book about looking after young children. Can you name some of the things in the picture?

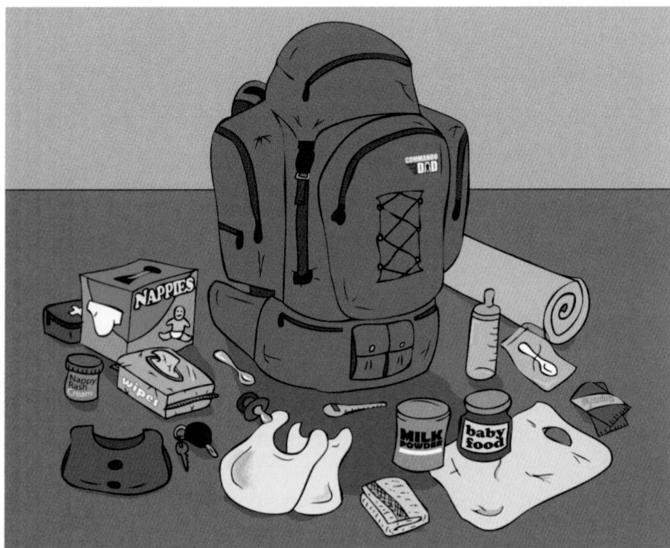

c Read the beginning of an article about the book. Why did Neil Sinclair write it? In what way is it different from other books about bringing up children?

d 2 23))) Listen to two men talking in the park about the book and mark the sentences **T** (true) or **F** (false).

1 Miranda is older than Stephen.
2 Miranda's father slept badly the night before.
3 Stephen's father recommends sleeping tablets.
4 Stephen's father hasn't read *Commando Dad*.
5 He likes the website because he enjoys reading about other men's experiences.
6 Stephen's father really likes the book because it helps him and makes him laugh.
7 In *Commando Dad*, BT means 'Baby Trooper' and 'Base Camp' means the kitchen.
8 The author of *Commando Dad* thinks that women are only better than men when the baby is small.

e Listen again and correct the wrong information.

f Do you think it's a good idea to have a book and a website on childcare especially for men? Why (not)?

COMMANDO DAD

For six years Neil Sinclair served as a commando with the British army. He had been in lots of dangerous situations, but nothing prepared him for the day when he brought his first baby home from hospital. 'I put the car seat containing my two-day-old son Samuel down on the floor and said to my wife, 'What do we do now?''

When he left the army, Sinclair and his wife agreed that he would stay at home and look after the baby, while his wife went back to work.

'I have done a lot of crazy things, but when I put that baby down I thought: I have a tiny baby and he is crying. What does he want? What does he need? I did not know. It was one of the most difficult days of my life.'

It was at that moment that Sinclair had an idea. 'I found myself thinking how much easier life would be if I had a basic training manual for my baby, like the manual you get when you join the army. I realized that somebody needed to write such a manual, and who better to write it than me? I had been a commando, but I was now a stay-at-home dad. I was the man for the job.'

His book, *Commando Dad: Basic Training*, is a set of instructions that explains with military precision and diagrams how new fathers should approach the first three years of their child's life to become a 'first-rate father'.

Adapted from The Times

Glossary
commando *noun* one of a group of soldiers who are trained to make quick attacks in enemy areas
stay-at-home dad *noun* a man who stays at home and looks after the children while his wife goes out to work

6 SPEAKING

a 2 24))) Listen to someone talking about men and women, and complete the gaps.

'Generally ________, I think women worry more about their appearance than men. They ________ to spend hours choosing what to wear, doing their hair, and putting on make-up. Women are also ________ better at making themselves look more attractive. But I think that in ________, men are more worried than women about their body image. They feel more insecure about their hair, for instance, especially when they're going bald.'

b In small groups discuss if the statements opposite about men and women are stereotypes or true. Try to use the highlighted expressions for generalizing from **a**.

MEN & WOMEN stereotypes or true?

- Women worry more about their appearance than men.
- Women spend more time than men on social networking sites.
- Men talk more about things; women talk more about people.
- Men are more interested than women in gadgets like phones and tablets.
- Women are better at multitasking than men.
- Men find it more difficult than women to talk to their friends or family if they have a problem.
- Women spend more time than men talking about celebrities and their lifestyles.
- Men are more interested than women in power.
- Women are less interested in sport than men.
- Men worry more about their health than women.

NEIL SINCLAIR
COMMANDO DAD
BASIC TRAINING
HOW TO BE AN ELITE DAD OR CARER
THE BASICS
Survive the first 24 hours
Prepare and plan to prevent poor parental performance
Maintain morale
Feed, clothe, transport and entertain your troops
FROM BIRTH TO 3 YEARS
Foreword by Dr Jan Mager-Jones MB ChB
COMMANDO DAD

7 VOCABULARY

collocation: verbs / adjectives + prepositions

a Cover the statements above. Can you remember the missing prepositions?

1 Men worry more ___ their health than women.
2 Women are better ___ multitasking than men.
3 Men are more interested than women ___ power.

b ➤ **p.156 Vocabulary Bank** *Dependent prepositions.*

When are prepositions stressed?
Prepositions are normally only stressed when they are the last word, e.g. in a question. Compare:

We **need** to **talk** about our **holiday**.
What are you **talking about**?

Freddie is **afraid** of **flying**.
What are you **afraid of**?

c Complete the questions with a preposition.

1 When you're with friends of the same sex, what do you usually talk ___?
2 Are there any sports or games that you're good ___?
3 Is there anything you're really looking forward ___?
4 Who in your family are you closest ___?
5 What kind of films are you keen ___?
6 Are there any animals or insects that you're afraid ___?
7 What's your town famous ___?
8 Are there any superstitions that you believe ___?

d 2 27))) Listen and check. Then ask and answer the questions with a partner.

Practical English A difficult celebrity

1 VIDEO ROB'S INTERVIEW

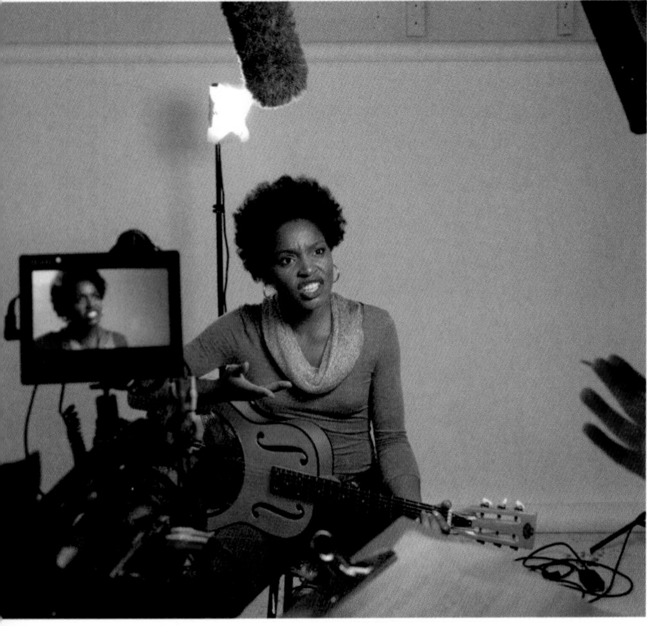

a 2 28 Watch or listen to Rob interviewing Kerri. What is she happy / not happy to talk about?

b Watch or listen again. Mark the sentences **T** (true) or **F** (false). Correct the **F** sentences.

1 Kerri's song is about love.
2 Kerri plays in a band.
3 She used to go out with a member of the band.
4 Only one of her parents was a musician.
5 Kerri started playing the guitar when she was six.
6 Her new album is very different from the previous ones.
7 She's been recording and touring recently.
8 She's going to give a big concert in New York.

2 VIDEO GIVING OPINIONS

a 2 29 Watch or listen to the conversation at lunch. What do they disagree about?

b Watch or listen again. Answer the questions.

1 What does Kerri think about...?
   a the waiters in New York compared to London
   b people in New York compared to London
2 Who agrees with Kerri? Who disagrees? What do they think?
3 Who phones Rob? What about?

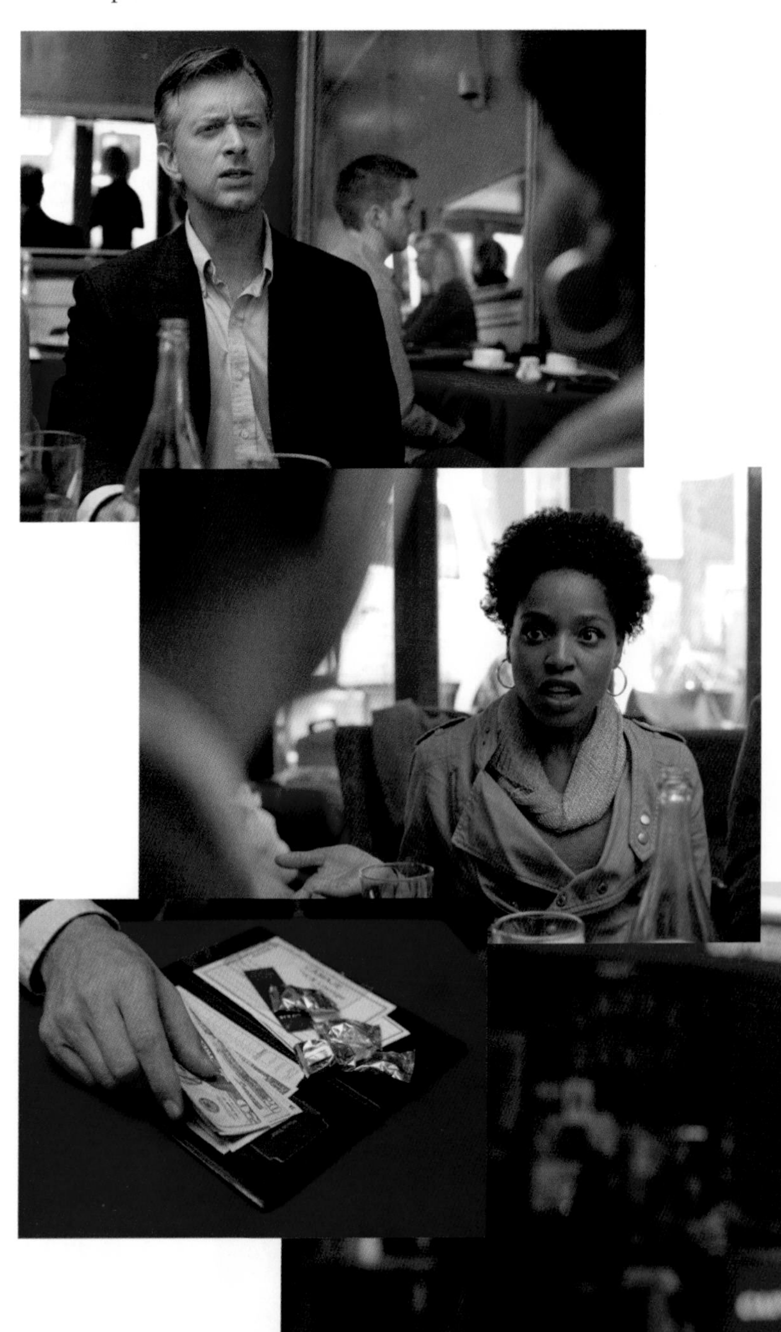

c 2 30 Look at some extracts from the conversation. Can you remember any of the missing words? Watch or listen and check.

1
Kerri ________, I think people in London are a lot more easy-going. London's just not as hectic as New York.
Don Sure, we all like peace and quiet. But in my ________, New York is possibly... well, no, is definitely the greatest city in the world. Don't you ________?
Kerri To be ________, I definitely prefer London.
Don Come on, Rob. You've lived in both. What do you ________?

2
Don OK, I ________, London has its own peculiar charm. But if you ________ me, nothing compares with a city like New York. The whole world is here!
Kerri But that's the problem. It's too big. There are too many people. Everybody's so stressed out. And nobody has any time for you.
Jenny I don't think that's ________, Kerri. New Yorkers are very friendly.
Kerri Oh ________, they can sound friendly with all that 'Have a nice day' stuff.

d 2 31 Watch or listen and repeat the highlighted phrases. Copy the rhythm and intonation.

e Practise the dialogues in **c** with a partner.

f In small groups, practise giving opinions. Discuss the following sentences.

- The best place to live is in a big city.
- Cycling is the most practical way to get round big cities.
- You only get good service in expensive restaurants.
- It's irritating when people in shops or restaurants say *Have a nice day!*

3 A SURPRISE FOR KERRI

VIDEO

a 2 32 Watch or listen to the end of the lunch. Why is Kerri surprised?

British and American English
cell phone = American English
mobile phone = British English

b Watch or listen again and complete the information.

1 Kerri thinks the waitress is friendly when they leave because Don...
2 Jenny is worried because she thinks Rob...
3 Kerri thinks that the taxi driver is very...

c Look at the **Social English phrases**. Can you remember any of the missing words?

Social English phrases

Jenny Did you ________ what you said in the restaurant, Rob?
Jenny It's ________ that... you seemed homesick in there.
Rob Oh, ________ on a minute.
Rob Our taxi's come ________.
Kerri That was so ________ of him!

d 2 33 Watch or listen and complete the phrases.

e Watch or listen again and repeat the phrases. How do you say them in your language?

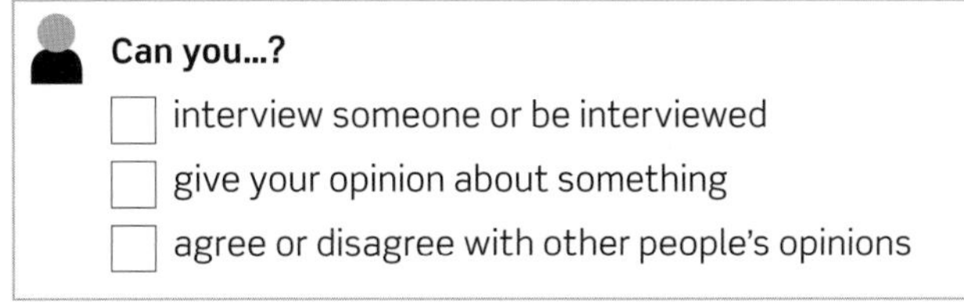
Can you...?
- [ ] interview someone or be interviewed
- [ ] give your opinion about something
- [ ] agree or disagree with other people's opinions

G *can, could, be able to*
V *-ed / -ing* adjectives
P sentence stress

Can you speak French?

No, I've never been able to learn a foreign language.

4A Failure and success

1 GRAMMAR *can, could, be able to*

a *'If at first you don't succeed, try, try, try again'* is a well-known English saying. What does it mean?

b More recently other people have invented different ways of continuing the saying. Which one do you like best?

If at first you don't succeed,
...give up
...blame your parents
...destroy all the evidence that you tried
...do it the way your mother told you to
...skydiving is not for you

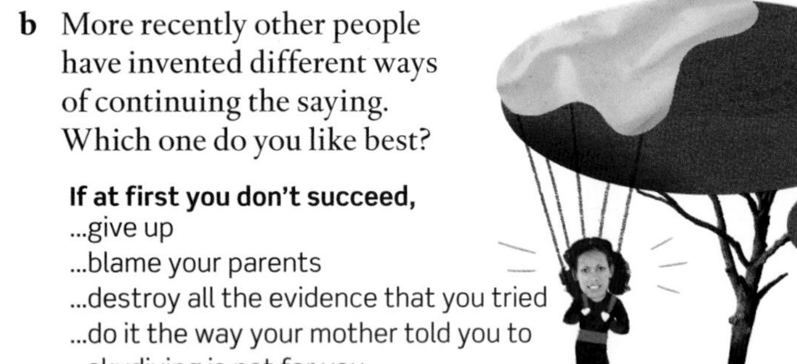

c Look at the definition of *be able to*. What other verb is it similar to?

be able to (do something) to have the ability, opportunity, time, etc. to do something: *Will you be able to come to the meeting next week?*

d Read about three people who have tried (but failed) to learn something, and complete the texts with A–G.

A I was able to
B Not being able to
C I just wasn't able to
D I will never be able to
E I would suddenly be able to
F I've always wanted to be able to
G we would never be able to

e Read the article again. Why did they have problems? Have they completely given up trying? Have you ever tried to learn something and given up? Why?

f Look at phrases **A–G** again. What tense or form is *be able to* in each one? What tenses or forms does *can* have?

g ➤ **p.138 Grammar Bank 4A.** Learn more about *can, could,* and *be able to*, and practise them.

h ➤ **Communication** *Guess the sentence* **A** *p.105* **B** *p.109.*

I've **never** been able to...

...scuba-dive

I really wanted to learn. Maybe it was because of that scene in one of the very first James Bond films, where a beautiful actress comes out of the sea looking fabulous, with oxygen bottles on her back – I could see myself looking just like her. So, two years ago I booked a holiday which included a week's intensive course. On the first day of the course I was incredibly excited. First we had two hours of theory, and then we went into the sea to put it into practice. But as soon as I went under the water I discovered that I suffered from claustrophobia. [1]__________ do it. After about half an hour I gave up. Every evening for the rest of my holiday I had to listen to my scuba-diving classmates talking about all the wonderful things they had seen that day on their diving excursions. [2]__________ join in the conversation was very frustrating.

I still love swimming and snorkelling, but I think that I have to accept that [3]__________ scuba-dive.

Bea, USA

[4] _______________ dance salsa, and when I was working in Ecuador there were free classes, so I joined. But the art of salsa is to keep your arms still and move your hips, and I just couldn't do it. When I hear music my arms start moving, but my hips don't. After about ten hours of classes [5] _______________ do the basic steps, but I was dancing like a robot! I didn't give up, but soon everyone in the class was dancing and I was just slowly moving from side to side and counting out loud 'one, two, three, four'. It was a bit embarrassing. I was sure that one day [6] _______________ do it – but that never happened. I can still remember the first two steps and I still try to dance when I hear a salsa tune – as long as nobody is watching!

Sean, UK

I love Manga – Japanese comics – and I tried to learn Japanese, but I found it incredibly difficult and I gave up after two years. I think oriental languages, which have symbols instead of words, are extremely hard to learn for people who are more used to Roman letters. Also my teacher, a Japanese woman, didn't speak Spanish very well, which didn't help! She was a very charming woman, but she was a bit disappointed with us, and you could see that she thought that [7] _______________ learn. However, one day she invited us to dinner and gave us some delicious traditional Japanese food, and since then I often go to Japanese restaurants. So I learnt to love the food, if not to speak the language!

Joaquin, Spain

2 PRONUNCIATION sentence stress

a 2 36 Listen and repeat the sentences. Copy the rhythm.

1. I'd **love** to be **able** to **ski.**
2. We **won't** be **able** to **come.**
3. I've **never** been **able** to **dance.**
4. She **hates not** being **able** to **drive.**

b 2 37 Listen again. Make new sentences with the verbs or verb phrases you hear.

I'd love to be able to ski. ***Ride a horse***
I'd love to be able to ride a horse.

We won't be able to come. ***Park***
We won't be able to park.

3 SPEAKING

a Look at the topics. Choose two or three and think about what you could say for them.

- Something you've tried to learn, but have never been able to do well.
- Something you learnt to do after a lot of effort.
- Something you can do, but you'd like to be able to do better.
- Something new that you would like to be able to do.
- Something you are learning to do and that you hope you'll soon be able to do well.
- Something you think all young people should be able to do before they leave school.

b Work with a partner. Tell him / her about the things you chose in **a**. Give reasons or explanations for each one.

I've never been able to ski, and now I don't think I'll ever learn. I always wanted to learn, but I don't live near mountains...

4 VOCABULARY *-ed / -ing* adjectives

a Look at the photo. Complete the sentences with *bored* or *boring*.

1 The film was _______.
2 The audience were _______.

> **-ed and -ing adjectives**
> Many adjectives for feelings have two possible forms, either ending in *-ed* or in *-ing*, e.g. ***frustrated*** and ***frustrating***.
> We use the adjective ending in *-ed* for the person who has the feeling (*I was very frustrated that I couldn't scuba-dive*). We use the adjective ending in *-ing* for a person or situation that produces the feeling (*I couldn't join in the conversation, which was very frustrating*).

b Read the information box. Then complete the adjectives with *-ed* or *-ing*.

1 What do you think is the most **excit**___ sport to watch?
2 What's the most **amaz**___ scenery you've ever seen?
3 What music do you listen to if you feel **depress**___?
4 Have you ever been **disappoint**___ by a birthday present?
5 Which do you find more **tir**___, speaking English or listening to English?
6 What's the most **embarrass**___ thing that's ever happened to you?
7 Are you **frighten**___ of heights?
8 Do you feel very **tir**___ in the morning?
9 Who's the most **bor**___ person you know?
10 Do you ever get **frustrat**___ by technology?

c **2 38** Listen and check. Underline the stressed syllable in the adjectives.

d Ask and answer the questions in pairs. Ask for more information.

5 READING & SPEAKING

a Do you know anybody who speaks more than two languages? Which languages do they speak? How did they learn?

b **2 39** You are going to read an article about Alex Rawlings, who speaks 11 languages. Before you read, match the languages below with words **1–11**. Then listen and check.

☐ English	☐ Greek	☐ German
☐ Spanish	☐ Russian	☐ Dutch
1 Afrikaans	☐ French	☐ Hebrew
☐ Catalan	☐ Italian	

c Read the article. Which language(s)...?

1 did he learn as a child
2 is he studying at university
3 does he like best
4 is he planning to learn next
5 did he wish he had been able to speak when he was a child
6 was the first one he taught himself
7 did he find the most difficult

He's English, but he can speak eleven languages

Alex Rawlings has been named the UK's most multilingual student, in a competition run by a dictionary publisher.

The German and Russian student from London, who is only 20 years old, can speak 11 languages fluently. In a video for the BBC News website he demonstrated his skills by speaking in all of them, changing quickly from one to another. Rawlings said that winning the competition was 'a bit of a shock'. He explained, 'I saw the competition advertised and I heard something about a free iPad. I never imagined that it would generate this amount of media attention.'

As a child, Rawlings' mother, who is half Greek, used to speak to him in English, Greek, and French, and he often visited his family in Greece.
He said that he has always been interested in languages. 'My dad worked in Japan for four years and I was always frustrated that I couldn't speak to the kids because of the language barrier.' After visiting Holland at the age of 14 he decided to learn Dutch with CDs and books. 'When I went back I could talk to people. It was great.'

d Look at the highlighted words and phrases related to language learning, and work out their meaning from the context. Then ask and answer the questions with a partner.

1 Can you or anyone in your family speak another language fluently?
2 Do you know any basic phrases in any other languages?
3 Do you have a personal link to another country or language? Why?
4 Have you ever travelled to another country and felt that there was a real language barrier?
5 What other languages would you like to be able to speak? Why?

He taught himself many of the languages with 'teach yourself' books, but also by watching films, listening to music, and travelling to the countries themselves.

Of all the languages he speaks, Rawlings says that Russian, which he has been learning for a year and a half, is the hardest. He said, 'There seem to be more exceptions than rules!' He added, 'I especially like Greek because I think it's beautiful and, because of my mother, I have a strong personal link to the country and to the language.'

'Everyone should learn languages, especially if they travel abroad. If you make the effort to learn even the most basic phrases wherever you go, it instantly shows the person you're speaking to that you respect their culture. Going around speaking English loudly and getting frustrated at people is tactless and rude.'

The next language Rawlings hopes to learn is Arabic, but 'only once I've finished my degree and got some more time on my hands. For now I need to concentrate on my German and Russian, so I can prepare for my finals.'

Glossary
finals the last exams that students take at university

e Read the grammar information box. Then complete 1–5 with a reflexive pronoun.

> **Reflexive pronouns**
> *He taught **himself** many of the languages with 'teach **yourself**' books.*
> We use reflexive pronouns (*myself, yourself, himself, herself, itself, ourselves, yourselves, themselves*) when the object of a verb is the same as the subject, e.g. *He taught himself Russian.* = he was his own teacher.
> We also use reflexive pronouns to emphasize the subject of an action, e.g. *We painted the kitchen ourselves.*

1 I always test ________ on new vocabulary – it's a good way to remember it.
2 My uncle built the house ________. It took him three years.
3 This light is automatic. It turns ________ on and off.
4 Did you fix the computer ________? Well done!
5 My sister's so vain! Every time she passes a mirror, she looks at ________ in it!

6 LISTENING & SPEAKING

a 2 40))) You're going to listen to six advanced students of English giving a tip which has helped them to learn. Listen once and complete their tip. Then compare your notes with a partner.

TIP 1: Change the language to English on all the ________ you have, for example on your ________, or ________, or ________.

TIP 2: Do things that you ________ ________, but in English.

TIP 3: Try to find an English-speaking ________ or ________.

TIP 4: Get a ________ ________ app for your phone.

TIP 5: Book yourself a ________ in an ________-________ ________.

TIP 6: Listen to as many ________ as possible in English, and then ________ ________ ________ them.

b Listen again. Try to add more details about each tip.

c Talk to a partner.

- Do you already do any of these things?
- Which do you think is the best tip?
- Which tip could you easily put into practice? Try it!
- What other things do you do to improve your English outside class (e.g. visit chat websites, listen to audio books)?

G modals of obligation: *must, have to, should*
V phone language
P silent consonants, linking

Do I have to bring a present?

Yes, I think you probably should.

4B Modern manners?

1 VOCABULARY & SPEAKING
phone language

a 2 41 Listen and match the phone sentences with the sounds.

A ☐ He's **dialling** a number.
B ☐ She's **texting / messaging** a friend.
C ☐ He's just **hung up**.
D ☐ She's choosing a new **ringtone**.
E ☐ He's **calling back**.
F ☐ She **left a message** on his **voicemail**.
G ☐ The line's **engaged / busy**.

b Can you explain what these are?

Skype a screensaver silent / vibrate mode quiet zones instant messaging

c Use the questionnaire to interview another student. Ask for more information.

YOU AND YOUR PHONE

- What make is your phone? How long have you had it?
- Would you like to get a new one? Why (not)?
- What ringtone do you have?
- What do you use your phone for (apart from talking)?
- Where and when do you normally switch off your mobile?
- Have you ever...?
  - lost your phone
  - sent a message to the wrong person
  - forgotten to turn your phone off (with embarrassing consequences)

2 GRAMMAR
modals of obligation: *must, have to, should*

a Read the extract from Debrett's guide to mobile phone etiquette. Then talk to a partner about questions 1–4.

1 Do you agree with what Debrett's says?
2 Do you ever do any of these things?
3 Are they a problem where you live?
4 Are there any other things people do with their phones that annoy you?

Debrett's, a well-known British publisher, has been producing guides on how people should behave since the 1900s, including *Debrett's Etiquette and Modern Manners* and *The English Gentleman*. Nowadays it still offers advice on what (and what not) to do in social situations.

DEBRETT'S
guide to mobile phone etiquette

1 *Think what your ringtone says about you*
If you're sometimes embarrassed by your ringtone, it's almost certainly the wrong one and you should change it.

2 *When in doubt, use silent or vibrate mode*
It may surprise your companions when you suddenly answer an invisible, silent phone, but at least they won't have to listen to your ringtone.

3 *Take notice of who is around you*
Make sure your conversation is not disturbing other people. Intimate conversations are never appropriate in front of others.

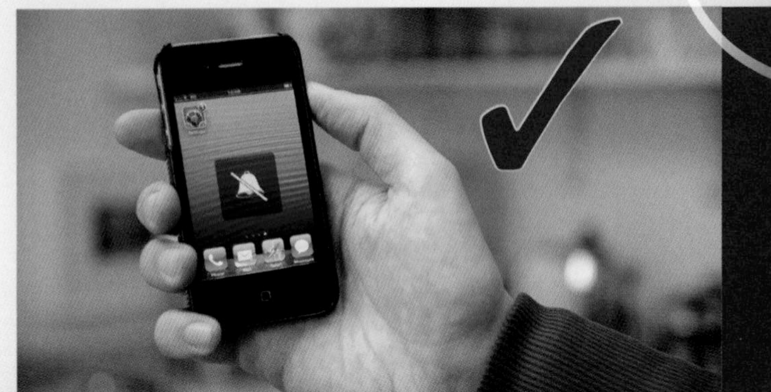

b Read the text again. Match the highlighted phrases with their meaning. Two of the phrases match the same meaning.

A You don't need to do this. It isn't necessary.
B Don't do this. It isn't allowed / permitted.
C It's necessary or compulsory to do this.
D It's a good idea to do this.

c ➤ **p.139 Grammar Bank 4B.** Learn more about *must*, *have to*, and *should*, and practise them.

4 *Respect quiet zones*
You must not use your phone in 'quiet zones' on trains or in hotels. That is the reason why they exist.

5 *Never shout*
Your phone is not a megaphone. You don't have to shout. And don't shout because you think reception is poor. It won't make any difference.

6 *People with you deserve more attention than those at the end of a phone*
Wherever possible, turn off your phone in social situations and at mealtimes, or put it on vibrate. If you have to keep your phone on because you are expecting an important call, apologize in advance.

7 *Don't carry on phone conversations when you are in the middle of something else*
This is especially true if you are in banks, shops, etc. It is insulting not to give the people who are serving you your full attention.

8 *Think about where you are calling from*
Don't make (or receive) calls in inappropriate places. Put your phone on vibrate in meetings, cinemas, etc. If you must take a call in the car, use a hands-free set.

Adapted from Debrett's Modern Manners

3 PRONUNCIATION & SPEAKING

silent consonants, linking

a Each of the words in the list has a silent consonant or consonants. With a partner, cross out the silent letters.

should ought mustn't talk wrong listen
half dishonest knowledge design whole
rhythm doubt foreign calm island

b 2 46 Listen and check.

c 2 47 Listen and repeat the sentences. Try to copy the rhythm and to link the marked words.

1 You must **switch off** your **phone** on a **plane**.
2 You should **only call him** in an **emergency**.
3 We **have** to **leave** at **eleven**.
4 You **mustn't open other people's emails**.
5 You **shouldn't talk loudly** on a **mobile phone**.

d Read the definition of *manners*. Then make sentences using *should* / *shouldn't* for something which you think is a question of manners, and with *must* / *mustn't* / *have to* for something which is a law or rule.

manners /ˈmænəz/ ***pl noun*** a way of behaving that is considered acceptable in your country or culture

- switch off your phone in a theatre
- talk loudly on your phone in public
- send text messages when you are driving
- reply to a message on your phone while you are talking to somebody face-to-face
- play noisy games on a phone in public
- use your phone at a petrol station
- video people on your phone without their permission
- set your phone to silent mode on a train
- send or receive texts in the cinema
- turn off your phone on a plane during take-off and landing

4 READING

a Imagine that you have been invited to stay for a weekend with your partner's family. Think of three things that you think it would be bad manners to do.

b Read the article. Did Heidi do any of those things? What did she do wrong (according to Mrs Bourne)? Now look at the title of the article. What do you think 'from hell' means in this context?

News online

Mother-in-law from hell... or daughter-in-law from hell?

By NEWS ONLINE **Reporter**

Everyone knows it can be difficult to get on with your in-laws, but for 29-year-old **Heidi Withers**, it may now be impossible. Heidi was invited to spend the weekend with her fiancé Freddie's family at their house in Devon, in south-west England. But soon after they returned to London, Heidi received a very nasty email from Carolyn Bourne, Freddie's stepmother, criticizing her manners.

Here are a few examples of your lack of manners:

- *When you are a guest in another's house, you should not declare what you will and will not eat – unless you are allergic to something.*
- *You should not say that you do not have enough food.*
- *You should not start before everyone else.*
- *You should not take additional helpings without being invited to by your host.*
- *You should not lie in bed until late morning.*
- *You should have sent a handwritten card after the visit. You have never written to thank me when you have stayed.*

Heidi was shocked, and immediately sent the email on to some of her close friends. Surprised and amused, the friends forwarded it to other people, and soon the email had been posted on several websites, with thousands of people writing comments about 'the mother-in-law from hell'.

Adapted from a news website

c Find words or phrases in the article which mean...

1 __________ *noun* a man to whom you are going to be married
2 __________ *adj* unpleasant
3 __________ *verb* saying what is bad or wrong with sb or sth
4 __________ *noun* not having enough of sth
5 __________ *noun* a person who you invite to your house
6 __________ *noun* a person who receives a visitor
7 __________ *verb* sent an email or message you received to another person

> ***should have***
> We use *should have* to talk about something that happened in the past that you think was wrong, e.g. *You should have written me a thank-you letter.* = you didn't write to me. I think this was wrong.

d Now read some of the comments that were posted on the internet. Write **H** next to the ones that support Heidi, and **C** next to the ones that support Carolyn.

1 Mrs Bourne says Heidi should have sent a handwritten thank-you note... however, she sends this letter by email! We are in the 21st century. Nobody sends handwritten letters any more. *13/07/2011 18:52*

2 Why do we hear nothing about Freddie's role in all this? Why didn't he prepare Heidi? He must know what his stepmother is like. He could also have prepared his family by telling them about any eating problems his girlfriend has. *13/07/2011 16:25*

3 The email was a private communication. I don't think Heidi should have sent it on to her friends. It makes me think that Mrs Bourne might be right about her bad manners. *13/07/2011 12:40*

4 The stepmother seems to be extremely jealous of Heidi, perhaps she wants to keep Freddie all to herself. If I were Heidi, I would leave him. *12/07/2011 10:15*

5 The mother-in-law may have a few good points but she should have spoken to Heidi face-to-face, not sent her an email. *11/07/2011 18:50*

6 I think that the one with the extremely bad manners is Mrs Bourne. *11/07/2011 14:10*

7 Mrs Bourne, I agree with every word you say. Young people just don't have any manners nowadays. I hope Freddie sees sense and finds someone better. *11/07/2011 09:48*

e Write your own comment. Then compare with a partner. Do you agree?

f ➤ **Communication** *The big day p.105.* Read about what Heidi and Freddie did next.

5 LISTENING

a 2 48 Listen to Miranda Ingram, who is married to Alexander Anichkin, talking about the difference between Russian manners and British manners. What was their problem? How have they managed to solve their differences?

b Listen again and mark the sentences **T** (true) or **F** (false).

1. In Russia you should say please (in Russian) when you ask someone to do something.
2. Before Miranda took Alexander to meet her parents she taught him about English manners.
3. When Alexander smiled at people in the UK, he felt ridiculous.
4. When Miranda went to Russia the first time Alexander's friends were delighted because she smiled all the time.
5. Alexander thinks that the English sometimes use very polite expressions unnecessarily.
6. Alexander thinks the English are too direct.
7. Miranda doesn't think her dinner guests should criticize her cooking.

c What would people from your country do in these situations?

6 SPEAKING

In groups, talk about each thing in the *Good Manners?* questionnaire. Do you think it's good manners, bad manners, or not important / not necessary. Why?

I think it is very rude to criticize the food if you are in somebody's house.

I think it depends. It's OK if you know the person very well or if it's a member of your family...

7 2 49 SONG *You Can't Hurry Love* ♫

WHEN YOU ARE INVITED TO SOMEBODY'S HOUSE...

- ☐ criticize the food (e.g. if it is too cold, salty, etc.)
- ☐ take a present
- ☐ write an email to say thank you
- ☐ arrive more than ten minutes late for lunch or dinner

WHEN GREETING PEOPLE...

- ☐ use more formal language when speaking to an older person
- ☐ kiss a woman on both cheeks when you meet her for the first time
- ☐ use your partner's parents' first names

WHEN YOU ARE HAVING A MEAL WITH FRIENDS IN A RESTAURANT...

- ☐ leave your mobile on silent on the table in front of you
- ☐ answer or send a text or message
- ☐ make a phone call
- ☐ kiss your partner

MEN AND WOMEN – A MAN'S ROLE...

- ☐ pay for the meal on a first date
- ☐ wait for a woman to go through the door first
- ☐ accompany a woman home

ON SOCIAL NETWORKING SITES...

- ☐ post a private message or conversation on an internet site
- ☐ post an embarrassing photo or video clip of a friend without asking their permission
- ☐ post all the details of your break-up with a partner

3&4 Revise and Check

GRAMMAR

Circle a, b, or c.

1 I walk to work. It's ______ than going by car.
a healthyer b as healthy c healthier
2 Cycling isn't ______ people think.
a as dangerous as b as dangerous than
c so dangerous than
3 This is ______ time of day for traffic jams.
a the most bad b the worse c the worst
4 My wife is a much safer driver than ______.
a I b me c my
5 What ______ beautiful day!
a a b – c an
6 I never drink coffee after ______ dinner.
a – b the c an
7 ______ are usually good language learners.
a The women b Women c Woman
8 We've decided to visit the UK ______.
a the next summer b next summer
c the summer next
9 We won't ______ come to the party.
a can b be able c be able to
10 When he was five he ______ already swim.
a can b could c was able
11 My mother has never ______ cook well.
a been able to b could c be able to
12 Entrance is free. You ______ pay anything.
a don't have to b mustn't c shouldn't
13 I'll ______ work harder if I want to pass.
a must b should c have to
14 I don't think I ______ have a dessert. I've already eaten too much!
a must b should c have to
15 You ______ switch on your phone until the plane has landed.
a don't have to b mustn't c shouldn't

VOCABULARY

a Complete with a preposition.

1 We arrived ______ Prague at 5.30.
2 I apologized ______ being late.
3 I'm not very keen ______ horror films.
4 My son is good ______ speaking languages.
5 This song reminds me ______ my holiday.

b Complete the compound nouns.

1 Slow down! The speed ______ on this road is 100, not 120.
2 I won't start the car until you have all put on your seat ______.
3 It's not a very good town for cyclists – there are very few cycle ______.
4 Try to avoid using the Tube during the ______ hour – between 8.00 and 9.30 in the morning.
5 There's a taxi ______ just outside the station.

c Complete with the right word.

1 We were late because we got **s**______ in a terrible traffic jam.
2 I'm moving into a new flat next week. I've hired a **v**______, so that I can take all my things there.
3 The next train to Bristol is now waiting at **pl**______ 5.
4 We're going to **s**______ off early because we want to get to the hotel before it gets dark.
5 How long does it **t**______ to get from here to the airport?

d Circle the right adjective.

1 The match ended 0–0. It was really *bored | boring*.
2 It was the most *frightened | frightening* experience I've ever had.
3 We're very *excited | exciting* about our holiday!
4 I'm a bit *disappointed | disappointing* with my exam results.
5 This programme is too *depressed | depressing*. Turn it off.

e Complete the missing words.

1 I'm not in at the moment. Please **l**______ a message.
2 The line's **eng**______. Please hold.
3 I was in the middle of talking to him and he just **h**______ up!
4 I love the **scr**______ on your phone. Is it a photo of your kids?
5 I hate it when people have really loud **r**______ on their mobiles!

PRONUNCIATION

a Circle the word with a different sound.

1	tram	want	manners	traffic
2	the moon	the sun	the beginning	the end
3	switch	cheap	machine	coach
4	should	crash	permission	gossip
5	carriage	message	argue	apologize

b Underline the stressed syllable.

1 mo|tor|way 3 pe|de|stri|an 5 em|ba|rra|ssing
2 di|sa|ppoin|ted 4 vi|brate

CAN YOU UNDERSTAND THIS TEXT?

a Read the article once. What kind of concert was it? What happened?

Turn it off!

Something historic happened at the New York Philharmonic on the evening of 10 January 2012, about an hour into Mahler's Ninth Symphony. During the beautiful fourth movement, an audience member's cellphone loudly rang. And rang. And rang again. It was the kind of marimba riff we've all heard on the street from a stranger's phone.

From my seat in Row L, I could see the horrified discomfort of the other audience members from their body language. We all wondered whether the conductor Alan Gilbert would react, and how. Suddenly there was silence. The orchestra had stopped playing. Mr Gilbert had halted the performance. He turned to the man, who was seated in the front row, and said:

'Are you going to turn it off? Will you do that?'

There was some 'discussion' between the conductor and the cellphone owner, but we couldn't hear it.

In the Avery Fisher Hall, many members of the audience stood and demanded that the man leave the hall. They were so furious that I could have imagined them dragging him from his seat on to the stage, tying him to a stake, and setting him alight!

When the 'power off' button on the man's phone had finally been located and put to use, Mr Gilbert turned to the audience. 'Usually, when there's a disturbance like this, it's best to ignore it,' he said. 'But this time I could not allow it.'

The audience applauded as if Mahler himself, the orchestra's conductor from 1909 to 1911, had suddenly been resurrected onstage. Mr Gilbert neither smiled nor acknowledged the cheers. Instead he turned to the orchestra, instructing the players to resume, several bars back from the point at which he had stopped the performance. Just before, he raised his baton and turned again to the audience and said, this time with a smile, 'We'll start again.' A few seconds later, the fourth movement resumed.

Mr Gilbert's brave decision that night brought new music to the Philharmonic.

Adapted from The New York Times

cellphone (*AmE*) mobile phone

b Read the text again and answer the questions.

1. In what part of the symphony did the phone ring? What kind of ringtone was it?
2. Did the owner turn it off immediately?
3. How did the audience react a) to the phone ringing, and b) to what the conductor did?
4. Did the audience really drag the man onto the stage?
5. Did Mr Gilbert restart the music from the same place where he had stopped?
6. Does the journalist think Mr Gilbert made the right decision?

c Choose five new words or phrases from the text. Check their meaning and pronunciation and try to learn them.

VIDEO CAN YOU UNDERSTAND THESE PEOPLE?

2 50 **In the street** Watch or listen to five people and answer the questions.

Christopher

Maria

Harry

Sean

Liz

1. Christopher likes using the subway because ______.
   a he only needs to take one train
   b he gets to work in less than half an hour
   c it runs all day and night
2. Maria thinks that women are better than men at looking after young children because ______.
   a they have had a lot of practice
   b they know when children are hungry
   c they know what to do when children are ill
3. Harry says that men in her family ______.
   a don't enjoy telling stories
   b talk about the same things as women
   c try to talk about things that interest them
4. Sean ______.
   a started learning yoga three years ago
   b can touch his toes
   c is thinking of giving up yoga
5. It annoys Liz when people ______.
   a make phone calls all the time
   b play games on their phones
   c use their phones when they are with other people

CAN YOU SAY THIS IN ENGLISH?

Do the tasks with a partner. Tick (✓) the box if you can do them.

Can you...?

1. ☐ compare different methods of public transport in your town / country
2. ☐ agree or disagree with this statement, and say why: *All towns and cities should have a lot more cycle lanes.*
3. ☐ talk about typical stereotypes about men and women, and say if you think they are true
4. ☐ describe something you would like to be able to do, but have never been able to
5. ☐ talk about things which are / aren't good manners in your country if you are staying with someone as a guest, and what you think is the right thing to do

VIDEO **Short films** Boris Bikes
Watch and enjoy this film
www.oup.com/elt/englishfile

Why did he lose the match?

Because he wasn't feeling very well in the last set.

5A Sporting superstitions

1 VOCABULARY sport

a Do the quiz in small groups.

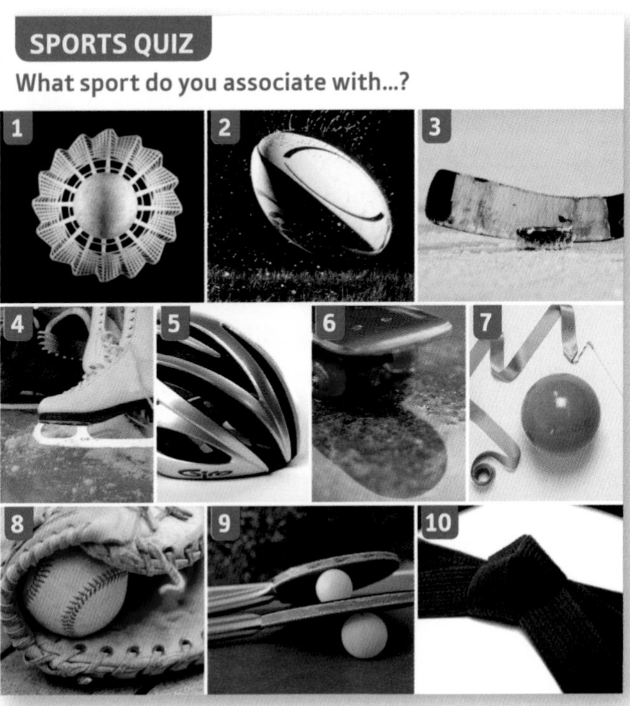

b ➤ **p.157 Vocabulary Bank** *Sport.*

2 PRONUNCIATION /ɔː/ and /ɜː/

a Write the words in the correct column. Be careful with *or* (there are two possible pronunciations).

ball caught court draw fought hurt score
serve shirt sport warm up world worse work out

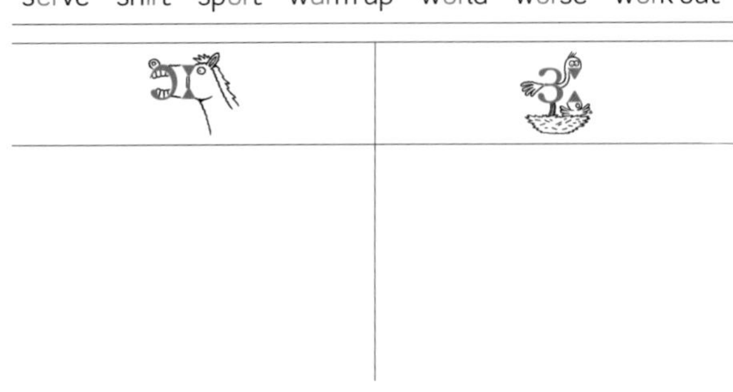

b 3 6 Listen and check.

c ➤ **p.166 Sound Bank.** Look at the typical spellings of these sounds.

d 3 7 Listen and write six sentences.

3 SPEAKING

In pairs, interview your partner about sport using the questionnaire. Ask for more information.

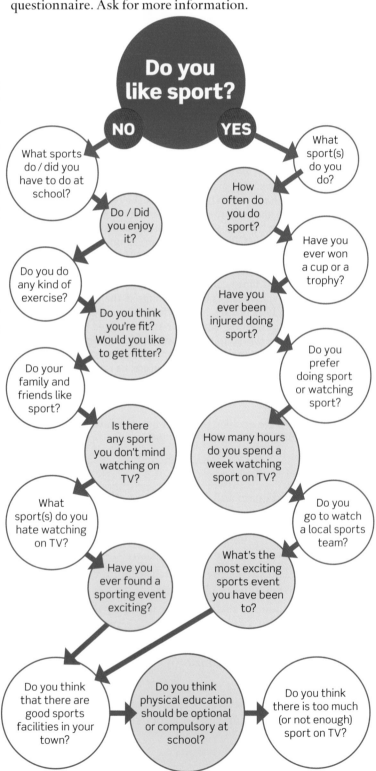

Do you like sport?

NO

- What sports do / did you have to do at school?
- Do / Did you enjoy it?
- Do you do any kind of exercise?
- Do you think you're fit? Would you like to get fitter?
- Do your family and friends like sport?
- Is there any sport you don't mind watching on TV?
- What sport(s) do you hate watching on TV?
- Have you ever found a sporting event exciting?

YES

- What sport(s) do you do?
- How often do you do sport?
- Have you ever won a cup or a trophy?
- Have you ever been injured doing sport?
- Do you prefer doing sport or watching sport?
- How many hours do you spend a week watching sport on TV?
- Do you go to watch a local sports team?
- What's the most exciting sports event you have been to?

Both

- Do you think that there are good sports facilities in your town?
- Do you think physical education should be optional or compulsory at school?
- Do you think there is too much (or not enough) sport on TV?

4 READING

a Do you know of any sports players who are superstitious? What do they do?

b Read an article about sport superstitions and complete it with **A–F**.

A It is not only the players who are superstitious
B A good example is Serena Williams
C Superstitions and rituals are very common among fans
D After my wife had left the room, Murray lost the fourth set
E The superstitions and rituals are not confined to the court
F ~~Tennis players are strange people~~

c Read the article again. Who does the article say are superstitious: sports players, sports fans, TV spectators, or all of them?

d Underline five words or phrases you want to remember from the article.

e Look at the photos of four more famous sports people who are superstitious. Do you know what any of their superstitions are or were?

Tiger Woods

Laurent Blanc

Kolo Touré

Alexander Wurz

f ➤ **Communication** *Other sporting superstitions* **A** *p.104* **B** *p.108*. Read and tell each other about the people in the photos.

g Do *you* have any superstitions, e.g. when you are playing or watching sport, or before an exam?

If I bounce the ball five times...

MATTHEW SYED writes about sporting superstitions

1 *Tennis players are strange people*. Have you noticed how they always ask for three balls instead of two; how they bounce the ball the same number of times before serving, as if any change from their routine might result in disaster?

2 ________________, the ex-world number 1 female tennis player. When she was once asked why she had played so badly at the French Open she answered, 'I didn't tie my shoe laces right and I didn't bounce the ball five times and I didn't bring my shower sandals to the court with me. I didn't have my extra dress. I just knew it was fate; it wasn't going to happen.'

3 ________________. Goran Ivanišević, Wimbledon champion in 2001, was convinced that if he won a match he had to repeat everything he did the previous day, such as eating the same food at the same restaurant, talking to the same people and watching the same TV programmes. One year this meant that he had to watch *Teletubbies* every morning during his Wimbledon campaign. 'Sometimes it got very boring,' he said.

4 ________________. As we were watching British tennis player Andy Murray play the fourth set at Wimbledon, my wife suddenly got up and went to the kitchen. 'He keeps losing games when I'm in the room,' she said. 'If I go out now, he'll win.'

5 ________________. Last year, a survey of British football supporters found that 21 per cent had a lucky charm (anything from a scarf to a lucky coin), while another questionnaire revealed that 70 per cent of Spanish football fans performed pre-match rituals (like wearing 'lucky' clothes, eating the same food or drink, or watching matches with the same people).

6 ________________. She returned, and he won the fifth. I laughed at her, and then remembered my football team, Spurs, who were losing 1–0 in the Carling Cup. 'If I leave the room now, Spurs will score,' I told my kids, after 27 minutes of extra time. I left the room and they scored. Twice.

Glossary
Teletubbies a British television series for very young children
Spurs Tottenham Hotspur, a London football team

Adapted from The Times

5 LISTENING

a In your country, are referees a) well-paid b) respected c) unpopular? Why do you think somebody would want to become a referee?

b 3 8 You're going to hear an interview with an ex-Champions League football referee from Spain. Listen to **Part 1** and choose a, b, or c.

Juan Antonio Fernandez Marin refereed 200 league and 50 international matches

1 Why did he become a referee?
   a His father was a referee.
   b He liked sport, but wasn't good at it.
   c He was always attracted by the idea.
2 What was the most exciting match he ever refereed?
   a His first professional match.
   b He can't choose just one.
   c Real Madrid against Barcelona.
3 The worst experience he ever had as a referee was when _______ attacked him.
   a a player   b a woman   c a child
4 Why does he think there is more cheating in football today?
   a Because football is big business.
   b Because the referees are worse.
   c Because footballers are better at cheating.
5 How does he say footballers often cheat?
   a They fall over when no one has touched them.
   b They accept money to lose matches.
   c They touch the ball with their hands.

c 3 9 Now listen to **Part 2**. Complete the sentences with one to three words.

1 The most difficult thing for him about being a referee is making _______________ during a match.
2 One of the reasons why it's difficult is because football today is so _______________.
3 Making correct decisions often depends on the referee's interpretation of _______________.
4 He thinks that players who cheat are still _______________.
5 A study that was done on Leo Messi shows that he can run exceptionally fast _______________.
6 He thinks Messi isn't the _______________ footballer.

d Do you agree with the referee that there is more cheating in football than before? Is it true in other sports as well? Would *you* like to be a sports referee (or umpire)? Why (not)?

6 GRAMMAR past tenses: simple, continuous, perfect

a In your country, is cheating considered a serious problem in sport? In what sports do you think cheating is most common? What kind of things do people do when they cheat?

b Read *Taking a short cut* about a marathon runner who cheated. How did she cheat?

c Look at the highlighted verbs in the text. Which of them are used for...?

1 a completed action in the past
2 an action that happened *before* the past time we are talking about
3 an action in progress (or not) at a particular moment in the past

d ➤ p.140 Grammar Bank 5A. Learn more about past tenses and practise them.

e Read *The hand of God?* and complete it with the verbs in the right tenses.

Famous (cheating) moments in sport

Although it isn't true that everybody in sport cheats, it is certainly true that there are cheats in every sport...

Taking a short cut

On 21 April 1980, 23-year-old Rosie Ruiz was the first woman to cross the finish line at the Boston Marathon. She finished the race in the third-fastest time for a female runner (two hours, 31 minutes, 56 seconds). But when the organizers congratulated Rosie after the race, they were surprised because she wasn't sweating very much. Some spectators who were watching the race told them what had really happened. During the last half mile Rosie suddenly jumped out of the crowd and sprinted to the finish line. The marathon organizers took Ruiz's title away and awarded it to the real winner, Jacqueline Gareau. It was later discovered that three months earlier Rosie had also cheated in the New York Marathon where she had taken the subway!

The hand of God?

It was 22 June 1986. Argentina 1 *were playing* (play) England in the quarter-finals of the World Cup and both teams 2 ________ (play) well. The score 3 ________ (be) 0–0. In the 51st minute the Argentinian captain, Diego Maradona, 4 ________ (score) a goal. The English players 5 ________ (protest), but the referee 6 ________ (give) the goal. However, TV cameras showed that Maradona 7 ________ (score) the goal with his hand! Maradona 8 ________ (say) the next day, 'It was partly the hand of Maradona, and partly the hand of God.'

Later in the game Maradona 9 ________ (score) another goal and Argentina 10 ________ (win) the match 2–1. They went on to win the World Cup.

7 SPEAKING

a You are going to tell your partner two anecdotes. Choose two of the topics below and plan what you are going to say. Ask your teacher for any words you need.

TELL YOUR PARTNER ABOUT...

- **a time you cheated (in a sport / game or in an exam)**
  When and where did this happen? What were you doing? Why did you cheat? What happened in the end?

- **a really exciting sports event you saw**
  Where and when was it? Who was playing? What happened? Why was it so exciting?
- **a time you had an accident or got a sports injury**
  When and where did this happen? What were you doing? How did the accident happen? What part of your body did you hurt? What happened next? How long did it take you to recover?

- **a time you saw or met a celebrity**
  When was this? Where were you? Who were you with? What was the celebrity doing? What was he / she wearing? Did you speak to him / her? What happened in the end?
- **a time you got lost**
  Where were you going? How were you travelling? Why did you get lost? What happened in the end?

b Work with a partner. Tell each other your two stories. Give as much detail as you can.

Starting an anecdote
I'm going to tell you about a time when...
This happened a few years ago...
When I was younger...

8 WRITING

➤ **p.116 Writing** *Telling a story.* Write a story about something that happened to you.

9 3 14)) SONG *We Are the Champions* ♫

G *usually* and *used to*
V relationships
P linking, the letter *s*

How do you usually get to work?

I used to take the bus, but now I cycle.

5B Love at Exit 19

1 READING

a How do you think people usually meet friends and partners nowadays? Number the phrases 1–5 (1 = the most popular). Then compare with a partner. Do you agree?

A ☐ at work
B ☐ at school or university
C ☐ on the internet (e.g. on forums, on social networking sites, etc.)
D ☐ in a bar, club, etc.
E ☐ through friends

b 3 15 Read and listen to an article about Sonya Baker and Michael Fazio. Why did their relationship nearly never happen?

❤ Love at Exit 19

He was a tollbooth operator, she was a soprano who sang in Carnegie Hall. Their eyes met at Exit 19 of the New York State Thruway, when he charged her 37¢. The romance that followed was even less likely than the plot of an opera!

Sonya Baker was a frequent commuter from her home in the suburbs to New York City. One day, when she was driving to an audition, she came off the Thruway and stopped at the tollbooth where Michael Fazio was working. She chatted to him as she paid to go through, and thought he was cute. For the next three months, they used to exchange a few words as she handed him the money, and he raised the barrier to let her pass. 'It was mostly "What are you doing today? Where are you going?"' she said. They learned more about each other, for example that Sonya loved Puccini and Verdi, while Michael's love was the New York Yankees. But their conversations suddenly came to an end when Michael changed his working hours. 'He used to work during the day,' said Sonya, 'but he changed to night shifts.' Although Michael still looked out for Sonya's white Toyota Corolla, he did not see her again for six months.

When Michael's working hours changed back to the day shift, he decided to put a traffic cone in front of his lane. He thought, 'It will be like putting a candle in a window.' Sonya saw it, and their romance started up again. 'I almost crashed my car on various occasions,' she said, 'trying to cross several lanes to get to his exit.' Finally, she found the courage to give Michael a piece of paper with her phone number as she passed through the toll. Michael called her and for their first date they went to see the film *Cool Runnings*, and then later they went to an opera, *La Bohème*, and to a Yankees game.

They are now married and living in Kentucky, where Sonya is a voice and music professor at Murray State College and Michael runs an activity centre at a nursing home. It turned out that she had given him her number just in time. A short while later she moved to New Jersey and stopped using the New York State Thruway. 'I might never have seen him again,' she said.

Glossary
a tollbooth a small building by the side of a road where you pay money to use the road
Carnegie Hall a famous concert hall in New York City
New York State Thruway a motorway
New York Yankees a baseball team based in the Bronx in New York
a traffic cone a plastic object, often red and white, used to show where vehicles can or can't go

Adapted from The Times

c Read the article again and number the events in the order they happened.

A ☐ Michael changed his working hours.
B ☐ Michael tried to find Sonya.
C ☐ They got married.
D ☐ Sonya moved to New Jersey.
E ☐ Sonya gave Michael her phone number.
F ☐ Michael changed his working hours again.
G *1* Sonya chatted to Michael.
H ☐ They stopped seeing each other.
I ☐ They had their first date.
J ☐ Sonya and Michael moved to Kentucky.

d Read the article again and look at the highlighted words and phrases. Try to work out what they mean. Then match them with 1–10 below.

1 __________ a period of time worked by a group of workers
2 __________ a person who travels into a city to work every day
3 __________ attractive, good-looking (*AmE*)
4 __________ what had happened was
5 __________ manages
6 __________ probable
7 __________ sth which is used to give light, made of wax
8 __________ have short conversations
9 __________ they looked at each other romantically
10 __________ was brave enough

2 GRAMMAR *usually* and *used to*

a Think of a couple you know well, e.g. your parents or friends. How did they meet? Do you know any couples who met in unusual circumstances?

b **3 16** Listen to four people talking about where they met their partner. Match each one with a place from **1a**.

Speaker 1 ☐ Speaker 2 ☐ Speaker 3 ☐ Speaker 4 ☐

c Listen to each story again and take notes on how the people met. Compare your notes with your partner and listen again if necessary. Which meeting do you think was the most romantic?

d Look at two extracts from the listening. Answer the questions with a partner.

We used to go to bars and clubs together on Saturday night.
It used to be quite difficult to meet people.

1 When do we use *used to*? How do you make negatives and questions?
2 How would you change these sentences (using *usually*) if you wanted to talk about present habits or situations?

e ➤ **p.141 Grammar Bank 5B.** Learn more about *usually* and *used to*, and practise them.

3 PRONUNCIATION & SPEAKING linking

used to
Remember that *used to* and *use to* are normally linked and pronounced /juːstə/.

a **3 18** Listen and repeat the sentences. Copy the linking and the sentence rhythm.

1 I **used**‿to **live**‿in **London**.
2 She **didn't use**‿to **wear glasses**.
3 **Where** did you **use**‿to **work before**?
4 They **used**‿to **see each**‿**other**‿a **lot**.
5 **Didn't** you **use**‿to **have**‿a **beard**?

b In pairs, tell each other about *three* of the following. Give as much information as you can. How do you feel about these people and things now?

- a kind of **food** or **drink** you didn't use to like at all, but which you now like?
- a **TV series** you used to be addicted to? Why did you like it?
- a **singer** or a **kind of music** you used to listen to a lot (but don't any more)?
- a **sport** or **game** you used to play a lot, but which you've given up?
- a **place** you used to go in the summer holidays, and which you'd like to go back to?
- a **machine** or **gadget** you used to use a lot, but which is now out of date?

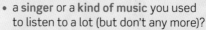

I used to hate most vegetables, especially spinach and cauliflower, but now I love them and usually eat a lot of vegetables every day...

4 **VOCABULARY** relationships

a Explain the difference between these pairs of phrases.

1 to meet somebody and to know somebody
2 a colleague and a friend
3 to argue with somebody and to discuss something with somebody

b ➤ **p.158 Vocabulary Bank** *Relationships.*

c Think of one of your close friends. In pairs, ask and answer the questions.

- How long have you known him / her?
- Where did you meet?
- Why do you get on well?
- What do you have in common?
- Do you ever argue? What about?
- How often do you see each other?
- How do you keep in touch?
- Have you ever lost touch? Why? When?
- Do you think you'll stay friends?

5 **PRONUNCIATION** the letter *s*

a **3 21** Listen to the words in the list. How is the *s* (or *se*) pronounced? Write them in the correct columns.

busy close (*adj*) close (*verb*) conversation decision discuss eyes friends lose music pleasure practise raise school somebody sport sugar summer sure unusual used to usually various

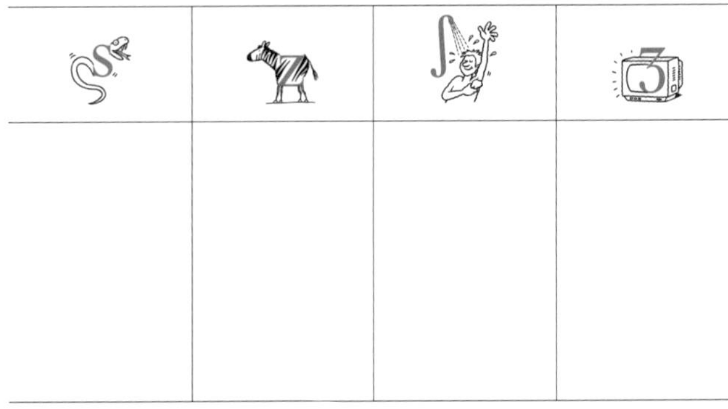

b **3 22** Listen and check.

c Answer with a partner.

1 How is *s* usually pronounced at the beginning of a word? What are the two exceptions?
2 What two ways can *s* (or *es*) be pronounced at the end of a word?
3 How is *s* pronounced in *-sion*?

6 LISTENING

a Talk to a partner. Do you think the following are **T** (true) or **F** (false)?

1 22-year-olds have an average of 1,000 friends.
2 Men have more online friends than women.
3 People who spend a lot of time on *Facebook* become more dissatisfied with their own lives.

b **3 23** Listen to the introduction to a radio programme. According to research, are 1–3 in **a** true or false?

c **3 24** Listen to four people who phone the programme, George, Beth, Caitlin, and Ned. Who is the most positive about *Facebook*? Who is the most negative?

d Listen again. Answer with **G**eorge, **B**eth, **C**aitlin, or **N**ed.

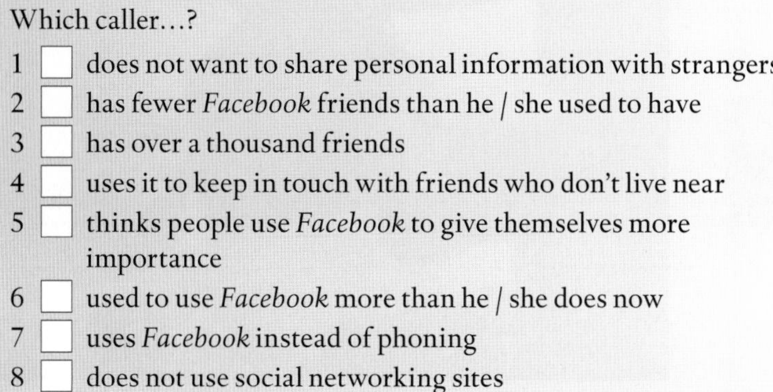

Which caller...?

1 ☐ does not want to share personal information with strangers
2 ☐ has fewer *Facebook* friends than he / she used to have
3 ☐ has over a thousand friends
4 ☐ uses it to keep in touch with friends who don't live near
5 ☐ thinks people use *Facebook* to give themselves more importance
6 ☐ used to use *Facebook* more than he / she does now
7 ☐ uses *Facebook* instead of phoning
8 ☐ does not use social networking sites

e Do you use *Facebook* or any other social networking sites? Do you agree with anything the speakers said?

7 SPEAKING

a Read sentences **A–F** below. Tick (✓) the ones you agree with and cross (✗) the ones you don't agree with. Think about your reasons.

A ☐ You can only have two or three close friends.
B ☐ Nowadays people are in touch with more people but have fewer close friends.
C ☐ Men keep their friends longer than women.
D ☐ You should never criticize your friend's partner.
E ☐ You should never lend money to a friend (or borrow money).
F ☐ It's impossible to stay good friends with an ex-partner.

b In groups, compare opinions. Try to give real examples from your own experience or of people you know. Use the phrases below to help you.

Giving examples

For example, I have a friend who I've known since I was five years old...

For instance, I once lent some money to a cousin...

Practical English Old friends

EPISODE 3

1 VIDEO JENNY HAS COFFEE WITH A FRIEND

a 3 25))) Watch or listen to Jenny and Monica. What's Monica's news?

b Watch or listen again and answer the questions.

1 Who's Scott?
2 When did they get engaged?
3 Who has Monica told the news to?
4 What did she use to do a lot at night? What does she do now?
5 Who's going to organize the wedding?
6 What does Jenny tell Monica about her relationship with Rob?
7 What does Monica think about Rob being British?

2 VIDEO PERMISSION AND REQUESTS

a 3 26))) Watch or listen. What two favours does Rob ask Jenny?

b Watch or listen again. Mark the sentences **T** (true) or **F** (false). Correct the **F** sentences.

1 Rob orders a cappuccino.
2 Rob says Monica looks different from her photos.
3 Monica gets a good impression of Rob.
4 Monica leaves because she has to go to work.
5 Jenny says that most of their friends are in serious relationships.
6 Paul is going to stay for a fortnight.
7 Paul used to be very quiet when they were younger.
8 Jenny is keen to meet Paul.

c 3 27 Look at some extracts from the conversation. Can you remember any of the missing words? Watch or listen and check.

Asking permission

1	**Rob**	Do you ________ if I join you?
	Monica	Of ________ not. Come on, sit down.
2	**Rob**	Is it ________ if we change our plans a bit this week?
	Jenny	Er...sure.

Requests: asking someone to do something

1	**Rob**	________ you pass the sugar?
	Jenny	________.
2	**Rob**	Could you do me a big ________? I have to work late this evening, so... would you mind ________ him at the airport?
	Jenny	________ at all. I'd like to meet him.
3	**Rob**	And do you think you ________ take him to my flat? I'll give you the keys.
	Jenny	No ________, Rob.

d Look at the highlighted phrases and answer the questions.

1 How do you respond to *Do you mind if...?* and *Would you mind...?* when you mean *OK, no problem?*

2 Which two forms of request should you use if you want to be very polite or are asking a very big favour?

e 3 28 Watch or listen and repeat the highlighted phrases. Copy the rhythm and intonation.

f Practise the dialogues in **c** with a partner.

g **Communication** *Could you do me a favour?* *p.105.*

3 PAUL ARRIVES

VIDEO

a 3 29 Watch or listen. How do Rob and Jenny feel about Paul's arrival?

b Watch or listen again and circle the right answer.

1 Paul's appearance *has changed a lot* | *hasn't changed much.*

2 His flight was *on time* | *late.*

3 On the journey from the airport Paul *talked a lot about himself* | *asked Jenny a lot of personal questions.*

4 Rob suggests *eating in* | *eating out.*

5 Paul feels *exhausted* | *full of energy.*

6 Jenny *feels like* | *doesn't feel like* going out.

c Look at the **Social English phrases**. Can you remember any of the missing words?

Social English phrases

Paul	Hey ________!
Paul	It's great to see you, ________.
Rob	How ________ you're so late?
Paul	No ________, man!
Jenny	Rob, I think I'll go home if you don't ________.
Rob	Just like the old ________!
Paul	Rob, we've got a lot to talk ________!

d 3 30 Watch or listen and complete the phrases.

e Watch or listen again and repeat the phrases. How do you say them in your language?

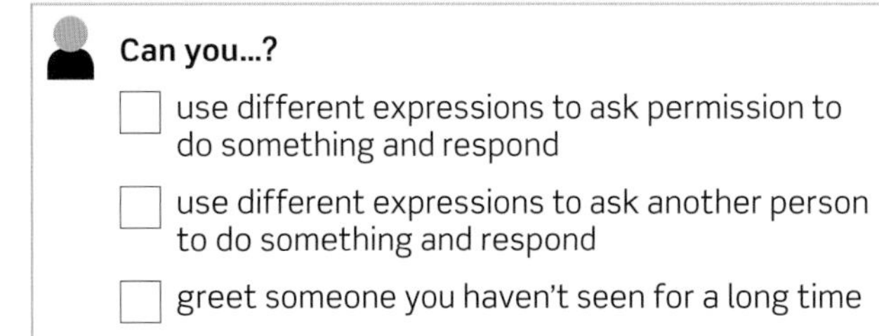

Can you...?

- [ ] use different expressions to ask permission to do something and respond
- [ ] use different expressions to ask another person to do something and respond
- [ ] greet someone you haven't seen for a long time

Communication

PE1 HOW AWFUL! HOW FANTASTIC! Student A

a Read your sentences 1–9 to **B**. **B** must react with a phrase, e.g. *You're kidding, Oh no!* etc.

1. I collect old English tea cups.
2. I spilled some coffee on my laptop last night and now it doesn't work.
3. I'm going to New York next weekend.
4. Someone stole my bike yesterday.
5. My dog can open the kitchen door by himself.
6. My father's going to be interviewed on TV tomorrow.
7. My grandmother's just bought a sports car.
8. My parents met when they were only 15.
9. I've just won €2,000 in the lottery!

b Listen to **B**'s sentences and react with a phrase.

c Tell **B** some real (or invented) news about you for **B** to react. React to **B**'s news.

5A OTHER SPORTING SUPERSTITIONS Student A

a Read about Tiger Woods and Kolo Touré.

TIGER WOODS always wears a red shirt on the last day of a golf tournament. It's a routine he has followed since he was eight and he believes it makes him play more aggressively.

When **KOLO TOURÉ** played for Arsenal, he always insisted on being the last player to leave the dressing room after the half-time break. This was never usually a problem. However, in one match when William Gallas, his teammate, was injured and needed treatment at half-time during a match, Touré stayed in the dressing room until Gallas had been treated. This meant that Arsenal had to start the second half with only nine players.

b Now cover the text and tell **B** about their superstitions from memory.

c Listen to **B** telling you about Laurent Blanc and Alexander Wurz's superstitions.

d Together decide which superstition you think is a) the strangest b) the most impractical.

2B ARE YOU HUNGRY? Student A

a Ask **B** your questions. He / she must respond with the phrase in brackets.

1. Is the water cold? (Yes, it's **freezing**.)
2. Was the film good? (Yes, it was **fantastic**.)
3. Were you tired after the exam? (Yes, I was **exhausted**.)
4. Was the room dirty? (Yes, it was **filthy**.)
5. Is it a big house? (Yes, it's **enormous**.)
6. Were you surprised? (Yes, I was **amazed**.)
7. Are you sure? (Yes, I'm **positive**.)

b Respond to **B**'s questions. Say *Yes, it's... / I'm...*, etc. + the strong form of the adjective which **B** used in the question. Remember to stress the strong adjective.

Are you afraid of flying? *Yes, I'm terrified.*

c Repeat the exercise. Try to respond as quickly as possible.

3A I'M A TOURIST – CAN YOU HELP ME? Student A

a Think of the town / city where you are, or the nearest big town. You are a foreign tourist and you are planning to get around using public transport. Ask **B** questions 1–5. Get as much information from **B** as you can.

1. What kind of public transport is there?
2. What's the best way for me to get around the city?
3. Can I hire a bike? Are there any cycle lanes?
4. Is it easy to find taxis? How expensive are they?
5. What's the best way to get to the airport from the town centre? How long does it take?

b Swap roles. **B** is a foreign tourist in the town, who has hired a car. You live in the town. Answer **B**'s questions and give as much information as you can.

PE3 COULD YOU DO ME A FAVOUR? Students A+B

a Look at the verb phrases below. Choose two things you would like somebody to do for you. Think about any details, e.g. what kind of dog it is, how much money you need, etc.

- **look after** (your children, your dog for the weekend, your flat while you're away, etc.)
- **lend you** (some money, their car, etc.)
- **give you a lift** (home, to the town centre, etc.)
- **help you** (with a problem, with your homework, to paint your flat, to choose some new clothes, etc.)

b Ask as many other students as possible. Be polite (*Could you do me a big favour? Would you mind...? Do you think you could...?*) and explain why you want the favour. How many people agree to help you?

4A GUESS THE SENTENCE Student A

a Look at sentences 1–6 and think of the correct form of *be able to* + a verb. **Don't write anything yet!**

1 I'm sorry I won't ________________ to your party next weekend.
2 It was August, but we ________________ a hotel without any problems.
3 I used to __________ a little Japanese, but I can't now.
4 I love ________________ in bed late at the weekend.
5 Will you ______________ the work before Saturday?
6 I've never __________________________ fish well.

b Read your sentence 1 to **B**. If it isn't right, try again until **B** tells you, 'That's right'. Then write it in. Continue with 2–6.

c Now listen to **B** say sentence 7. If it's the same as your sentence 7 below, say 'That's right'. If not, say 'Try again' until **B** gets it right. Continue with 8–12.

7 It must be fantastic to **be able to speak** a lot of languages.
8 I won't **be able to see** you tonight. I'm too busy.
9 My grandmother can't walk very well, but luckily we **were able to park** just outside the restaurant.
10 They haven't **been able to find** a flat yet. They're still looking.
11 You should **be able to do** this exercise. It's very easy.
12 We really enjoy **being able to eat** outside in the summer.

4B THE BIG DAY Students A+B

Read a newspaper article about what happened at Heidi and Freddie's wedding. Do you think they behaved well or badly? Why?

News online

Mother-in-law from hell... What happened next...

By NEWS ONLINE **Reporter**

Yesterday Heidi Withers married Freddie Bourne in a £25,000 ceremony at St Mary the Virgin Church in Berkeley, Gloucestershire. It was followed by a reception at 900-year-old Berkeley Castle. However, there was no sign of Carolyn, Freddie's stepmother, the woman who was ridiculed for the email she sent Heidi. She and her husband Edward, Freddie's father, were not invited.

Heidi arrived almost 25 minutes late for the ceremony, which was due to begin at 2.45 p.m. Perhaps, as Carolyn suggested was her habit, she had been in bed until the last possible minute. She arrived at the church with security guards holding umbrellas to prevent onlookers from catching sight of her, and with her head covered. This is a well-known tactic for celebrities, but for a 29-year-old secretary it seemed, in the words of one onlooker, 'a bit ridiculous'.

Edward and Carolyn admitted being disappointed at not receiving an invitation. They spent the weekend on a walking holiday with friends. They have had no contact with the couple since the saga began, and did not even know the date of the wedding.

5A OTHER SPORTING SUPERSTITIONS Student B

a Read about Laurent Blanc and Alexander Wurz.

LAURENT BLANC, the French football captain, kissed the head of the goalkeeper Fabien Barthez before each game at the 1998 World Cup. France won, but Blanc was suspended and didn't play in the final.

ALEXANDER WURZ, an Austrian racing driver, used to race with odd-coloured shoes, the left one red and the right one blue. It came about when he lost a shoe before a big race and had to borrow one of a different colour. After winning the race, he decided it was a lucky omen.

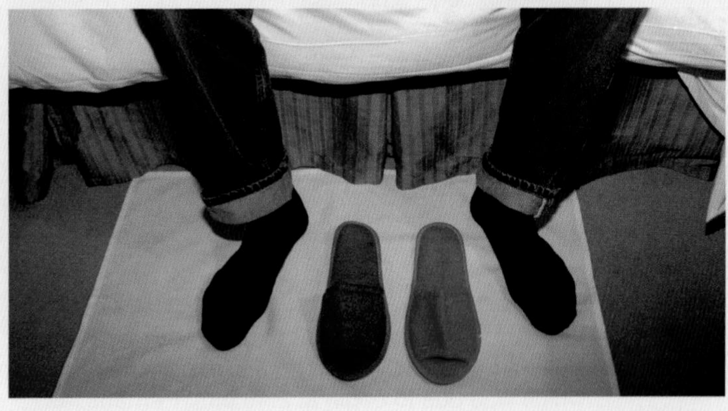

b Now listen to **A** telling you about Tiger Woods and Kolo Touré's superstitions.

c Cover the text and tell **B** about Laurent Blanc and Alexander Wurz's superstitions from memory.

d Together decide which superstition you think is a) the strangest b) the most impractical.

1B PERSONALITY Students A+B

Read the explanation and compare with a partner. Do you agree with your results?

The activity you have just done is a personality test. The first adjective you wrote down is how you see yourself, the second is how other people see you, and the third is what you are really like.

2A SPENDER OR SAVER? Students A+B

Check your results, then compare with a partner. Do you agree with your results?

Mostly 'a' answers
You can't be trusted with your own money! You definitely need someone to help you to manage your finances better. Why not speak to an organized friend about how to plan? This will help you to make your money go further and stop you getting into debt.

Mostly 'b' answers
Although you understand how to manage your money, sometimes you need to be a bit more organized. Try setting yourself a weekly or monthly budget, then keep to it. You will then know how much money you have, what you spend it on, and how much you can save.

Mostly 'c' answers
Congratulations! It sounds like you really know what you are doing when it comes to managing your money. You know how important it is to keep track of your spending and are responsible with your money.

PE1 HOW AWFUL! HOW FANTASTIC! Student B

a Listen to **A**'s sentences and react with a phrase, e.g. *You're kidding, Oh no!* etc.

b Read your sentences 1–9 for **A** to react.

1. I failed my driving test yesterday.
2. I lost my wallet on the way to class.
3. I met George Clooney at a party last week.
4. I think I saw a ghost last night.
5. I won a salsa competition last weekend.
6. I'm going to be on a new edition of Big Brother.
7. My dog died yesterday.
8. My grandfather has a black belt in karate.
9. My uncle is 104.

c Tell **A** some real (or invented) news about you for **A** to react. React to **A**'s news.

2B ARE YOU HUNGRY? Student B

a Respond to **A**'s questions. Say *Yes, it's... / I'm...*, etc. + the strong form of the adjective which **A** used in the question. Remember to stress the strong adjective.

Is the water cold? *Yes, it's freezing.*

b Ask **A** your questions. He / she must respond with the phrase in brackets.

1. Are you afraid of flying? (Yes, I'm **terrified**.)
2. Is the soup hot? (Yes, it's **boiling**.)
3. Was the teacher angry? (Yes, he / she was **furious**.)
4. Is the bedroom small? (Yes, it's **tiny**.)
5. Are the children hungry? (Yes, they're **starving**.)
6. Is the chocolate cake nice? (Yes, it's **delicious**.)
7. Was she happy with the present? (Yes, she was **delighted**.)

c Repeat the exercise. Try to respond as quickly as possible.

3A I'M A TOURIST - CAN YOU HELP ME? Student B

a Think of the town / city where you are, or the nearest big town. **A** is a foreign tourist who is planning to get around using public transport. You live in the town. Answer **A**'s questions and give as much information as you can.

b Swap roles. You are a foreign tourist in the town. You have hired a car. Ask **A** questions 1–5. Get as much information from **A** as you can.

1. What time is the rush hour in this town?
2. Where are there often traffic jams?
3. What's the speed limit in the town? Are there speed cameras anywhere?
4. What will happen if I park somewhere illegal?
5. Where's the nearest tourist attraction outside the city? How long does it take to drive there from here?

4A GUESS THE SENTENCE Student B

a Look at sentences 7–12 and think of the correct form of *be able to* + a verb. **Don't write anything yet!**

7. It must be fantastic to ________________ a lot of languages.
8. I won't ________________ you tonight. I'm too busy.
9. My grandmother can't walk very well, but luckily we ________________ just outside the restaurant.
10. They haven't ________________ a flat yet. They're still looking.
11. You should ________________ this exercise. It's very easy.
12. We really enjoy ________________ outside in the summer.

b Now listen to **A** say sentence 1. If it's the same as your sentence 1 below, say 'That's right'. If not, say 'Try again' until **A** gets it right. Continue with 2–6.

1. I'm sorry I won't **be able to come** to your party next weekend.
2. It was August, but we **were able to find** a hotel without any problems.
3. I used to **be able to understand** a little Japanese, but I can't now.
4. I love **being able to stay** in bed late at the weekend.
5. Will you **be able to finish** the work before Saturday?
6. I've never **been able to cook** fish well.

c Read your sentence 7 to **A**. If it isn't right, try again until **A** tells you, 'That's right'. Then write it in. Continue with 8–12.

Writing

1 A DESCRIPTION OF A PERSON

a Read the two *Facebook* messages once and answer the questions.

1 Why has Angela written to Sofia?
2 Does Sofia recommend her friend to Angela?

Messages

+ New Message

Angela Vernon

Hi Sofia,

I hope you're well.

I'm looking for an au pair to look after Mike and Sally, and I remembered your Polish friend Kasia, who I met last summer. She said she might be interested in working in England as an au pair, so I thought I would write and ask her. The thing is, I don't really know her, so before I write and suggest it, could you tell me a bit about her (age, personality, etc., and what she likes doing) so that I can see if she would fit in with the family? Please be honest!

Angela

Sofia Lugo

Hi Angela,

Kasia is one of my best friends, so of course I know her very well. She's 22 and she's just finished economics at university, but she doesn't have a job yet and I'm sure she would be interrested in going to the UK. Her parents are both doctors, and she has two younger brothers. She gets on very well with them and they are a very close family.

Kasia's an intelligent girl and very hard-working. She can be quite shy at first, but when she gets to know you she's incredibly friendly. She loves children – she often looks after her brothers – so she has a lot of experience, and she's also very responsable.

In her free time she likes going to the cinema, listening to music, and she's also very good at fotography – she always has her camera with her. She's really independant and happy to do things on her own, so you won't have to worry about taking her to places.

The only problem with Kasia is that she's a bit forgetfull... she sometimes loses things, like her keys, or her phone. Also, to be honest her English isn't fantastic, but I'm sure she'll improve very quickly. I think Mike and Sally will love her.

I hope this helps! Let me know if you need anything else.

Love,

Sofia

b The computer has found five spelling mistakes in Sofia's email. Can you correct them?

c Read both emails again. Then cover them and answer the questions from memory.

1 What five  adjectives describe Kasia's personality?
2 What does she like doing in her free time?
3 What negative things does Sofia say about Kasia?
4 Does Sofia think Kasia will get on with Angela's family?

d Look at the highlighted expressions we use to modify adjectives. Put them in the correct place in the chart.

Kasia is ______ / ______ / *very* / ______ / ______ forgetful.

Useful language: describing a person

He's quite / very, etc. + positive adjective (e.g. *friendly, outgoing*, etc.)
She's a bit + negative adjective (e.g. *untidy, shy*, etc.)
He likes / loves / doesn't mind + verb + *-ing*
She's happy to + infinitive
He's good **with** *children*
at *making new friends*

e Imagine you received Angela's message asking about a friend of yours. **Write** an email to answer it. **Plan** what you're going to write using the paragraph headings below. Use the **Useful language** box and **Vocabulary Bank** *Personality p.153* to help you.

Paragraph 1	age, family, work / study
Paragraph 2	personality (good side)
Paragraph 3	hobbies and interests
Paragraph 4	any negative things?

f **Check** your email for mistakes (grammar, vocabulary, punctuation, and spelling).

p.11

2 AN INFORMAL EMAIL

a Kasia went to Britain and stayed for six months with a couple, Angela and Matt, working as an au pair. After going back to Poland, she sent them an email. Look at the list of things she says in her email. Number them in a logical order 1–6.

- ☐ She promises to send some photos.
- ☐ She thanks them for her stay and says how much she enjoyed it.
- ☐ She talks about what she's been doing recently.
- ☐ She apologizes for not writing before.
- ☐ She thanks them again and invites them to stay.
- ☐ She talks about the nice things that happened when she was with them.

b Now read Kasia's email and check your answers to **a**.

c Correct eight mistakes in the email (grammar, vocabulary, punctuation, and spelling.)

> **Useful language: informal emails**
>
> **Beginnings**
>
> *Hi* + name (or *Dear* + name if you want to be a bit more formal)
>
> *Sorry for not writing earlier, but...*
>
> *Thank you / Thanks* (so much) *for* (*your letter, having me to stay*, etc.)...
>
> *It was great to hear from you...*
>
> **Endings**
>
> *That's all for now.*
>
> *Hope to hear from you soon. / Looking forward to hearing from you soon.*
>
> (*Give my*) *regards / love to...*
>
> *Best wishes / Love* (*from*)
>
> *PS* (when you want to add a short message at the end of an email) *I've attached a photo...*

d Imagine you have some British friends in the UK, and you stayed with them for a week last month. **Write** an email to say thank you. **Plan** what you're going to say. Use 1–6 in **a** and the **Useful language** box to help you.

e **Check** your email for mistakes (grammar, vocabulary, punctuation, and spelling).

◀ p.21

From: Kasia [kasia_new@redmail.com]
To: Angela [angelav1970@yahoo.com]
Subject: Thanks

Hi Angela,

I'm really sorry for not writing earlier, but I am very busy since I got back!

Thanks for a wonderful six months. I loved being in Chichester, and I had a great time. I also think my english got a bit better... dont you think?

It was so nice to look after Mike and Sally. I thought they were adorable, and I think we had a fantastic time together. I have really good memories – for example our travel to the Isle of Wight and the zoo there!

I've been a bit stressed these last few weeks, because I've started working at a restaurant, while I look for a proper job. Be a waitress is very hard work, but I can now afford to rent a flat with Sofia and two other friends, and I'm saving for to buy a car! I've also spent a lot of time with my family – my brothers have changed so much over the past six months!

I've had several mesages from Mike and Sally since I've been back! Please tell them from me that I miss them and that I send them some photos very soon.

That's all for now. Thanks again for everything. And I hope you know you're welcome in Gdansk at any time – my family would love to meet you. Summer here is usually lovely.

Hope to hear from you soon. Give my regards to Matt!

Best wishes,

Kasia

PS I've attached a photo I took of me with the kids. I hope you like it!

3 AN ARTICLE FOR A MAGAZINE

a Look at the four forms of public transport in London. Which one do you think is probably...?

- the most expensive
- the healthiest
- the best if you want to see the sights of London
- the safest to use late at night

the Tube

double-decker bus

Boris Bike

black taxi

b Read an article from an online magazine for foreign students about public transport in London and check your answers to **a**. Then answer these questions from memory.

1 What can you use an Oyster card for?
2 Why are the bikes you can hire called 'Boris Bikes'?
3 What's the difference between a black taxi and a mini-cab?

c Read the article again and complete the gaps with a preposition from the list.

~~around~~ at in next to off on (x2) on the top of with

> **Useful language: transport in your town**
> *You can buy Oyster cards at tube stations.*
> *You must have a ticket or card before you get on a bus.*
> (*You* = people in general)
>
> **Comparatives and superlatives**
> *Buses aren't as quick as trams.*
> *Cycling is the cheapest way to get around.*

d **Write** an article about transport in your nearest town or city for foreign students. **Plan** what headings you're going to use, and what to say about each form of transport.

e **Check** your article for mistakes (grammar, vocabulary, punctuation, and spelling).

p.27

Transport in London

London Underground (The Tube)

This is the quickest way to get [1]*around* the city and there are many underground stations all over London. The cheapest way to use the underground is to get an Oyster card. This is like a phone card. You put money on it, and then top it up when you need to, and then you use it every time you get [2]________ or [3]________ the Tube. You can buy Oyster cards at tube stations and in newsagents.

Buses

They can be quicker than the underground if there isn't too much traffic. The easiest way to use the buses, like the underground, is to just use your Oyster card. You can also buy tickets from machines [4]________ bus stops. On some buses you can buy a ticket with cash when you get [5]________ the bus. Some of the buses operate 24 hours a day, so you can also use them late at night. Travelling [6]________ a double-decker bus is also a good way to see London.

Bikes

Bikes are now more popular than ever in London, especially [7]________ tourists and people who want to be fit. There are quite a lot of cycle lanes, and bikes that you can hire, nicknamed 'Boris Bikes' after Boris Johnson, the mayor of London. You can use your credit card to hire a bike, and the first 30 minutes are free.

Taxis and Mini-cabs

London's black taxis are expensive, but they are comfortable and the taxi drivers know London very well. You normally tell the driver where you want to go before you get [8]________ the taxi. Mini-cabs are normal cars which work for a company, and which you have to phone. They are much cheaper, but make sure you use a licensed company. Taxis or mini-cabs are probably the safest way to travel late [9]________ night.

4 TELLING A STORY

a A magazine asked its readers to send in stories of a time they got lost. Read the story once. Why did Begoña and her husband get lost? What else went wrong?

b Read the story again and complete it with a connecting word or phrase from the list.

although as soon as because but instead of so ~~then~~ when

Useful language: getting lost

We were going in the wrong direction.
We took the wrong exit / turning.
We turned right instead of left.
We didn't know where we were.
We had to turn round and go back in the opposite direction.

c **Write** about a journey where you got lost (or invent one) to send to the magazine. **Plan** what you're going to write using the paragraph headings below. Use the **Useful language** to help you.

Paragraph 1	When was the journey? Where were you going? Who with? Why?
Paragraph 2	How did you get lost? What happened?
Paragraph 3	What happened in the end?

d **Check** your story for mistakes (grammar, vocabulary, punctuation, and spelling).

p.47

DISASTROUS JOURNEYS!

We asked you to tell us about a time you got lost. Begoña from Spain wrote to us...

This happened a few years ago. I live in Alicante, in Spain and my husband and I had rented a house in Galicia for the summer holiday. We were going to first drive to Tarragona, to stay for a few days with some friends, and [1] *then* drive from Tarragona to Galicia.

The first part of the journey was fine. We were using our new satnav for the first time, and it took us right to the door of our friends' house. Three days later, [2] ________ we continued our journey, we put in the name of the small town in Galicia, Nigrán, which was our final destination. We started off, obediently following the instructions, but after a while we realized that [3] ________ driving west towards Lleida, we were going north. In fact, soon we were quite near Andorra. I was sure we were going in the wrong direction, [4] ________ my husband wanted to do what the satnav was telling us – it was his new toy! It was only when we started seeing mountains that even he admitted this couldn't be the right way. [5] ________ we stopped, got out an old map, and then turned round! We had wasted nearly two hours going in the wrong direction!

It was an awful journey [6] ________ as well as getting lost, when we were nearly at our destination we had another problem. We stopped for a coffee at a little bar, but [7] ________ we got back onto the motorway we realized that we had left our dog under the table in the café! For the second time that day we had to turn round and go back. Luckily, the dog was still there! However, [8] ________ the beginning of our trip was a disaster, we had a wonderful holiday!

Listening

1 6

A I usually have meat or seafood. Usually prawns or something as a starter and then maybe lamb for the main course.

B I quite often have ready-made vegetable soups that you only have to heat up – in fact they're the only vegetables I ever eat! And I usually have a couple of frozen pizzas in the freezer for emergencies. I don't really order take-away when I'm on my own, but if I'm with friends in the evening, we sometimes order Chinese food for dinner.

C Eggs and Coke. I have eggs for breakfast at least twice a week and I drink a couple of cans of Coke every day.

D If I'm feeling down, chicken soup, with nice big pieces of chicken in it. It's warm and comforting. I usually have a banana before going to the gym. If I know I'm going to have a really long meeting, I usually have a coffee and a cake because I think it will keep me awake and give me energy.

E Fruit – cherries, strawberries, raspberries and apples. Vegetables – peppers, tomatoes, and cucumbers. The only thing I really don't like is beetroot. I can't even stand the smell of it.

1 7

Part 1

Interviewer What was your favourite food when you were a child?

Steve Well, I always liked unusual things, at least things that most English children at the time didn't like. For instance, when I was six or seven my favourite things were snails, oh and prawns with garlic.

Interviewer Funny things for a six-year-old English boy to like!

Steve Well, the thing is my parents liked travelling and eating out a lot, and I first tried snails in France, and the prawns, my first prawns I had at a Spanish restaurant in the town where we lived.

Interviewer So you were keen on Spanish food right from the start. Is that why you decided to come to Spain?

Steve Partly, but of course, I suppose like a lot of British people I wanted to see the sun! The other thing that attracted me when I got here were all the fantastic ingredients. I remember going into the market for the first time and saying 'Wow!'

Interviewer When you opened your restaurant, how did you want it to be different from typical Spanish restaurants?

Steve Well, when I came to Spain, all the good restaurants were very formal, very traditional. In London then, the fashion was for informal places where the waiters wore jeans, but the food was amazing. So I wanted a restaurant a bit like that. I also wanted a restaurant where you could try more international food, but made with some of these fantastic local ingredients. For example, Spain's got wonderful seafood, but usually here it's just grilled or fried. I started doing things in my restaurant like cooking Valencian mussels in Thai green curry paste.

Interviewer What do you most enjoy cooking?

Steve What I most enjoy cooking, I think, are those traditional dishes which use quite cheap ingredients, but they need very long and careful cooking, and then you turn it into something really special... like a really good casserole, for example.

Interviewer And is there anything you don't like cooking?

Steve Maybe desserts. You have to be very very precise when you're making desserts. And that's not the way I am.

1 8

Part 2

Interviewer What's the best thing about running a restaurant?

Steve I think the best thing is making people happy. That's why even after all this time I still enjoy it so much.

Interviewer And the worst thing?

Steve That's easy, it has to be the long hours. This week for example I'm cooking nearly every day. We usually close on Sundays and Mondays, but this Monday is a public holiday, when lots of people want to eat out, so we're open.

Interviewer Seu Xerea is in all the British restaurant guides now. Does that mean you get a lot of British customers?

Steve Yes, we get a lot of British people, especially at the weekends, but then we get people from other countries too.

Interviewer And are the British customers and the Spanish customers very different?

Steve Yes, I think they are. The British always say that everything is lovely, even if they've only eaten half of it. The Spanish, on the other hand, are absolutely honest about everything. They tell you what they like, they tell you what they don't like. I remember when I first opened, I had sushi on the menu, which was very unusual at that time, and I went into the dining room and I said to people, 'So what do you think of the sushi?' And the customers, who were all Spanish, said 'Oh, it was awful! It was raw fish!' Actually, I think I prefer that honesty, because it helps us to know what people like.

Interviewer What kind of customers do you find difficult?

Steve I think customers who want me to cook something in a way that I don't think is very good. Let's see, a person who asks for a really well-done steak, for instance. For me that's a difficult customer. You know, they'll say 'I want a really really well-done steak' so I give them a really really well-done steak and then they say 'It's tough'. And I think well, of course it's tough. It's well done! Well-done steak is always tough.

Interviewer People say that the Mediterranean diet is very healthy. Do you think people's eating habits in Spain are changing?

Steve Well, I think they are changing – unfortunately I think they're getting worse. People are eating more unhealthily.

Interviewer How do you notice that?

Steve I see it with, especially with younger friends. They often eat in fast food restaurants, they don't cook... and actually the younger ones come from a generation where their mothers don't cook either. That's what's happening now, and it's a real pity.

1 27

Interviewer This morning we're talking about family and family life and now Danielle Barnes is going to tell us about a book she has just read called *Birth Order* by Linda Blair. So what's the book about Danielle?

Danielle Well, it's all about how our position in the family influences the kind of person we are. I mean whether we're first born, a middle child, a youngest child or an only child. Linda Blair argues that our position in the family is possibly the strongest influence on our character and personality.

Interviewer So tell us more about this, Danielle. What about the oldest children in a family, the first-born?

Danielle Well first-born children often have to look after their younger brothers and sisters, so they're usually sensible and responsible as adults. They also tend to be ambitious and they make good leaders. Many US Presidents and British Prime Ministers, including for example Winston Churchill were oldest children.
On the negative side oldest children can be insecure and anxious. This is because when the second child was born they lost some of their parents' attention and maybe they felt rejected.

Interviewer That's all very interesting. What about the middle child?

Danielle Middle children are usually more relaxed than oldest children. That's probably because the parents are more relaxed themselves by the time the second child arrives. They're usually very sociable – the kind of people who get on with everybody and they're also usually sensitive to what other people need. Now this is because they grew up between older and younger brothers and sisters. For the same reason they are often quite good at sorting out arguments, and they're always sympathetic to the ones on the losing side, or in general to people who are having problems. On the other hand, middle children can sometimes be unambitious, and they can lack direction in life.

Interviewer And youngest children?

Danielle I was very interested in this part of the book as I'm a youngest child myself. It seems that youngest children are often very outgoing and charming. This is the way they try to get the attention of both their parents and their older brothers and sisters.
They are often more rebellious, and this is probably because it's easier for the youngest children to break the rules – by this time their parents are more relaxed about discipline.
On the negative side, youngest children can be immature, and disorganized, and they often depend too much on other people. This is because they have always been the baby of the family.

Interviewer Fascinating. And finally, what about only children?

Danielle Only children usually do very well at school because they have a lot of contact with adults. They get a lot of love and attention from their parents so they're typically self-confident. They're also independent, as they're used to being by themselves. And because they spend a lot of time with adults they're often very organized.

Interviewer I'm an only child myself and people always think that I must be spoilt. Is that true, according to Linda Blair?

Danielle Well, it's true that only children can sometimes be spoilt by their parents because they're given everything they ask for. Also, on the negative side, only children can be quite selfish, and they can also be impatient, especially when things go wrong. This is because they're not used to sorting out problems with other brothers and sisters.

1 28

Jenny My name's Jenny Zielinski. And New York is my city. I live here and I work for a magazine, *NewYork24seven*.

Rob My name's Rob Walker. I'm a writer on *NewYork24seven*. You can probably tell from my accent that I'm not actually from New York. I'm British, and I came over to the States a few months ago.

Jenny I met Rob in London when I was visiting the UK on a work trip. He was writing for the London edition of *24seven*. We got along well right away. I really liked him.

Rob So why am I in New York? Because of Jenny, of course. When they gave me the opportunity to work here for a month, I took it immediately. It gave us the chance to get to know each other better. When they offered me a permanent job I couldn't believe it!

Jenny I helped Rob find an apartment. And now here we are. Together in New York. I'm so happy. I just hope Rob's happy here, too.

Rob I really loved living in London. A lot of my friends and family are there, so of course I still miss it. But New York's a fantastic city. I've got a great job and Jenny's here too.

Jenny Things are changing pretty fast in the office. We have a new boss, Don Taylor. And things are changing in my personal life, too. This evening's kind of important. I'm taking Rob to meet my parents for the very first time. I just hope it goes well!

1 29

Jenny I can't believe we got here so late.

Rob I'm sorry, Jenny. I had to finish that article for Don.

Jenny Don't forget the chocolates.

Rob OK.

Rob Oh no!

Jenny I don't believe it. Don't tell me you forgot them!?

Rob I think they're still on my desk.

Jenny You're kidding.

Rob You know what my desk's like.

Jenny Yeah, it's a complete mess. Why don't you ever tidy it?

Rob We could go and buy some more.

Jenny How can we get some more? We're already late!

Jenny Hi there!

Harry You made it!

Jenny Sorry we're late. So, this is my mom and dad, Harry and Sally. And this, of course, is Rob.

Rob Hello.

Sally It's so nice to meet you at last.

Harry Yes, Jenny's finally decided to introduce you to us.

Sally Come in, come in!

Jenny Mom, I'm really sorry – we bought you some chocolates but we left them at the office.

Sally What a pity. Never mind.

Harry Yeah, don't worry about it. We know what a busy young woman you are. And your mom has made way too much food for this evening anyway.

Sally Oh Harry.

Jenny But I also have some good news.

Sally Really? What's that?

Jenny Well, you know we have a new boss? He's still new to the job and needs support, so today he made me the managing editor of the magazine.

Sally So you've got a promotion? How fantastic!

Harry That's great news! Hey, does that mean Jenny's going to be your boss, Rob?

Rob Er... yes, I guess so.

Jenny Well, not exactly. I'm a manager, but I'm not Rob's manager.

Sally Let's go and have dinner.

Jenny What a great idea!

1 32

Harry You know, our Jenny has done incredibly well, Rob. She's the first member of our family to study at Harvard. She's a very capable and ambitious young woman.

Jenny Oh Dad.

Rob No, it's true, Jenny.

Harry But what about you, Rob? How do you see your career? Do you see yourself going into management?

Rob Me? No. Not really. I'm more of a... a writer.

Harry Really? What kind of things do you write?

Rob Oh... you know, interviews, reviews... things like that... and I'm doing a lot of work for the online magazine...

Jenny Rob's a very talented writer, Dad. He's very creative.

Harry That's great but being creative doesn't always pay the bills.

Jenny You know, my dad's a very keen photographer. He took all of these photos.

Harry Oh, Rob won't be interested in those.

Rob But I am interested. I mean, I like photography. And I think I recognize some of these people...

Harry That's because most of them are of Jenny.

Rob But there are some great jazz musicians, too. That's Miles Davis... and isn't that John Coltrane? And that's Wynton Marsalis.

Harry You know about Wynton Marsalis?

Rob Know about him? I've interviewed him!

Harry How incredible! I love that guy. He's a hero of mine.

Rob Well, he's a really nice guy. I spent a whole day with him, chatting and watching him rehearse.

Harry Really? I want to hear all about it.

Sally Have a cookie, Rob.

Harry Go ahead, son! Sally makes the best cookies in New York!

1 40

1 I'm a spender, I think. I try to save, but something always seems to come along that I need to buy and I finish up broke. I can get by with very little money for myself when I need to, but I don't seem to be good at holding on to it. Also, if my kids ask to borrow some money, I always say yes.

2 I would say that I'm spender. I spend money on things like concerts, or on trips because I like having the experience and the memories. I know that I should spend my money on things that last, or save for the future, but I don't want to miss all those good things that are happening right now.

3 I consider myself a spender. I don't have much money, but when I do have some there's always something I need or want to spend it on. I love computers and computer games, so I often buy things to make sure my computer is always up to date. I know it's not very sensible, but it's important to me.

4 That's difficult to say. I can save money if there's something I really, really want, but usually my money disappears as soon as I get it. I get some money from my parents every week so I have just enough money to go to the cinema with my friends and to buy something for myself, maybe a book or a DVD or some makeup... I usually end up buying something. But for example if I want to go on a trip with my friends, then I can make an effort and save some money for a few weeks.

5 Since I was very small, I've always saved about a third of the money I get. I would never think of spending all the money I have. You could say that I'm careful about money. When I want to buy something which is expensive I don't use a credit card, I take the money out of the bank and so I never have to worry about getting into debt.

6 I'd say a saver, definitely. I like having some money saved in case I have an emergency. I also think very carefully before I buy something and I always make sure it's the best I can buy for that price. But I wouldn't describe myself as mean. I love buying presents for people, and when I do spend my money I like to buy nice things, even if they're more expensive.

1 45

Part 1

Interviewer Jane, you're a primary school teacher, and a writer. What kind of books do you write?

Jane Well, I write books for children who are learning English as a foreign language.

Interviewer How long have you been a writer?

Jane Er, let me see, since 1990. So for about 22 years.

Interviewer Tell us about the trip that changed your life. Where were you going?

Jane Well, it was in the summer of 2008, and my family – my husband and I and our three children, decided to have a holiday of a lifetime, and to go to Africa. We went to Uganda and Ruanda, to see the mountain gorillas. It was something we'd always wanted to do. Anyway about half way through the trip we were in Uganda, and we were travelling in a lorry when the lorry broke down. So the driver had to find a mechanic to come and help fix it.

Interviewer And then what happened?

Jane Well, as soon as we stopped, lots of children appeared and surrounded us. I could see some long buildings quite near, so I asked the children what they were, and they said in English 'That's our school.' And I was very curious to see what a Ugandan school was like, so I asked them to show it to me.

Interviewer What was it like?

Jane I was shocked when I first saw it. The walls were falling down, the blackboards were broken, and there weren't many desks. But the children were so friendly, and I asked them if they would like to learn a song in English. They said yes, and I started teaching them some songs, like 'Heads, shoulders, knees and toes', a song I've used all over the world to teach children parts of the body. Almost immediately the classroom filled up with children of all ages and they all wanted to learn. I was just amazed by how quickly they learned the song!

Interviewer Did you meet the teachers?

Jane Yes, we did, and the headmaster too. He explained that the school was called St Josephs, and it was a community school for orphans, very poor children and refugees. I asked him what the school needed. I thought that he might say 'we need books, or paper,' and then later we could send them to him. But actually he said 'What we need is a new school'. And I thought yes, of course he's right. These children deserve to have better conditions than this to learn in. So when I got back home, my husband and I, and other people who were with us on the trip decided to set up an organization to get money to build a new school.

1 46

Part 2

Interviewer So Adelante África was born. Why did you decide to call it that?

Jane Well, we wanted a name that gave the idea of Africa moving forward, and my husband is Spanish, and he suggested Adelante África, because in Spanish Adalante means 'go forward', and Adelante África sort of sounded better than 'Go forward, Africa'.

Interviewer How long did it take to raise the money for the new school?

Jane Amazingly enough, not long really, only about two years. The school opened on the 14th March 2010 with 75 children. Today it has nearly 500 children.

Interviewer That's great! I understand that since the new school opened you've been working on other projects for these children.

Jane Yes. When we opened the school we realised that although the children now had a beautiful new school, they couldn't really make much progress because they were suffering from malnutrition, malaria, things like that. So we've been working to improve their diet and health, and at the moment we're building a house where children who don't have families can live.

Interviewer And are your children involved in Adelante Africa too?

Jane Yes, absolutely! They all go out to Uganda at least once a year. My daughter Tessie runs the Facebook page, and my other daughter Ana runs a project to help children to go to secondary school, and Georgie, my son, organizes a football tournament there every year.

Interviewer And how do you think you have most changed the children's lives?

Jane I think the school has changed the children's lives because it has given them hope. People from outside came and listened to them and cared about them. But it's not only the children whose lives have changed. Adelante África has also changed me and my family. We have been very lucky in life. I feel that life has given me a lot. Now I want to give something back. But it's not all giving. I feel that I get more from them than I give! I love being there. I love their smiles and how they have such a strong sense of community, and I love feeling that my family and the other members of Adelante África are accepted as part of that community.

Interviewer And do you have a website?

Jane Yes, we do. It's www.adelanteafrica.com. We've had the website for about four years. It was one of the first things we set up. If you'd like to find out more about Adelante África, please go there and have a look. There are lots of photos and even a video my son took of me teaching the children to sing on that first day. Maybe it will change your life too, who knows?

1 52

Phone call 4

I haven't had any music for the last three days, because my iPod broke, so paddling has been getting more boring. To pass the time I count or I name countries in my head and sometimes I just look up at the sky. Sometimes the sky is pink with clouds that look like cotton wool, other times it's dark like the smoke from a fire and sometimes it's bright blue. The day that I reached the half way point in my trip the sky was bright blue. I'm superstitious so I didn't celebrate – there's still a very long way to go.

Phone call 5

This week the mosquitoes have been driving me mad. They obviously think I'm easy food! They especially like my feet. I wake up in the night when they bite me and I can't stop scratching my feet.

But I'm feeling happier now than I've been feeling for weeks. I've seen a lot of amazing wildlife this week. One day I found myself in the middle of a group of dolphins. There were about six pairs jumping out of the water. I've also seen enormous butterflies, iguanas, and vultures which fly above me in big groups. Yesterday a fish jumped into my kayak. Maybe it means I'm going to be lucky. I am starting to feel a bit sad that this adventure is coming to an end.

And finally on the news, BBC presenter Helen Skelton has successfully completed her 3,200 kilometre journey down the Amazon River in a kayak. She set off from Nauta in Peru six weeks ago on a journey which many people said would be impossible. But yesterday she crossed the finish line at Almeirim in Brazil to become the first woman to paddle down the Amazon. Here's Helen: 'It's been hard but I've had an amazing time. The only thing I've really missed is my dog Barney. So the first thing I'm going to do will be to pick him up and take him for a nice long walk.'

2 9

The Stig was using public transport, for the first time in his life! He saw a big red thing coming towards him. A bus! He got on it, and used his Oyster Card to pay. Ten minutes later he got off and got the tube at Acton Town to take the District line to Monument. 18 stops!

The train now approaching is a District line train to West Ham. Please mind the gap between the train and the platform.

The Stig noticed that everyone was reading a newspaper, so he picked up a free one that was on a seat and started reading.

The next station is Monument. Change here for the Central line and the Docklands Light Railway.

He got off the tube and ran to the platform for the Docklands Light Railway. After a few minutes a train arrived. Now it was just ten stops and he would be there!

2 15

Host And on tonight's programme we talk to Tom Dixon, who is an expert on road safety. Tom, new technology like satnav has meant new distractions for drivers, hasn't it?

Tom That's right, Nicky, but it isn't just technology that's the problem. Car drivers do a lot of other things while they're driving which are dangerous and which can cause accidents. Remember, driver distraction is the number one cause of road accidents.

Host Now I know you've been doing a lot of tests with simulators. According to your tests, what's the most dangerous thing to do when you're driving?

Tom The tests we did in a simulator showed that the most dangerous thing to do while you're driving is to send or receive a text message. This is incredibly dangerous and it is of course illegal. In fact, research done by the police shows that this is more dangerous than drinking and driving.

Host Why is that?

Tom Well, the reason is obvious – many people use two hands to text, one to hold the phone and the other to type. Which means that they don't have their hands on the wheel, and they are looking at the phone, not at the road. Even for people who can text with one hand, it is still extremely dangerous. In the tests we did in the simulator two of the drivers crashed while texting.

Host And which is the next most dangerous?

Tom The next most dangerous thing is to set or adjust your sat nav. This is extremely hazardous too because although you can do it with one hand, you still have to take your eyes off the road for a few seconds.

Host And number three?

Tom Number three was putting on make-up or doing your hair. In fact this is something that people often do, especially women of course, when they stop at traffic lights, but if they haven't finished when the lights change, they often carry on when they start driving again. It's that fatal combination of just having one hand on the steering wheel, and looking in the mirror, not at the road.

Host And number four?

Tom In fourth place, there are two activities which are equally dangerous. One of them is making a phone call on a mobile. Our research showed that when people talk on the phone they drive more slowly (which can be just as dangerous as driving fast) but their control of the car gets worse, because they're concentrating on the phone call and not on what's happening on the road. But the other thing, which is just as dangerous as talking on your mobile, is eating and drinking. In fact if you do this, you double your chance of having an accident because eating and drinking always involves taking at least one hand off the steering wheel. And the worrying thing here is that people don't think of this as a dangerous activity at all and it isn't even illegal.

Host And in fifth, well actually sixth place. It must be listening to music, but which one?

Tom Well, it's listening to music you know.

Host Oh, that's interesting.

Tom We found in our tests that when drivers were listening to music they knew and liked, they drove either faster or slower depending on whether the music was fast or slow.

Host So fast music made drivers drive faster.

Tom Exactly. And a study in Canada also found that if the music was very loud then drivers' reaction time was 20% slower. If you're listening to very loud music you're twice as likely to go through a red light.

Host So the safest of all of the things in the list is to listen to music we don't know.

Tom Exactly. If we don't know the music then it doesn't distract us. In this part of the tests all drivers drove safely.

2 23

A Excuse me, is this seat free?

B Yes, sure sit down. Ah, he's lovely. Is he yours?

A Yes, yes. He's a she actually. Miranda.

B Oh. Three months?

A Three and a half. How about yours?

B Stephen. He's four months. Did you have a bad night?

A Yes, Miranda was crying all night. You know, that noise gets to you. It drives me mad.

B Do you know what you need? These.

A What are they? Earplugs?

B Yes. Earplugs! When the baby starts crying you just put these in. You can still hear the crying, but the noise isn't so bad and it's not so stressful.

A That's a great idea! Who told you to do that?

B It's all in this book I've read. You should get it.

A Yeah? What's it called?

B It's called 'Commando Dad'. It was written by an ex-soldier. He was a commando in the army and it's especially for men with babies or small children. It's brilliant.

A Really? So what's so good about it?

B Well, it's like a military manual. It tells you exactly what to do with a baby in any situation. It makes everything easier. There's a website too that you can go to – commandodad.com. It has lots of advice about looking after babies and small kids and I really like the forums where men can write in with their problems, or their experiences.

A What sort of things does it help you with?

B All sorts of things. How to change nappies – he has a really good system, how to dress the baby, how to get the baby to sleep, the best way to feed the baby, how to know if the baby is ill. It's really useful and it's quite funny too, I mean he uses sort of military language, so for example he calls the baby a BT which means a baby trooper, and the baby's bedroom is base camp, and taking the baby for a walk is manoeuvres, and taking the nappies to the rubbish is called bomb disposal.

A What else does it say?

A And what does he think about men looking after children? Does he think we do it well?

B He thinks that men are just as good as women at looking after children in almost everything.

A Almost everything?

B Yeah, he says the one time when women are better than men is when the kids are ill. Women sort of understand better what to do. They have an instinct. Oh. Now it's my turn. Right, I know exactly what that cry means. It means he's hungry.

A Wow! What was that book called?

2 28

Kerri You work hard but your money's all spent
Haven't got enough to pay the rent
You know it's not right and it makes no sense
To go chasing, chasing those dollars and cents
Chasing, chasing those dollars and cents...

Rob That was great, Kerri.

Kerri Thanks.

Rob Kerri, you used to be in a band, now you play solo. Why did you change?

Kerri What happened with the band is private. I've already said I don't want to talk about it in interviews. All I'll say is that I have a lot more freedom this way. I can play – and say – what I want.

Rob Did your relationship with the band's lead guitarist affect the break up?

Kerri No comment. I never talk about my private life.

Rob Your Dad was in a famous punk band and your Mum's a classical pianist, have they influenced your music?

Kerri Of course they have – what do you think? Isn't everyone influenced by their parents?

Rob When did you start playing?

Kerri I started playing the guitar when I was about four.

Rob Four? That's pretty young.
Kerri Yeah, the guitar was nearly as big as me!
Rob I think that your new album is your best yet. It's a lot quieter and more experimental than your earlier albums.
Kerri Thank you! I think it's my best work.
Rob So what have you been doing recently?
Kerri Well, I've been writing and recording some new songs. And I've played at some of the summer festivals in the UK.
Rob And what are you doing while you're in the States?
Kerri I'm going to play at some clubs here in New York, then I'm doing some small gigs in other places. I just want to get to know the country and the people. It's all very new to me.
Jenny Good job, Rob. She isn't the easiest person to interview.
Rob She's OK. And this video clip will work great online.
Don Well, thank you for coming in today, Kerri. Now I suggest we have some lunch. Rob, could you call a taxi?
Rob Er, sure.

2 29

Don So when will you be coming back to New York, Kerri?
Kerri Oh, I don't know.
Waitress Hi guys, is everything OK?
Don Yes, it's delicious, thank you.
Waitress That's great!
Kerri New York waiters never leave you alone! I really don't like all this 'Hi guys! Is everything OK?' stuff.
Don What? You mean waiters aren't friendly in London?
Rob Oh, they're very friendly!
Kerri Yes, they're friendly but not too friendly. They don't bother you all the time.
Waitress Can I get you anything else? More drinks, maybe?
Don No thanks. We're fine.
Waitress Fantastic.
Kerri See what I mean? Personally, I think people in London are a lot more easy-going. London's just not as hectic as New York.
Don Sure, we all like peace and quiet. But in my opinion, New York is possibly... well, no, is definitely the greatest city in the world. Don't you agree?
Kerri To be honest, I definitely prefer London.
Don Come on, Rob. You've lived in both. What do you think?
Rob Erm, well, I have to say, London's very special. It's more relaxed, it's got great parks and you can cycle everywhere. It's dangerous to cycle in New York!
Don Why would you cycle when you can drive a car?
Kerri You can't be serious.
Don OK, I agree, London has its own peculiar charm. But if you ask me, nothing compares with a city like New York. The whole world is here!
Kerri But that's the problem. It's too big. There are too many people. Everybody's so stressed out. And nobody has any time for you.
Jenny I don't think that's right, Kerri. New Yorkers are very friendly...
Kerri Oh sure, they can sound friendly with all that 'Have a nice day' stuff. But I always think it's a little bit... fake.
Don You've got to be kidding me!
Rob I'm sorry. I'll just have to take this... Hello?... Yes... You're who?... The taxi driver?... What did she leave? ... Her cell phone... right. OK. Yes, we're still at the restaurant. See you in about five minutes.

2 32

Kerri Thank you for a nice lunch, Don.
Don You're welcome.
Waitress Thanks for coming, guys! Have a nice day.
Don See? Nice, friendly service.
Kerri Maybe. But I think she saw the big tip you left on the table!
Jenny Did you mean what you said in the restaurant, Rob?
Rob Did I mean what?
Jenny About missing London?
Rob Sure, I miss it, Jenny.
Jenny Really?
Rob But hey, not that much! It's just that moving to a new place is always difficult.
Jenny But you don't regret coming here, do you?
Rob No ... no ... not at all.
Jenny It's just that... you seemed homesick in there. For the parks, the cycling ...
Rob Well there are some things I miss but – Oh, hang on a minute. Look over there. Our taxi driver's back.
Taxi driver Excuse me, Ma'am.
Kerri Who me? What is it?
Taxi driver I believe this is your cell phone. You left it in my cab.
Kerri What?... Oh, wow... thank you!
Taxi driver Have a nice day!
Kerri That was so kind of him!
Don See? New Yorkers are really friendly people.

2 40

1 One very easy thing you can do is just change the language to English on all the gadgets you have, for example on your phone, or laptop, or tablet. That way you're reading English every day and without really noticing you just learn a whole lot of vocabulary, for example the things you see on your screen like *Are you sure you want to shut down now*, things like that.
2 My tip is to do things that you like doing, but in English. So for example, if you like reading, then read in English, if you like the cinema, watch films in English with subtitles, if you like computer games, play them in English. But don't do things you don't enjoy in your language, I mean if you don't like reading in your language, you'll enjoy it even less in English, and so you probably won't learn anything.
3 What really helped me to improve my English was having an Australian boyfriend. He didn't speak any Hungarian – well, not many foreigners do – so we spoke English all the time, and my English improved really quickly. We broke up when he went back to Australia but by then I could speak pretty fluently. We didn't exactly finish as friends, but I'll always be grateful to him for the English I learned. So my tip is try to find an English-speaking boyfriend or girlfriend.
4 I've always thought that learning vocabulary is very important, so I bought a vocabulary flash card app for my phone. I write down all the new words and phrases I want to remember in Polish and in English and then when I get a quiet moment I test myself. It really helps me remember new vocabulary. So that's my tip. Get a vocabulary learning app for your phone.
5 I think one of the big problems when you're learning something new is motivation, something to make you carry on and not give up. So my tip is to book yourself a holiday in an English-speaking country or a country where people speak very good English, like Holland, as a little reward for yourself and so you can actually practise your English. It's really motivating when you go somewhere and find that people understand you and you can communicate! Last year I went to Amsterdam for a weekend and I had a great time and I spoke a lot of English.
6 If you love music, which I do, my tip is to listen to as many songs as possible in English and then learn to sing them. It's so easy nowadays with YouTube. First I download the lyrics and try to understand them. Then I sing along with the singer and try to copy the way he or she sings – this is fantastic for your pronunciation. Then once I can do it well, I go back to YouTube and get a karaoke version of the song, and then I sing it. It's fun and your English will really improve as a result.

2 48

I always thought that good manners were always good manners, wherever you were in the world. But that was until I married Alexander. We met in Russia, when I was a student there, and I always remember when I first met him. He came to my flat one afternoon, and as soon as he came in he said to me, in Russian, *Nalei mnye chai* – which means 'pour me some tea'. Well, I got quite angry and I said, 'Pour it yourself'. I couldn't believe that he hadn't used a 'Could you…?' or a 'please'. To me it sounded really rude. But Alexander explained that in Russian it was fine – you don't have to add any polite words.

Some months later I took Alexander home to meet my parents in the UK. But before we went I had to give him an intensive course in 'pleases' and 'thank yous'. He thought they were completely unnecessary. I also told him how important it was to smile all the time.

Poor Alexander – he complained that when he was in England he felt really stupid, 'like the village idiot' he said, because in Russia if you smile all the time people think that you're mad. And in fact, this is exactly what my husband's friends thought of me the first time I went to Russia because I smiled at everyone, and translated every 'please' and 'thank you' from English into Russian!

Another thing that Alexander just couldn't understand was why people said things like, 'Would you mind passing me the salt, please?' He said, 'It's only the salt, for goodness sake! What do you say in English if you want a real favour?'

He was also amazed when we went to a dinner party in England, and some of the food was…well, it wasn't very nice, but everybody – including me – said, 'Mmm…this is delicious'.

In Russia, people are much more direct. The first time Alexander's mother came to our house for dinner in Moscow, she told me that my soup needed more salt and pepper, that it didn't really taste of anything. I was really annoyed, and later after she left Alexander and I argued about it. Alexander just couldn't see my point. He said, 'Do you prefer your dinner guests to lie?' Actually you know, I think I do. I'd prefer them to say 'that was lovely' even if they didn't mean it.

Anyway, at home we now have an agreement. If we're speaking Russian, he can say 'Pour me some tea', and not say 'thank you' when I give it to him. But when we're speaking English, he has to add a 'please', a 'thank you', and... a smile.

3 8

Part 1

Interviewer What made you want to become a referee?
Juan My father was a referee but that didn't influence me – in fact the opposite because I saw all the problems that he had as a referee. But as a child I was always attracted by the idea of being a referee and at school I used to referee all kinds of sports, basketball, handball, volleyball and of course football. I was invited to join the Referee's Federation when I was only 14 years old.
Interviewer Were you good at sport yourself?
Juan Yes, I was a very good handball player. People often think that referees become referees because they are frustrated sportsmen, but this is just not true in most cases in my experience.
Interviewer What was the most exciting match you ever refereed?
Juan It's difficult to choose one match as the most exciting. I remember some of the Real Madrid–Barcelona matches, for example the first one I ever refereed. The atmosphere was incredible in the stadium. But really it's impossible to pick just one – there have been so many.
Interviewer What was the worst experience you ever had as a referee?

Juan The worst? Well, that was something that happened very early in my career. I was only 16 and I was refereeing a match in a town in Spain and the home team lost. After the match, I was attacked and injured by the players of the home team and by the spectators. After all these years I can still remember a mother, who had a little baby in her arms, who was trying to hit me. She was so angry with me that she nearly dropped her baby. That was my worst moment, and it nearly made me stop being a referee.

Interviewer Do you think that there's more cheating in football than in the past?

Juan Yes, I think so.

Interviewer Why?

Juan I think it's because there's so much money in football today that it's become much more important to win. Also football is much faster than it used to be, so it's much more difficult for referees to detect cheating.

Interviewer How do footballers cheat?

Juan Oh, there are many ways, but for me the worst thing in football today is what we call 'simulation'. Simulation is when a player pretends to have been fouled when in fact he hasn't. For example, sometimes a player falls over in the penalty area when, in fact, nobody has touched him and this can result in the referee giving a penalty when it wasn't a penalty. In my opinion, when a player does this he's cheating not only the referee, not only the players of the other team, but also the spectators, because spectators pay money to see a fair contest.

3 9

Part 2

Interviewer What's the most difficult thing about being a referee?

Juan The most difficult thing is to make the right decisions during a match. It's difficult because you have to make decisions when everything's happening so quickly – football today is very fast. You must remember that everything is happening at 100 kilometres an hour. Also important decisions often depend on the referee's interpretation of the rules. Things aren't black and white. And of course making decisions would be much easier if players didn't cheat.

Interviewer Do you think that the idea of fair play doesn't exist any more.

Juan Not at all. I think fair play does exist – the players who cheat are the exceptions.

Interviewer Finally, who do you think is the best player in the world at the moment?

Juan I think most people agree that the best footballer today is Leo Messi.

Interviewer Why do you think he's so good?

Juan It's hard to say what makes him so special, but a study was done on him which showed that Messi can run faster with the ball than many footballers can do without the ball. Apart from his great ability, what I also like about him is that he isn't the typical superstar footballer. You can see that he enjoys playing football and he behaves in public and in his personal life in a very normal way. That's unusual when you think how famous he is. And what's more he doesn't cheat – he doesn't need to!

3 23

Presenter Hello and welcome to Forum, the programme that asks you what you think about current topics. Today Martha Park will be talking about the social networking site Facebook, how we use it, how much we like it – or dislike it. So get ready to call us or text us and tell us what you think. The number as always is 5674318. Martha.

Martha Hello. Since Facebook was first launched in 2004, a lot of research has been done to find out what kind of people use it, what they use it for, and what effect it has on their lives. According to a recent study by consumer research specialist Intersperience the average 22 year old in Britain has over 1,000 online friends. In fact, 22 seems to be the age at which the number of friends peaks. It also appears that women have slightly more online friends than men. And another study from an American university shows that people who spend a lot of time on Facebook reading other people's posts tend to feel more dissatisfied with their own lives, because they feel that everyone else is having a better time than they are. So, over to you. Do you use Facebook? How do you feel about it? Can you really have 1,000 friends? Are social networking sites making us unhappy? Phone in and share your experiences…

3 24

Presenter And our first caller is George. Go ahead George.

George Hi. Er yeah, I use Facebook a lot, every day really. I think it's a great way to, er, organize your social life and keep in touch with your friends. I have loads of friends.

Martha How many friends do you have George?

George At the moment I have 1,042.

Martha And how many of them do you know personally?

George About half maybe?

Martha And what do you use Facebook for?

George For me, it's a good way to get in touch with my friends without having to use the phone all the time. When I'm having a busy week at university, I can change my status so I can let my friends know I can't go out. That's much easier than wasting time telling people 'sorry I'm too busy to meet up'. It's just easier and quicker than using the phone.

Presenter Thanks George. We have another caller. It's Beth. Hello, Beth.

Beth Hi. Er, I don't use Facebook or any other social networking site.

Martha Why's that Beth?

Beth Two reasons really. First, I don't spend much time online anyway. I do a lot of sport – I'm in a hockey team, so I meet my teammates almost every day, and we don't need to communicate on Facebook.

Martha And the other reason?

Beth I just don't really like the whole idea of social networking sites. I mean, why would I want to tell the whole world everything that I'm doing? I don't want to share my personal information with the world, and become friends with people I don't even know. And I don't want to read what other people had for breakfast or lunch or dinner or what they're planning to do this weekend.

Presenter Thanks for that Beth. Our next caller is Caitlin. It's your turn Caitlin.

Martha Hi Caitlin

Caitlin Hi Martha.

Martha And do you use Facebook Caitlin?

Caitlin I use it from time to time but not very much. I only really use it to keep up with friends who have moved abroad or live too far away for us to meet regularly. For example, one of my best friends recently moved to Canada and we often chat on Facebook. But I never add 'friends' who are people I hardly know. I just can't understand those people who collect hundreds or even thousands of Facebook friends! I think it's just competition, people who want to make out that they're more popular than everybody else.

Martha So you think the Facebook world is a bit unreal?

Caitlin Absolutely. I think people write things and post photos of themselves just to show everyone they know what a fantastic time they're having and what exciting lives they lead. But they're probably just sitting at home in front of the computer all the time.

Presenter Thanks for that Caitlin. We've just got time for one more caller before the news and it's Ned. Hi Ned. You'll have to be quick.

Martha Hi Ned.

Ned Hi. When I started off with Facebook I thought it was great, and I used it to communicate with close friends and with family, and I got back in touch old friends from school. It was good because all the people I was friends with on Facebook were people I knew, and I was interested in what they were doing. But then I started adding friends, people I hardly knew who were friends of friends, people like that – in the end I had more than a 1,000 – and it just became too much. There were just too many people leaving updates, writing messages on my wall. So last month I decided to delete most of them. It took me about half an hour to delete and in the end the only people I left were actual, real-life friends and family, and old school friends. I got it down to 99. It was really liberating.

Presenter Thanks Ned and we'll be back after the news, so keep those calls coming.

3 25

Jenny Monica!

Monica Jenny!

Jenny Wow! How are you? You look great!

Monica Thanks, Jenny! You look really good, too.

Jenny Hey, why don't we get some coffee?

Monica I'd love to, but I'm on the way to meet… oh, come on. Five minutes!

Jenny So, how is everything?

Monica Oh great. Things couldn't be better actually. Scott and I … we're getting married!

Jenny You're what? Congratulations!

Monica Thank you!

Jenny When did you get engaged?

Monica Only a few days ago. I'm glad I saw you actually. I was going to call you. We've only told family so far.

Jenny I can't believe it. Monica the wife! And to think you used to go clubbing every night!

Monica Well, that was a few years ago! All I want to do now is stay in and read wedding magazines.

Jenny And how are the plans coming along?

Monica I haven't done anything yet. My mom and Scott's mom want to organize the whole thing themselves!

Jenny That's what mothers are for!

Monica True. But what about you? You look fantastic.

Jenny Well, I guess I'm kind of happy, too.

Monica Uh huh. What's his name?

Jenny Rob.

Monica You've been keeping him very quiet! Is it serious?

Jenny Erm, it's kind of, you know…

Monica So it is!

Jenny It's still early. We haven't been together for long. He only moved here from London a few months ago…

Monica What? He's British? And you think you can persuade him to stay in New York? That won't be easy!

Jenny I think he likes it here. You know how guys are, you never know what they're thinking.

Monica When can I meet him?

Jenny Er… that's him now.

3 26

Rob Do you mind if I join you?

Monica Of course not. Come on, sit down.

Rob Thank you.

Monica I have to leave in a minute anyway.

Rob Could I have a large latte, please?

Waiter Of course.

Jenny Rob, this is Monica.

Monica Nice to meet you, Rob.

Rob You too, Monica. You know, Jenny talks about you a lot. And I've seen college photos of you two together. At Jenny's parents' house.

Jenny Of course you have. My dad's photos.

Rob You've hardly changed at all.

Monica What a nice man! I can see why you like him, Jenny. The perfect English gentleman.

Waiter Your latte.

Rob Oh, thanks. Can you pass the sugar?

Jenny Sure.

Monica Sorry guys, but I have to go.

Rob You're sure I haven't interrupted anything?

Monica Not at all. It's just that I have to meet someone. But let's get together very soon.

Jenny We will!
Monica Bye, Rob. Nice meeting you.
Rob Bye.
Jenny Bye. Talk soon.
Rob She seems like a happy person.
Jenny She is, especially right now - she's getting married.
Rob That's fantastic news!
Jenny Yeah, it is. I guess we're at that age now. When most of our friends are settling down and getting married.
Rob Yeah... Oh, speaking of friends, I want to ask you a favour. Is it OK if we change our plans a bit this week?
Jenny Er... sure. What's up?
Rob I've just had a call from an old friend of mine, Paul. I haven't seen him since we were at university and he's travelling around the States at the moment. Anyway, he's arriving in New York this evening and, er... I've invited him to stay for the week.
Jenny Cool! It'll be fun to meet one of your old friends! What's he like?
Rob Oh, Paul's a laugh. He used to be a bit wild, but that was a long time ago. He's probably changed completely.
Jenny Well, I'm looking forward to meeting him.
Rob Just one other thing. Could you do me a big favour? I have to work late this evening so... would you mind meeting him at the airport?
Jenny Not at all. I'd like to meet him.
Rob And do you think you could take him to my flat? I'll give you the keys.
Jenny No problem, Rob.
Rob Thanks so much, Jenny. You're a real star.

3 29

Paul Hey man!
Rob Paul!
Paul It's great to see you, mate.
Rob You too, Paul. It's been years. You haven't changed at all.
Paul Just got better looking!
Rob How come you're so late?
Jenny Paul's flight from LA was delayed. And then the traffic coming back was just awful.
Paul But that gave us time to get to know each other.
Jenny Yeah. Paul told me all about his travels. Every detail.
Paul And look at this. Your own New York flat. How cool is that?
Rob It's good. Really good. But – do you want something to eat? I got some things on my way home.
Paul Stay in? It's my first night in the Big Apple! Let's go out and have a pizza or something.
Rob I thought you'd be tired after the flight.
Paul No way, man! I'm ready for action.
Rob Great! I'll get my jacket...
Jenny Rob, I think I'll go home if you don't mind. I, uh, I'm exhausted.
Rob Oh, OK then.
Paul So it's a boys' night out!
Rob Just like the old days!
Paul And after the pizza we can go on somewhere else. Rob, we've got a lot to talk about!

1A

present simple and continuous, action and non-action verbs

present simple: *I live, he works*, etc.

1 I **work** in a bank. She **studies** Russian. 1 10
We **don't have** any pets. Jack **doesn't wear** glasses.
Where **do** you **live**? **Does** your brother **have** a car?
2 She usually **has** cereal for breakfast.
I'**m** never late for work.
We only **eat out** about once a month.

1 We use the present simple for things that are always true or happen regularly.
- Remember the spelling rules for third person singular, e.g. *lives, studies, watches.*
- Use **ASI** (**A**uxiliary, **S**ubject, **I**nfinitive) or **QUASI** (**Qu**estion word, **A**uxiliary, **S**ubject, **I**nfinitive) to help you with word order in questions. *Do you know David? What time does the film start?*

2 We often use the present simple with adverbs of frequency, e.g. *usually, never,* or expressions of frequency, e.g. *every day, once a week.*
- Adverbs of frequency go before the main verb, and after *be.*
- Expressions of frequency usually go at the end of the sentence or verb phrase.

present continuous: *be* + verb + *-ing*

A Who **are** you **waiting** for? 1 11
B I'**m waiting** for a friend.
A **Is** your sister still **going out** with Adam?
B No, they broke up. She **isn't going out** with anyone at the moment.

- We use the present continuous (not the present simple) for actions in progress at the time of speaking, e.g. things that are happening now or around now. These are normally temporary, not habitual actions.
- Remember the spelling rules, e.g. *living, studying, getting.*
- We also use the present continuous for future arrangements (see **1B**).

action and non-action verbs

A What **are** you **cooking**? 1 12
B I'**m making** pasta.
A Great! I **love** pasta.
A What **are** you **looking** for?
B My car keys.
A I'll help you in a moment.
B But I **need** them now!

- Verbs which describe **actions**, e.g. *cook, make,* can be used in the present simple or continuous. ***I'm making** the lunch. I usually **make** the lunch at the weekend.*
- Verbs which describe **states** or **feelings** (not actions), e.g. *love, need, be,* are **non-action verbs**. They are not usually used in the present continuous, even if we mean 'now'.
- Common non-action verbs are *agree, be, believe, belong, depend, forget, hate, hear, know, like, love, matter, mean, need, prefer, realize, recognize, remember, seem, suppose.*

Verbs that can be both action and non-action
A few verbs have an action and a non-action meaning, e.g. *have* and *think.*
I have a cat now. = possession (non-action)
I can't talk now. I'm having lunch. = an action
I think this music's great. = opinion (non-action)
What are you thinking about? = an action

a Complete the sentences with the present simple or present continuous forms of the verbs in brackets.

We *don't go* to Chinese restaurants very often. (not go)
1 These days, most children ________ too many fizzy drinks. (have)
2 ________ you ________ any vitamins at the moment? (take)
3 Don't eat that spinach if you ________ it. (not like)
4 ________ your boyfriend ________ how to cook fish? (know)
5 We ________ takeaway pizzas during the week. (not get)
6 What ________ your mother ________? It smells great! (make)
7 You look sad. What ________ you ________ about? (think)
8 The diet in my country ________ worse. (get)
9 How often ________ you ________ seafood? (eat)
10 I ________ usually ________ fish. (not cook)

b Circle the correct form, present simple or continuous.

I don't believe | *I'm not believing* that you cooked this meal yourself.
1 Come on, let's order. The waiter *comes* | *is coming.*
2 Kate *doesn't want* | *isn't wanting* to have dinner now. She isn't hungry.
3 The head chef is ill, so he *doesn't work* | *isn't working* today.
4 The bill *seems* | *is seeming* very high to me.
5 We've had an argument, so we *don't speak* | *aren't speaking* to each other at the moment.
6 My mum *thinks* | *is thinking* my diet is awful these days.
7 *Do we need* | *Are we needing* to go shopping today?
8 Can I call you back? *I have* | *I'm having* lunch right now.
9 I didn't use to like oily fish, but now *I love* | *I'm loving* it!
10 What *do you cook* | *are you cooking*? It smells delicious!

◄ p.7

1B

future forms

be going to + infinitive

future plans and intentions 1 17

My sister's **going to adopt** a child.
Are you **going to buy** a new car or a second-hand one?
I'm not going to go to New York tomorrow. The meeting is cancelled.

predictions 1 18

Barcelona **are going to win**. They're playing really well.
Look at those black clouds. I think it's **going to rain**.

- We use *going to* (NOT *will* / *won't*) when we have already decided to do something. NOT ~~*My sister will adopt a child.*~~
- We also use *going to* to make a prediction about the future, especially when you can see or have some evidence (e.g. black clouds).

present continuous: *be* + verb + *-ing*

future arrangements 1 19

Lorna and Jamie **are getting** married in October.
We**'re meeting** at 10.00 tomorrow in Jack's office.
Jane**'s leaving** on Friday and **coming back** next Tuesday.

- We often use the present continuous for future arrangements.
- There is very little difference between the present continuous and *going to* for future plans / arrangements, and often you can use either.
  - *going to* shows that you have made a decision. *We're going to get married next year.*
  - the present continuous emphasizes that you have made the arrangements. *We're getting married on October 12th.* (= we've booked the church, etc.)
- We often use the present continuous with verbs relating to travel arrangements, e.g. *go, come, arrive, leave*, etc. *I'm going to Paris tomorrow and coming back on Tuesday.*

will / *shall* + infinitive

instant decisions, promises, offers, predictions, future facts, suggestions 1 20

1 I**'ll have** the steak. (instant decision)
I **won't tell** anybody where you are. (promise)
I'**ll carry** that bag for you. (offer)
You'**ll love** New York! (prediction)
I'**ll be** at home all afternoon. (future fact)
2 **Shall I help** you with your homework? (offer)
Shall we **eat** out tonight? (suggestion)

1 We use *will* / *won't* (NOT the present simple) for instant decisions, promises, offers, and suggestions. NOT ~~*I carry that bag for you.*~~
- We can also use *will* / *won't* for predictions, e.g. *I think Barcelona will win,* and to talk about future facts, e.g. *The election will be on 1st March.*

2 We use *shall* (NOT *will*) with *I* and *we* for offers and suggestions when they are questions.

a Circle the correct form. Tick ✓ the sentence if both are possible.

My grandparents *are going to retire* / *will retire* next year. ✓

1 *Will we* / *Shall we* invite your parents for Sunday lunch?
2 *I'm going to make* / *I'll make* a cake for your mum's birthday, if you want.
3 *I'm not having* / *I'm not going to have* dinner with my family tonight.
4 The exam *will be* / *is being* on the last Friday of term.
5 You can trust me. *I'm not telling* / *I won't tell* anyone what you told me.
6 My cousin *is arriving* / *will arrive* at 5.30 p.m.
7 I think the birth rate *will go down* / *shall go down* in my country in the next few years.
8 *I'm not going to go* / *I won't go* to my brother-in-law's party next weekend.
9 *Shall I* / *Will I* help you with the washing-up?

b Complete **B**'s replies with a correct future form.

A What's your stepmother going to do about her car?
B She*'s going to buy* a second-hand one. (buy)

1 **A** I'm going to miss you.
B Don't worry. I promise I ________ every day. (write)
2 **A** What are Alan's plans for the future?
B He ________ a degree in engineering. (do)
3 **A** Can I see you tonight?
B No, I ________ late. How about Saturday? (work)
4 **A** What would you like for starters?
B I ________ the prawns, please. (have)
5 **A** There's nothing in the fridge.
B OK. ________ we ________ a takeaway? (get)
6 **A** I don't have any money, so I can't go out.
B No problem, I ________ you some. (lend)
7 **A** Shall we have a barbecue tomorrow?
B I don't think so. On the radio they said that it ________. (rain)
8 **A** We land at about eight o'clock.
B ________ I ________ you ________ from the airport? (pick up)

◄ p.9

2A

present perfect and past simple

present perfect simple: *have / has* + past participle (*worked, seen,* etc.)

1 **past experiences** 1 42
I**'ve been** to London, but I **haven't been** to Oxford.
Have you ever **lost** your credit card?
Sally **has** never **met** Bill's ex-wife.

2 **recent past actions**
I**'ve cut** my finger!
Too late! Our train **has** just **left**!

3 **with *yet* and *already* (for emphasis)**
I**'ve** already **seen** this film twice. Can't we watch another one?
My brother **hasn't found** a new job yet. He's still looking.
Have you **finished** your homework yet? No, not yet.

1 We use the present perfect for past experiences, when we don't say exactly when they happened.
- We often use *ever* and *never* when we ask or talk about past experiences. They go before the main verb.

2 We use the present perfect for recent past actions, often with *just*.
- *just* goes before the main verb.

3 We also use the present perfect with *yet* and *already*.
- *already* is used in [+] sentences and goes before the main verb.
- *yet* is used with [-] sentences and [?]. It goes at the end of the phrase.
- For irregular past participles see **Irregular verbs** *p.165*.

past simple (*worked, stopped, went, had,* etc.)

They **got** married last year. 1 43
What time **did** you **wake up** this morning?
I **didn't have** time to do my homework.

- Use the past simple for finished past actions (when we say, ask, or know when they happened).

present perfect or past simple?

I**'ve been** to Madrid twice. 1 44
(= in my life up to now)
I **went** there in 1998 and 2002.
(= on two specific occasions)
I**'ve bought** a new computer.
(= I don't say exactly when, where, etc.)
I **bought** it last Saturday. (= I say when)

- Use the present perfect (NOT the past simple) to talk about past experiences and recent past actions **when we don't specify a time**.
- Use the past simple (NOT the present perfect) to ask or talk about finished actions in the past, **when the time is mentioned or understood**. We often use a past time expression, e.g. *yesterday, last week,* etc.

a Complete the mini dialogues with the present perfect form of the verb in brackets and an adverb from the list. You can use the adverbs more than once.

already ever just never yet

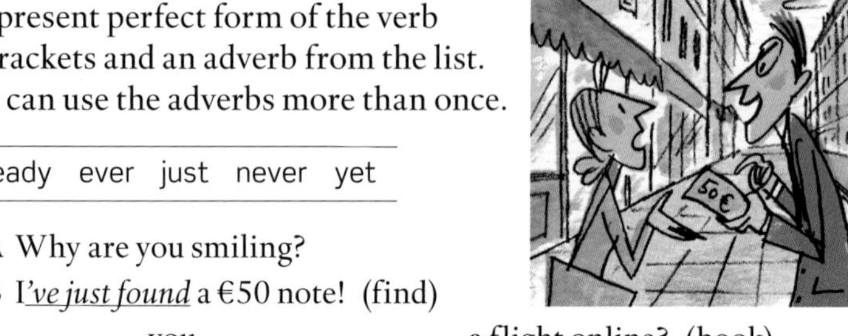

A Why are you smiling?
B I*'ve just found* a €50 note! (find)

1 **A** ________ you ________ ________ a flight online? (book)
B Yes, of course. I've done it loads of times.

2 **A** When are you going to buy a motorbike?
B Soon. I ________ ________ ________ nearly €1,000. (save)

3 **A** ________ you ________ the electricity bill ________? (pay)
B No, sorry. I forgot.

4 **A** ________ your parents ________ ________ you money? (lend)
B Yes, but I paid it back as soon as I could.

5 **A** How does eBay work?
B I don't know. I ________ ________ ________ it. (use)

6 **A** What are you celebrating?
B We ________ ________ ________ a prize in the lottery! (win)

7 **A** Why haven't you got any money?
B I ________ ________ ________ my salary. I bought a new tablet last week. (spend)

8 **A** Would you like a coffee?
B No, thanks. I ________ ________ ________ one. (have)

b Right or wrong? Tick ✓ or cross ✗ the sentences. Correct the wrong sentences.

I've never been in debt. ✓
How much has your new camera cost? ✗
How much did your new camera cost?

1 Dean has just inherited €5,000 from a relative.
2 Did your sister pay you back yet?
3 We booked our holiday online a month ago.
4 When have you bought that leather jacket?
5 They've finished paying back the loan last month.
6 We haven't paid the gas bill yet.
7 Have you ever wasted a lot of money on something?
8 I'm sure I haven't borrowed any money from you last week.
9 I spent my salary really quickly last month.
10 Have you seen the Batman film on TV yesterday?

◀ *p.16*

2B

present perfect + *for / since*, present perfect continuous

present perfect + *for / since*

1 47))

They**'ve known** each other for ten years.
Julia **has had** that bag since she was at university.

A How long **have** you **worked** here?
B Since 1996.

A How long **has** your brother **had** his motorbike?
B For about a year.

- We use the present perfect + *for* or *since* with **non-action verbs** (e.g. *like, have, know*, etc.) to talk about something which started in the past and is still true now.
  They've known each other for ten years. (= they met ten years ago and they still know each other today)
- We use *How long…?* + present perfect to ask about an unfinished period of time (from the past until now).
- We use *for* + a period of time, e.g. *for two weeks*, or *since* + a point of time, e.g. *since 1990*.
- Don't use the present simple with *for / since*, NOT ~~*They know each other for a long time*~~.

present perfect continuous: *have / has been* + verb + *-ing*

1 48))

1 How long **have** you **been learning** English?
Nick **has been working** here since April.
They**'ve been going out** together for about three years.
2 Your eyes are red. **Have** you **been crying?**
No, **I've been cutting** onions.

1 We use the present perfect continuous with *for* and *since* with **action verbs** (e.g. *learn, work, go*, etc.) to talk about actions which started in the past and are still true now.
- Don't use the present continuous with *for / since*, NOT ~~*I am working here for two years*~~.

2 We can also use the present perfect continuous for continuous or repeated actions which have been happening very recently. The actions have usually just finished.

I**'ve** (I **have**) You**'ve** (You **have**) He / She / It**'s** (He **has**) We**'ve** (We **have**) They**'ve** (They **have**)	**been working** here for two years.

I **haven't** (I **have not**) You **haven't** He / She / It **hasn't** We **haven't** They **haven't**	**been working** here for two years.

Have you **been working** here for two years?	Yes, I **have**.	No, I **haven't**.
Has she **been working** here for two years?	Yes, she **has**.	No, she **hasn't**.

work* and *live
Work and *live* are often used in either present perfect simple or present perfect continuous with the same meaning.
I've lived *here since 1980.*
I've been living *here since 1980.*

a Correct the mistakes.

Harry is unemployed since last year.
Harry has been unemployed since last year.

1 We've had our new flat since six months.
2 Hi Jackie! How are you? I don't see you for ages!
3 How long are you knowing your husband?
4 Emily has been a volunteer for ten years ago.
5 Paul doesn't eat anything since yesterday because he's ill.
6 It hasn't rained since two months.
7 How long has your parents been married?
8 They're having their dog since they got married.
9 I haven't had any emails from my brother for last Christmas.
10 My grandmother lives in the same house all her life.

b Make sentences with the present perfect simple or present perfect continuous (and *for / since* if necessary). Use the present perfect continuous if possible.

I / work for a charity / eight years
I've been working for a charity for eight years.

1 we / know each other / we were children
2 the children / play computer games / two hours
3 your sister / have that hairstyle / a long time?
4 I / love her / the first day we met
5 my internet connection / not work / yesterday
6 how long / you / wait?
7 I / be a teacher / three years
8 it / snow / five o'clock this morning
9 Sam / not study enough / recently
10 you / live in London / a long time?

◄ p.19

3A

comparatives and superlatives: adjectives and adverbs

comparing two people, places, things, etc.

1 My sister is a bit **taller than** me. 2 11
London is **more expensive than** Edinburgh.
This test is **less difficult than** the last one.
Olive oil is **better** for you **than** butter.
2 The new sofa isn't **as comfortable as** the old one.
I don't have **as many** books **as** I used to.

1 We use comparative **adjectives** to compare two people, places, things, etc.
- Regular comparative adjectives: spelling rules
  *old > old**er*** *big > bigg**er*** *easy > easi**er***
  *modern > **more** modern* *difficult > **more** difficult*
- Irregular comparative adjectives:
  good > better *bad > worse* *far > further*
- One-syllable adjectives ending in *-ed*:
  *bored > **more** bored* *stressed > **more** stressed*
  *tired > **more** tired*

2 We can also use (*not*) *as* + adjective + *as* to make comparisons.

Object pronouns (*me, him*, etc.) after *than* and *as*
After *than* or *as* we can use an object pronoun (*me, him, her*, etc.) or a subject pronoun (*I, he, she*, etc.) + auxiliary verb.
She's taller than me. OR *She's taller than I am.* NOT ~~*She's taller than I.*~~
They're not as busy as us. OR *They're not as busy as we are.* NOT ~~*They're not as busy as we.*~~

the same as
We use *the same as* to say that two people, places, things, etc. are identical.
Her dress is the same as mine.

comparing two actions

1 My father drives **faster than** me. 2 12
You walk **more quickly** than I do.
Liverpool played worse today **than** last week.
2 Max doesn't speak English **as well as** his wife does.
I don't earn **as much as** my boss.

1 We use comparative **adverbs** to compare two actions.
- Regular comparative adverbs: spelling rules
  *fast > fast**er*** *slowly > **more** slowly* *carefully > **more** carefully*
- Irregular comparatives:
  well > better *badly > worse*

2 We can also use (*not*) *as* + adverb + *as* to make comparisons.

superlatives

Kevin is **the tallest** player in the team. 2 13
Oslo is **the most expensive** capital city in Europe.
The small bag is **the least expensive**.
Lucy is **the best student** in the class.
Who dresses **the most stylishly** in your family?
That's **the worst** we've ever played.

- We use superlative **adjectives** and **adverbs** to compare people, things, or actions with all of their group.
- Form superlatives like comparatives, but use *-est* instead of *-er* and *most* / *least* instead of *more* / *less*.
- We normally use *the* before superlatives, but you can also use possessive adjectives, e.g. ***my** best friend*, ***their** most famous song*.
- We often use a superlative with present perfect + *ever*, e.g. *It's the best book I've ever read.*

***in* after superlatives**
Use *in* (NOT *of*) before places after a superlative.
*It's the longest bridge **in** the world.* NOT ~~*of the world*~~
*It's the best beach **in** England.* NOT ~~*of England*~~

a Complete with the comparative or superlative of the **bold** word (and *than* if necessary).

What's <u>*the fastest*</u> way to get across London? **fast**
1 I think skiing is ________ horse-riding. **easy**
2 A motorbike is ________ a scooter. **powerful**
3 I think that travelling by train is ________ form of transport. **relaxing**
4 You walk ________ I do. **slowly**
5 ________ time to travel is on holiday weekends. **bad**
6 ________ I've ever driven is from London to Edinburgh. **far**
7 The London Underground is ________ the subway in New York. **old**
8 This is ________ coach I've ever been on. **hot**
9 Of all my family, my mum is ________ driver. **good**

b Complete with one word.

Going by motorboat is <u>*more*</u> exciting than travelling by ferry.
1 A coach isn't as comfortable ______ a train.
2 It's ______ most expensive car we've ever bought.
3 The traffic was worse ______ we expected.
4 This is the longest journey I've ______ been on.
5 He gets home late, but his wife arrives later than ______.
6 The ______ interesting place I've ever visited is Venice.
7 I leave home at the same time ______ my brother.
8 He drives ______ carefully than his girlfriend – he's never had an accident.
9 We don't go abroad ______ often as we used to.
10 What's the longest motorway ______ the UK?

◀ p.26

3B

articles: *a / an, the,* no article

a / an

1 I saw **an old man** with **a dog**. 2 17
2 It's **a nice house**. She's **a lawyer**.
3 What **an awful day**!
4 I have classes three times **a week**.

- We use *a / an* with singular countable nouns:
  1 the first time you mention a thing / person.
  2 when you say what something is or what somebody does.
  3 in exclamations with *What…!*
  4 in expressions of frequency.

the

1 I saw an old man with **a dog**. 2 18
The dog was barking.
2 My father opened **the door**.
The children are at school.
3 **The moon** goes round **the Earth**.
4 I'm going to **the cinema** tonight.
5 It's **the best** restaurant in town.

- We use *the*:
  1 when we talk about something we've already mentioned.
  2 when it's clear what you're referring to.
  3 when there's only one of something.
  4 with places in a town, e.g. *cinema* and *theatre*.
  5 with superlatives.

no article

1 **Women** usually talk more than **men**. 2 19
Love is more important than **money**.
2 She's not **at home** today.
I get back **from work** at 5.30.
3 I never have **breakfast**.
4 See you **next Friday**.

- We don't use an article:
  1 when we are speaking in general (with plural and uncountable nouns). Compare:
  *I love **flowers**.* (= flowers in general)
  *I love **the flowers** in my garden.* (= the specific flowers in my garden)
  2 with some nouns, (e.g. *home, work, school, church*) after *at / to / from*.
  3 before meals, days, and months.
  4 before *next / last* + day, week, etc.

a Circle the correct answers.

I love *weddings* / *the weddings*!

1 Jess is *nurse* / *a nurse* in a hospital. *A hospital* / *The hospital* is a long way from her house.
2 What *a horrible day* / *horrible day*! We'll have to eat our picnic in *the car* / *a car*.
3 My wife likes *love stories* / *the love stories*, but I prefer *the war films* / *war films*.
4 We go to *theatre* / *the theatre* about *once a month* / *once the month*.
5 I'm having *dinner* / *the dinner* with some friends *the next Friday* / *next Friday*.
6 My boyfriend is *chef* / *a chef*. I think he's *the best cook* / *best cook* in the world.
7 I'm not sure if I closed *the windows* / *windows* before I left *the home* / *home* this morning.
8 In general, I like *dogs* / *the dogs*, but I don't like *dogs* / *the dogs* that live next door to me.
9 I got to *the school* / *school* late every day *the last week* / *last week*.
10 I think *happiness* / *the happiness* is more important than *success* / *the success*.

b Complete with *a / an, the,* or – (= no article).

A We're lost. Let's stop and buy *a* map.
B No need. I'll put *the* address in *the* satnav.

1 **A** How often do you go to _____ gym?
B About three times _____ week. But I never go on _____ Fridays.
2 **A** What time does _____ train leave?
B In ten minutes. Can you give me _____ lift to _____ station?
3 **A** What _____ lovely dress!
B Thanks. I bought it in _____ sales _____ last month.
4 **A** What's _____ most interesting place to visit in your town?
B Probably _____ castle. It's _____ oldest building in town.
5 **A** What shall we do _____ next weekend?
B Let's invite some friends for _____ lunch. We could eat outside in _____ garden.
6 **A** Do you like _____ dogs?
B Not really. I prefer _____ cats. I think they're _____ best pets.
7 **A** Is your mum _____ housewife?
B No, she's _____ teacher. She's always tired when she finishes _____ work.
8 **A** Have you ever had _____ problem in your relationship?
B Yes, but we got over _____ problem and we got married _____ last year.
9 **A** When is _____ meeting?
B They've changed _____ date. It's _____ next Tuesday now.

◀ p.29

4A

can, could, be able to (ability and possibility)

can / could

I **can** speak three languages fluently. 2 34
Jenny **can't** come tonight. She's ill.
My cousin **could** play the violin when she was three.
They **couldn't** wait because they were in a hurry.
Could you open the door for me, please?

Could you open the door for me, please?

- *can* is a modal verb. It only has a present form (which can be used with future meaning) and a past or conditional form (*could*).
- For all other tenses and forms, we use *be able to* + infinitive.

be able to + infinitive

1 Luke **has been able to** swim since he was three. 2 35
I'd like **to be able to** ski.
I love **being able to** stay in bed late on Sunday morning.
You**'ll be able to** practise your English in London.
2 Fortunately, I **am able to** accept your invitation.
My colleagues **weren't able to** come to yesterday's meeting.

1 We use *be able to* + infinitive for ability and possibility, especially where there is no form of *can*, e.g. future, present perfect, infinitive and gerund, etc.
2 We sometimes use *be able to* in the present and past (instead of *can / could*), usually if we want to be more formal.

a Complete with the correct form of *be able to* (+, -, or ?).

I*'ve* never *been able to* scuba dive.

1 Her mobile has been switched off all morning, so I ______________ talk to her yet.
2 I don't like noisy bars. I like ______________ have a conversation without shouting.
3 I ______________ leave home when I get a job.
4 We're having a party next Saturday. ______________ you ______________ come?
5 You need ______________ swim before you can go in a canoe.
6 I'm going to France next week, but I don't speak French. I hate ______________ communicate with people.
7 Fortunately, firefighters ______________ rescue all of the people trapped inside the burning house.
8 I'm very sorry, but we ______________ go to your wedding next month. We'll be on holiday.
9 I'm feeling a bit worse. ______________ you ______________ contact the doctor yet?
10 The manager ______________ see you right now because he's in a meeting.

b Circle the correct form. Tick ✓ if both are possible.

I've always wanted to *can* | *be able to* dance salsa.

1 My little boy *couldn't* | *wasn't able to* speak until he was nearly two years old.
2 She's much better after her operation. She'll *can* | *be able to* walk again in a few months.
3 He hasn't *could* | *been able to* mend my bike yet. He'll do it tomorrow.
4 It's the weekend at last! I love *can* | *being able to* go out with my friends.
5 When we lived on the coast, we used to *can* | *be able to* go to the beach every day.
6 I *can't* | *'m not able to* send any emails at the moment. My computer isn't working.
7 I *could* | *was able to* read before I started school.
8 We won't *can* | *be able to* go on holiday this year because we need to spend a lot of money on the house.
9 Linda's really pleased because she's finally *could* | *been able to* find a part-time job.
10 Alex *can* | *is able to* speak Portuguese fluently after living in Lisbon for ten years.

◄ p.34

have to, must, should

have to / must (+ infinitive)

2 42

1 You **have to** wear a seatbelt in a car.
Do you **have to** work on Saturdays?
I **had to** wear a uniform at my primary school.
I'll have to get up early tomorrow. My interview is at 9.00.
2 You **must** be on time tomorrow because there's a test.
You **must** remember to phone Emily – it's her birthday.
3 I love the Louvre! You **have to** go when you're in Paris.
You **must** see this film – it's amazing!

- *have to* and *must* are normally used to talk about obligation or something that it is necessary to do.

1 *have to* is a normal verb and it exists in all tenses and forms, e.g. also as a gerund or infinitive.
2 *must* is a modal verb. It only exists in the present, but it can be used with a future meaning.
3 You can also use *have to* or *must* for strong recommendations.

have to or must?
Have to and *must* have a very similar meaning, and you can usually use either form.
Have to is more common for general, external obligations, for example rules and laws.
Must is more common for specific (i.e. on one occasion) or personal obligations. Compare:
I have to wear a shirt and tie at work. (= It's the rule in this company.)
I must buy a new shirt – this one is too old now. (= It's my own decision.)

have got to
Have got to is often used instead of *have to* or *must* in spoken English, e.g. *I've got to go now. It's very late.*

don't have to

2 43

You **don't have to** pay – this museum is free.
You **don't have to** go to the party if you don't want to.

mustn't

2 44

You **mustn't** park here.
You **mustn't** eat that cake – it's for the party.

- We use *don't have to* when there is no obligation to do something, and *mustn't* when something is prohibited.
- *don't have to* and *mustn't* are completely different. Compare:
  You don't have to drive – we can get a train. (= You can drive if you want to, but it's not necessary / obligatory.)
  You mustn't drive along this street. (= It's prohibited, against the law, NOT ~~*You don't have to drive along this street.*~~)
- You can often use *can't* or *not allowed to* instead of *mustn't*.
  You ***mustn't*** */* ***can't*** */* ***'re not allowed to*** *park here.*

should / shouldn't (+ infinitive)

2 45

You **should** take warm clothes with you to Dublin. It might be cold at night.
You **shouldn't** drink so much coffee. It isn't good for you.
I think the government **should** do something about unemployment.

- *should* is not as strong as *must* / *have to*. We use it to give advice or an opinion – to say if we think something is the right or wrong thing to do.
- *should* is a modal verb. The only forms are *should* / *shouldn't*.
- You can use *ought to* / *ought not to* instead of *should* / *shouldn't*.
  You ought to take warm clothes with you to Dublin.
  You ought not to drink so much coffee.

a Complete with the correct form of *have to* ([+], [-], or [?]).

I'll have to call back later because the line's engaged. [+]

1 Passengers ________ switch off their laptops during take-off. [+]
2 ________ you ________ do a lot of homework when you were at school? [?]
3 My sister is a nurse, so some weeks she ________ work nights. [+]
4 ________ you ever ________ have an operation? [?]
5 Saturdays are the best day of the week. I love ________ get up early. [-]
6 I ________ leave a message on her voicemail because she wasn't in. [+]
7 In the future, people ________ go to school; they'll all study at home. [-]
8 With old mobile phones, you used to ________ charge the battery more often. [+]
9 ________ your boyfriend ________ answer his work emails at weekends? [?]
10 The exhibition was free, so I ________ pay. [-]

b Circle the correct form. Tick ✓ if both are possible.

You *don't have to* / *mustn't* use your phone in quiet zones.

1 Do you think we *should* / *ought to* text Dad to tell him we'll be late?
2 You *don't have to* / *mustn't* send text messages when you are driving.
3 A pilot *has to* / *must* wear a uniform when he's at work.
4 You *shouldn't* / *mustn't* talk on your mobile when you're filling up with petrol.
5 I *have to* / *must* speak to my phone company. My last bill was wrong.
6 We *don't have to* / *mustn't* hurry. We have plenty of time.

◀ p.39

5A

past tenses

past simple: *worked, stopped, went, had*, etc.

She **was** born in Berlin. 3 10
They **got** married last year.
On the way to Rome we **stopped** in Florence for the night.
The plane **didn't arrive** on time.
What time **did** you **get up** this morning?

- We use the past simple for finished actions in the past (when we say, ask, or know when they happened).
- Remember **Irregular verbs** *p.165*.

past continuous: *was / were* + verb + *-ing*

1 What **were** you **doing** at six o'clock last night? 3 11
2 I **was driving** along the motorway when it started snowing.
3 While I **was doing** the housework the children **were playing** in the garden.
4 It was a cold night and it **was raining**. I **was watching** TV in the sitting room...

1 We use the past continuous to talk about an action in progress at a specific time in the past.
2 We often use the past continuous to describe a past action in progress which was interrupted by another action (expressed in the past simple).
3 We often use the past continuous with *while* for two actions happening at the same time.
4 We often use the past continuous to describe the beginning of a story or anecdote.

past perfect: *had* + past participle

When they turned on the TV, the match **had** already **finished**. 3 12
As soon as I shut the door, I realized that **I'd left** my keys on the table.
We couldn't get a table in the restaurant because we **hadn't booked**.

- We use the past perfect when we are talking about the past and we want to talk about an earlier past action. Compare:
  When John arrived, they ***went out***. (= first John arrived and then they went out)
  When John arrived, they ***had gone out***. (= they went out before John arrived)

using narrative tenses together

It was a cold night and it **was raining**. I **was watching** TV in the sitting room. Suddenly I **heard** a knock at the door. I **got up** and **opened** the door. But there was nobody there. The person who **had knocked** on the door **had disappeared**... 3 13

- Use the past continuous (*was raining, was watching*) to set the scene.
- Use the past simple (*heard, got up*, etc.) to say what happened.
- Use the past perfect (*had knocked, had disappeared*) to say what happened before the previous past action.

a Circle the correct form.

The teacher gave Robbie a zero because he *cheated* | *had cheated* in the exam.

1 They didn't win the match although they *were training* | *had trained* every evening.
2 Mike had an accident while he *cycled* | *was cycling* to work.
3 I *cleaned* | *had cleaned* the house when I got home. It looked great.
4 When we arrived, the match *started* | *had started*. We got there just in time and saw the whole match!
5 The captain *didn't score* | *hadn't scored* any goals when the referee sent him off.
6 My son got injured while he *played* | *was playing* basketball last Saturday.
7 Luckily, we *stopped* | *had stopped* skiing when the snowstorm started. We were already back at the hotel.
8 England *weren't losing* | *hadn't lost* any of their games when they played in the quarter-finals.
9 The referee suspended the match because it *was raining* | *rained* too hard to play.

b Complete with the past simple, past continuous, or past perfect.

The marathon runner *was sweating* when she *crossed* the finish line. (sweat, cross)

1 The accident ________ when they ________ home. (happen, drive)
2 The crowd ________ when the referee ________ the final whistle. (cheer, blow)
3 I ________ her at first because she ________ so much. (not recognize, change)
4 The police ________ her on the motorway because she ________ a seat belt. (stop, not wear)
5 Some of the players ________ while the coach ________ to them. (not listen, talk)
6 We ________ use the ski slope because it ________ enough. (not can, not snow)
7 They ________ play tennis because they ________ a court. (not able to, not book)
8 The player ________ a yellow card because he ________ his shirt. (get, take off)

◀ p.46

present and past habits and states: *usually* and *used to*

3 17

1 I **usually get up** at 8.00 during the week.
I **don't normally go out** during the week.
English houses **usually have** gardens.
Do you **normally walk** to work?
2 We **used to go** to France for our holidays when I was a child.
He **didn't use to do** any exercise, but now he runs marathons.
I **never used to like** football, but I watch it every week now.
We **used to be** close friends, but we don't talk to each other any more.
That building **used to be** a restaurant, but it closed down last year.
Did they **use to live** in the city centre?
Didn't you **use to have** long hair?

1 For present habits we can use *usually* or *normally* + present simple. NOT ~~*I used to get up at 8.00.*~~
2 For past habits we use *used to* / *didn't use to* + infinitive.
- *used to* does not exist in the present tense. NOT ~~*I use to get up at 8.00 during the week.*~~
- We use *used to* for things that were true over a period of time in the past. *Used to* often refers to something which is not true now.
  I used to do a lot of sport. (= I did a lot of sport for a period of time in the past, but now I don't.)
- We often use *never used to* instead of *didn't use to*.
- *used to* / *didn't use to* can be used with action verbs (e.g. *go, do*) and non-action verbs (e.g. *be, have*).
- We can also use the past simple to describe past habits (often with an adverb of frequency).
  We (often) went to France for our holidays when I was a child.
  I lived in the city centre until I got married.

used to or past simple?
We can use *used to* or past simple for repeated actions or states, and the meaning is the same.
I used to live in Leeds as a child. / I lived in Leeds as a child.
But if the action happened only once, or we mention exact dates or number of times, we have to use past simple.
I went to Paris last year. NOT ~~*I used to go to Paris last year.*~~
Jack caught the train to London four times last week. NOT ~~*Jack used to catch the train to London four times last week.*~~

any more and _any longer_
We often use *not...any more / any longer* (= not now) with the present simple to contrast with *used to*.
I used to go to the gym, but I don't (go) any more / any longer.

be used to and _get used to_
Don't confuse *used to / didn't use to* (do sth) with *be used to* or *get used to* (doing sth).
*I **am used to getting up** early every day.*
(= I am accustomed to it. I always do it so it is not a problem for me.)
*Lola can't **get used to living** in the UK.*
(= She can't get accustomed to it. It is a problem for her.)

a Complete with *used to* (+, –, or ?) and a verb from the list.

argue be get on go out have like ~~live~~ speak spend wear work

Sonya *used to live* in New York City, but later she moved to New Jersey. +
1 We ________ a lot in common, but now we're completely different. +
2 I ________ much time online, but now I'm addicted to *Facebook*. –
3 ________ your fiancé ________ glasses? He looks different now. ?
4 I ________ with my classmates, but now I spend all my time with my boyfriend. +
5 Where ________ your husband ________ before he got the job in the bank? ?
6 My sister has lost a lot of weight. She ________ so slim. –
7 ________ you ________ a lot with your parents when you were a teenager? ?
8 I ________ Japanese food, but now I eat a lot of sushi. –
9 Laura ________ well with her flatmate, but now they've fallen out. +
10 My ex ________ to me, but now he calls me quite often. –

b Are the highlighted verb forms right ✓ or wrong ✗? Correct the wrong ones.

Sonya use to see Michael every day. ✗ *used to see*
1 His parents used to split up after he was born.
2 Do you usually tell a close friend about your problems?
3 My sister didn't use to want children, but now she's got four!
4 I didn't used to like my maths teacher when I was at school.
5 They used to go on holiday every year.
6 That couple have three kids, so they don't use to go out at night.
7 Where did your parents use to meet when they first went out?
8 My husband use to work for a bank, but now he's unemployed.
9 We love the theatre. We usually go to a play at least once a month.

◀ p.49

Food and cooking

1 FOOD

a Match the words and pictures.

Fish and seafood

1 crab /kræb/
mussels /ˈmʌslz/
prawns /prɔːnz/
salmon /ˈsæmən/
squid /skwɪd/
tuna /ˈtjuːnə/

Meat

beef /biːf/
chicken /ˈtʃɪkɪn/
duck /dʌk/
lamb /læm/
pork /pɔːk/

Fruit and vegetables

aubergine /ˈəʊbəʒiːn/ (*AmE* eggplant)
beetroot /ˈbiːtruːt/
cabbage /ˈkæbɪdʒ/
cherries /ˈtʃeriz/
courgette /kɔːˈʒet/ (*AmE* zucchini)
cucumber /ˈkjuːkʌmbə/
grapes /greɪps/
green beans /griːn biːnz/
lemon /ˈlemən/
mango /ˈmæŋgəʊ/
melon /ˈmelən/
peach /piːtʃ/
pear /peə/
raspberries /ˈrɑːzbəriz/
red pepper /red ˈpepə/

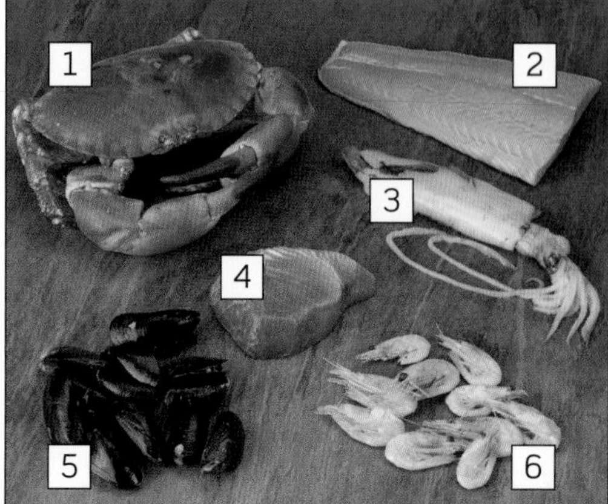

b 1 2 Listen and check.

c Are there any things in the list that you...?

a love
b hate
c have never tried

d Are there any other kinds of fish, meat, or fruit and vegetables that are very common in your country?

2 COOKING

a Match the words and pictures.

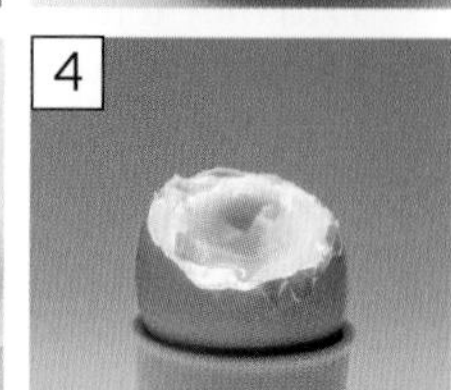

4 boiled /bɔɪld/
roast /rəʊst/
baked /beɪkt/
grilled /grɪld/
fried /fraɪd/
steamed /stiːmd/

b 1 3 Listen and check.

c How do you prefer these things to be cooked?

eggs	chicken
potatoes	**fish**

Phrasal verbs

Learn these phrasal verbs connected with food and diet.

*I **eat out** a lot because I often don't have time to cook.* (= eat in restaurants)

*I'm trying to **cut down on** coffee at the moment. I'm only having one cup at breakfast.* (= have less)

*The doctor told me I had very high cholesterol and that I should completely **cut out** all high-fat cheese and dairy products from my diet.* (= eliminate)

◄ p.4

Personality

1 WHAT ARE THEY LIKE?

a Complete the definitions with the adjectives.

affectionate /ə'fekʃənət/ aggressive /ə'gresɪv/ ambitious /æm'bɪʃəs/ anxious /'æŋkʃəs/ bossy /'bɒsi/ charming /'tʃɑːmɪŋ/ competitive /kəm'petətɪv/ independent /ɪndɪ'pendənt/ jealous /'dʒeləs/ moody /'muːdi/ rebellious /rɪ'belɪəs/ reliable /rɪ'laɪəbl/ ~~selfish~~ /'selfɪʃ/ sensible /'sensəbl/ sensitive /'sensətɪv/ sociable /'səʊʃəbl/ spoilt /spɔɪlt/ stubborn /'stʌbən/

1 *Selfish* people think about themselves and not about other people.
2 A __________ person always wants to win.
3 __________ children behave badly because they are given everything they want.
4 An __________ person gets angry quickly and likes fighting and arguing.
5 __________ people have an attractive personality and make people like them.
6 A __________ person has common sense and is practical.
7 A __________ person is friendly and enjoys being with other people.
8 __________ people are often worried or stressed.
9 A __________ person is happy one minute and sad the next, and is often bad-tempered.
10 __________ people like doing things on their own, without help.
11 A __________ person likes giving orders to other people.
12 An __________ person shows that they love or like people very much.
13 A __________ person thinks that someone loves another person more than them, or wants what other people have.
14 A __________ person can be easily hurt or offended.
15 An __________ person wants to be successful in life.
16 A __________ person is someone who you can trust or depend on.
17 A __________ person doesn't like obeying rules.
18 A __________ person never changes his (or her) opinion or attitude about something.

b 1 23 Listen and check.

c Cover the definitions and look at the adjectives. Remember the definitions.

2 OPPOSITES

a Match the adjectives and their opposites.

hard-working /hɑːd 'wɜːkɪŋ/ mean /miːn/ outgoing /aʊt'gəʊɪŋ/ self-confident /self 'kɒnfɪdənt/ stupid /'stjuːpɪd/ talkative /'tɔːkətɪv/

	Opposite
clever	__________
generous	__________
insecure	__________
lazy	__________
quiet	__________
shy	__________

b 1 24 Listen and check. Then cover the opposites and test yourself.

c With a partner, look at the adjectives again in **1** and **2**. Do you think they are positive, negative, or neutral characteristics?

3 NEGATIVE PREFIXES

a Which prefix do you use with these adjectives? Put them in the correct column.

~~ambitious~~ friendly honest imaginative kind mature organized patient reliable responsible selfish sensitive sociable tidy

un- / dis-	im- / ir- / in-
unambitious	

b 1 25 Listen and check. Which of the new adjectives has a positive meaning?

c Cover the columns. Test yourself.

False friends

Some words in English are very similar to words in other languages, but have different meanings.

Sensible looks very similar to *sensible* in Spanish and French, but in fact in English it means someone who has common sense and is practical. The Spanish / French word *sensible* translates as ***sensitive*** in English (to describe a person who is easily hurt).

Sympathetic does not mean the same as *sympatyczny* in Polish or *sempatik* in Turkish (which mean ***nice, friendly***). In English, ***sympathetic*** means a person who understands other people's feelings, e.g. *My best friend was very sympathetic when I failed my exam last week.*

◀ p.11

Money

1 VERBS

a Complete the sentences with a verb from the list.

be worth /bi wɜːθ/ borrow /ˈbɒrəʊ/ can't afford /kɑːnt əˈfɔːd/ charge /tʃɑːdʒ/ cost /kɒst/ earn /ɜːn/ ~~inherit~~ /ɪnˈherɪt/ invest /ɪnˈvest/ lend /lend/ owe /əʊ/ raise /reɪz/ save /seɪv/ waste /weɪst/

1	My uncle is going to leave me £2,000.	I'm going to *inherit* £2,000.
2	I put some money aside every week for a holiday.	I ________ money every week.
3	My brother has promised to give me €50 until next week.	He has promised to ________ me €50.
4	I need to ask my mum to give me £20 until Friday.	I need to ________ £20 from my mum.
5	I often spend money on stupid things.	I often ________ money.
6	I don't have enough money to buy that car.	I ________ to buy that car.
7	I usually have to pay the mechanic £100 to service my car.	The mechanic ________ me £100.
8	These shoes are quite expensive. They are $200.	They ________ $200.
9	Jim gave me £100. I haven't paid it back yet.	I ________ Jim £100.
10	I want to put money in a bank account. They'll give me 5% interest.	I want to ________ some money.
11	I work in a supermarket. They pay me £1,000 a month.	I ________ £1,000 a month.
12	I could sell my house for about €200,000.	My house ________ about €200,000.
13	We need to get people to give money to build a new hospital.	We want to ________ money for the new hospital.

b 1 35 Listen and check. Cover the sentences on the right. Try to remember them.

2 PREPOSITIONS

a Complete the **Preposition** column with a word from the list.

back by for (x2) from in (x2) into on to

	Preposition
1 Would you like to pay ___ cash or ___ credit card?	*in, by*
2 I paid ___ the dinner last night. It was my birthday.	
3 I spent £50 ___ books yesterday.	
4 My uncle invested all his money ___ property.	
5 I don't like lending money ___ friends.	
6 I borrowed a lot of money ___ the bank.	
7 They charged us €60 ___ a bottle of wine.	
8 I can only lend you the money if you pay me ___ next week.	
9 I never get ___ debt. I hate owing people money.	

b 1 36 Listen and check.

c Cover the **Preposition** column. Look at the sentences and remember the prepositions.

3 NOUNS

a Match the nouns and definitions.

bill /bɪl/ cash machine (*AmE* ATM) /kæʃ məˈʃiːn/ coin /kɔɪn/ loan /ləʊn/ mortgage /ˈmɔːɡɪdʒ/ ~~note~~ /nəʊt/ salary /ˈsæləri/ tax /tæks/

1 *note* a piece of paper money
2 ________ a piece of money made of metal
3 ________ a piece of paper which shows how much money you have to pay for something
4 ________ the money you get for the work you do
5 ________ money that you pay to the government
6 ________ money that somebody (or a bank) lends you
7 ________ money that a bank lends you to buy a house
8 ________ a machine where you can get money

b 1 37 Listen and check. Cover the words and look at the definitions. Try to remember the words.

Phrasal verbs

*I **took out** €200 from a cash machine.* (= took from my bank account)

*When can you **pay** me **back** the money I lent you?* (= return)

*I have to **live off** my parents while I'm at university.* (= depend on financially)

*It's difficult for me and my wife to **live on** only one salary.* (= have enough money for basic things you need to live)

◄ p.14

Transport

1 PUBLIC TRANSPORT AND VEHICLES

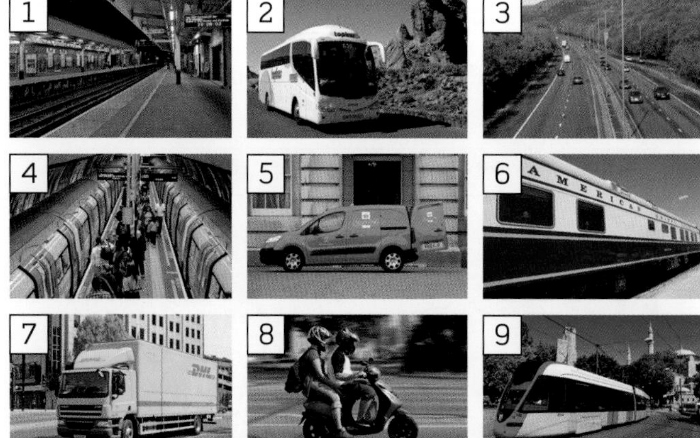

a Match the words and pictures.

- [ ] carriage /ˈkærɪdʒ/
- [ ] coach /kəʊtʃ/
- [ ] lorry /ˈlɒri/(*AmE* truck)
- [ ] motorway /ˈməʊtəweɪ/
- 1 platform /ˈplætfɔːm/
- [ ] scooter /ˈskuːtə/
- [ ] the underground /ˈʌndəgraʊnd/ (*AmE* subway)
- [ ] tram /træm/
- [ ] van /væn/

b 2 2 Listen and check.

c Cover the words and look at the pictures. Try to remember the words.

2 ON THE ROAD

Compound nouns

Compound nouns are two nouns together where the first noun describes the second, e.g. *a child seat* = a seat for a child, *a bus stop* = a place for buses to stop, etc. In compound nouns the first noun is stressed more strongly than the second. There are many compound nouns related to road travel.

a Complete the compound nouns.

belt /belt/ camera /ˈkæmərə/ ~~crash~~ /kræʃ/ crossing /ˈkrɒsɪŋ/ fine /faɪn/ hour /ˈaʊə/ jam /dʒæm/ lane /leɪn/ lights /laɪts/ limit /ˈlɪmɪt/ rank /ræŋk/ station /ˈsteɪʃn/ works /wɜːks/ zone /zəʊn/

1 car *crash*

2 cycle ________

3 parking ________

4 pedestrian ________

5 petrol ________

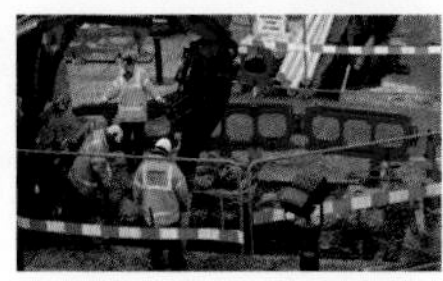

6 road ________

7 rush ________

8 seat ________

9 speed ________

10 speed ________

11 taxi ________

12 traffic ________

13 traffic ________

14 zebra ________

b 2 3 Listen and check. Then cover the compound nouns and look at the pictures. Remember the compound nouns.

3 HOW LONG DOES IT TAKE?

How long does it take?

It **takes** about an hour to get from London to Oxford by train.

It **took (me)** more than an hour to get to work yesterday.

How long does it take (you) to get to school?

Use *take* (+ person) + time (+ *to get to*) to talk about the duration of a journey, etc.

Read the information box above. Then ask and answer with a partner.

1 How do you get to work / school? How long does it take?

2 How long does it take to get from your house to the town centre?

Phrasal verbs

Learn these phrasal verbs connected with transport and travel.

*We **set off** at 7.00 in the morning to try to avoid the traffic.* (= leave on a journey)

*I arrive at 8.15. Do you think you could **pick** me **up** at the station?* (= collect sb, in a car, etc.)

*I got on the wrong bus, and I **ended up** on the opposite side of town.* (= find yourself in a place / situation that you did not expect)

*We're **running out of** petrol. Let's stop at the next petrol station.* (= finish your supply of sth)

***Watch out!** / **Look out!** You're going to crash!* (= be careful or pay attention to sth dangerous)

◀ p.24

Dependent prepositions

1 AFTER VERBS

a Complete the **Preposition** column with a word from the list.

about at between for in of on to with

He apologized to the policeman for driving fast.

b 2 25 Listen and check.

c Cover the **Preposition** column. Say the sentences with the correct preposition.

		Preposition
1	He apologized ___ the policeman ___ driving fast.	*to*, *for*
2	We're arriving ___ Milan on Sunday.	___
3	We're arriving ___ Malpensa airport at 3.45.	___
4	Who does this book belong ___ ?	___
5	I never argue ___ my husband ___ money.	___, ___
6	Could you ask the waiter ___ the bill?	___
7	Do you believe ___ ghosts?	___
8	I can't choose ___ these two bags.	___
9	We might go out. It depends ___ the weather.	___
10	I dreamt ___ my childhood last night.	___
11	Don't laugh ___ me! I'm doing my best!	___
12	I'm really looking forward ___ the party.	___
13	If I pay ___ the meal, can you get the drinks?	___
14	This music reminds me ___ our honeymoon in Italy.	___
15	I don't spend a lot of money ___ clothes.	___

2 AFTER ADJECTIVES

a Complete the **Preposition** column with a word from the list.

about at for from in of on to with

My brother is afraid of* bats.

*also *scared of* and *frightened of*

b 2 26 Listen and check.

c Cover the **Preposition** column. Say the sentences with the correct preposition.

		Preposition
1	My brother is afraid* ___ bats.	*of*
2	She's really angry ___ her boyfriend ___ last night.	___ ___
3	I've never been good ___ sport.	___
4	Eat your vegetables. They're good ___ you.	___
5	I'm very close ___ my elder sister.	___
6	This exercise isn't very different ___ the last one.	___ (or *to*)
7	We're really excited ___ going to Brazil.	___
8	I'm fed up ___ listening to you complaining.	___
9	Krakow is famous ___ its main square.	___
10	My sister is very interested ___ astrology.	___
11	I'm very fond ___ my little nephew. He's adorable.	___
12	She's very keen ___ cycling. She does about 50 kilometres every weekend.	___
13	I don't like people who aren't kind ___ animals.	___
14	She used to be married ___ a pop star.	___
15	I'm really pleased ___ my new motorbike.	___
16	My dad was very proud ___ learning to ski.	___
17	Why are you always rude ___ waiters and shop assistants?	___
18	Rachel is worried ___ losing her job.	___
19	I'm tired ___ walking. Let's stop and have a rest.	___

Gerunds after prepositions
Remember that after a preposition we use a verb in the gerund (+ *-ing*).
We're really excited ***about going*** *to Brazil.*
I'm tired ***of walking***.

◀ p.31

Sport

1 PEOPLE AND PLACES

a Match the words and pictures.

- captain /ˈkæptɪn/
- coach /kəʊtʃ/
- 1 fans /fænz/
- players /ˈpleɪəz/
- referee /refəˈriː/ / umpire /ˈʌmpaɪə/
- spectators /spekˈteɪtəz/ / the crowd /kraʊd/
- team /tiːm/
- stadium /ˈsteɪdiəm/
- sports hall /spɔːts hɔːl/ / arena /əˈriːnə/

b 3 2 Listen and check. Cover the words and look at the pictures. Test yourself.

c Match the places and sports.

circuit /ˈsɜːkɪt/ course /kɔːs/ ~~court~~ /kɔːt/ pitch /pɪtʃ/ pool /puːl/ slope /sləʊp/ track /træk/

1 tennis / basketball *court*
2 football / rugby / hockey ________
3 swimming / diving ________
4 athletics ________
5 Formula 1 / motorcycling ________
6 golf ________
7 ski ________

d 3 3 Listen and check. Then test a partner.

A (book open) say a sport, e.g. *tennis*.
B (book closed) say where you do it, e.g. *tennis court*.

2 VERBS

win* and *beat
You *win* a match, competition, medal, or trophy.
You *beat* another team or person NOT ~~*Milan won Chelsea*~~.

a Complete with the past tense and past participles.

beat	*beat*	________
win	________	________
lose	________	________
draw	________	________

b Complete the **Verb** column with the past tense of a verb from **a**.

	Verb
1 Milan ▢ Chelsea 3–0.	________
2 Milan ▢ the match 3–0.	________
3 The Chicago Bulls ▢ 78–91 to the Boston Celtics.	________
4 Spain ▢ with Brazil 2–2.	________

c 3 4 Listen and check **a** and **b**.

d Complete the **Verb** column with a verb from the list.

do get fit get injured go kick score throw ~~train~~

	Verb
1 Professional sportspeople have to ▢ every day.	*train*
2 Don't play tennis on a wet court. You might ▢.	________
3 A footballer has to try to ▢ the ball into the goal.	________
4 I've started going to the gym because I want to ▢.	________
5 Our new striker is going to ▢ a lot of goals.	________
6 Would you like to ▢ swimming this afternoon?	________
7 My brothers ▢ yoga and tai-chi.	________
8 In basketball, players ▢ the ball to each other.	________

e 3 5 Listen and check. Cover the **Verb** columns in **b** and **d**. Test yourself.

Phrasal verbs
It's important to ***warm up*** *before you do any vigorous exercise.* (= do light exercise to get ready, e.g. for a match)
My daughter ***works out*** *every afternoon.* (= does exercise at a gym)
The player got a red card and was ***sent off*** *after committing a foul.* (= told to leave the pitch / court, etc.)
My team was ***knocked out*** *in the semi-finals.* (= eliminated)

◄ p.44

Relationships

1 PEOPLE

a Match the words and definitions.

classmate /ˈklɑːsmeɪt/
close friend /kləʊs frend/
colleague /ˈkɒliːɡ/ ~~couple~~ /ˈkʌpl/
ex /eks/ fiancé /fiˈɒnseɪ/ (*female* fiancée)
flatmate /ˈflætmeɪt/ partner /ˈpɑːtnə/

1 *couple* ______ two people who are married or in a romantic relationship
2 ______ your husband, wife, boyfriend, or girlfriend
3 ______ the person that you are engaged to be married to
4 ______ a person that you share a flat with
5 ______ a person that you work with
6 ______ (*colloquial*) a person that you used to have a relationship with
7 ______ a very good friend that you can talk to about anything
8 ______ a friend from school or college

b 3 19 Listen and check. Cover the definitions and look at the words. Remember the definitions.

2 VERBS AND VERB PHRASES

a Complete the sentences with a verb or verb phrase in the past tense.

be together become friends break up get in touch get married get on
get to know go out together have (sth) in common lose touch ~~meet~~ propose

1 I *met* ______ Mark when I was studying at York University.
2 We ______ each other quickly because we went to the same classes.
3 We soon ______, and we discovered that we ______ a lot ______. For example, we both liked art and music.
4 We ______ in our second term and we fell in love.
5 We ______ for two years, but we argued a lot and in our last term at university we ______.
6 After we left university, we ______ because I moved to London and he stayed in York.
7 Five years later we ______ again on *Facebook*. We were both still single, and Mark had moved to London too.
8 This time we ______ better than before, maybe because we were older.
9 After two months Mark ______ and I accepted.
10 We ______ last summer. A lot of our old university friends came to the wedding!

b 3 20 Listen and check.

c Look at the pictures. Try to remember the story.

Colloquial language

I went out last night with some ***mates****.* (= friends)
I really ***fancy*** *a girl I met in class last week.* (= I'm attracted to her)
Jane ***dumped*** *her boyfriend last night!* (= told him that their relationship was over)
My younger sister ***has a crush on*** *Justin Bieber!* (= be madly in love with when you are young)

Phrasal verbs

My sister and her boyfriend ***broke up*** */* ***split up*** *last month.* (= ended their relationship)
My daughter has ***fallen out with*** *her best friend. They aren't speaking to each other at the moment.* (= had an argument with and stopped being friends)

◄ p.50

Irregular verbs

5 45

Infinitive	Past simple	Past participle
be /bi/	was /wɒz/ were /wɜː/	been /biːn/
beat /biːt/	beat	beaten /'biːtn/
become /bɪ'kʌm/	became /bɪ'keɪm/	become
begin /bɪ'gɪn/	began /bɪ'gæn/	begun /bɪ'gʌn/
bite /baɪt/	bit /bɪt/	bitten /'bɪtn/
break /breɪk/	broke /brəʊk/	broken /'brəʊkən/
bring /brɪŋ/	brought /brɔːt/	brought
build /bɪld/	built /bɪlt/	built
buy /baɪ/	bought /bɔːt/	bought
can /kæn/	could /kʊd/	–
catch /kætʃ/	caught /kɔːt/	caught
choose /tʃuːz/	chose /tʃəʊz/	chosen /'tʃəʊzn/
come /kʌm/	came /keɪm/	come
cost /kɒst/	cost	cost
cut /kʌt/	cut	cut
do /duː/	did /dɪd/	done /dʌn/
draw /drɔː/	drew /druː/	drawn /drɔːn/
dream /driːm/	dreamt /dremt/ (dreamed /driːmd/)	dreamt (dreamed)
drink /drɪŋk/	drank /dræŋk/	drunk /drʌŋk/
drive /draɪv/	drove /drəʊv/	driven /'drɪvn/
eat /iːt/	ate /eɪt/	eaten /'iːtn/
fall /fɔːl/	fell /fel/	fallen /'fɔːlən/
feel /fiːl/	felt /felt/	felt
find /faɪnd/	found /faʊnd/	found
fly /flaɪ/	flew /fluː/	flown /fləʊn/
forget /fə'get/	forgot /fə'gɒt/	forgotten /fə'gɒtn/
get /get/	got /gɒt/	got
give /gɪv/	gave /geɪv/	given /'gɪvn/
go /gəʊ/	went /went/	gone /gɒn/
grow /grəʊ/	grew /gruː/	grown /grəʊn/
hang /hæŋ/	hung /hʌŋ/	hung
have /hæv/	had /hæd/	had
hear /hɪə/	heard /hɜːd/	heard
hit /hɪt/	hit	hit
hurt /hɜːt/	hurt	hurt
keep /kiːp/	kept /kept/	kept
know /nəʊ/	knew /njuː/	known /nəʊn/

Infinitive	Past simple	Past participle
learn /lɜːn/	learnt /lɜːnt/	learnt
leave /liːv/	left /left/	left
lend /lend/	lent /lent/	lent
let /let/	let	let
lie /laɪ/	lay /leɪ/	lain /leɪn/
lose /luːz/	lost /lɒst/	lost
make /meɪk/	made /meɪd/	made
mean /miːn/	meant /ment/	meant
meet /miːt/	met /met/	met
pay /peɪ/	paid /peɪd/	paid
put /pʊt/	put	put
read /riːd/	read /red/	read /red/
ride /raɪd/	rode /rəʊd/	ridden /'rɪdn/
ring /rɪŋ/	rang /ræŋ/	rung /rʌŋ/
run /rʌn/	ran /ræn/	run
say /seɪ/	said /sed/	said
see /siː/	saw /sɔː/	seen /siːn/
sell /sel/	sold /səʊld/	sold
send /send/	sent /sent/	sent
set /set/	set	set
shine /ʃaɪn/	shone /ʃɒn/	shone
shut /ʃʌt/	shut	shut
sing /sɪŋ/	sang /sæŋ/	sung /sʌŋ/
sit /sɪt/	sat /sæt/	sat
sleep /sliːp/	slept /slept/	slept
speak /spiːk/	spoke /spəʊk/	spoken /'spəʊkən/
spend /spend/	spent /spent/	spent
stand /stænd/	stood /stʊd/	stood
steal /stiːl/	stole /stəʊl/	stolen /'stəʊlən/
swim /swɪm/	swam /swæm/	swum /swʌm/
take /teɪk/	took /tʊk/	taken /'teɪkən/
teach /tiːtʃ/	taught /tɔːt/	taught
tell /tel/	told /təʊld/	told
think /θɪŋk/	thought /θɔːt/	thought
throw /θrəʊ/	threw /θruː/	thrown /θrəʊn/
understand /ʌndə'stænd/	understood /ʌndə'stʊd/	understood
wake /weɪk/	woke /wəʊk/	woken /'wəʊkən/
wear /weə/	wore /wɔː/	worn /wɔːn/
win /wɪn/	won /wʌn/	won
write /raɪt/	wrote /rəʊt/	written /'rɪtn/

Vowel sounds

	usual spelling		! but also
fish	i	dish bill pitch fit ticket since	pretty women busy decided village physics
tree	ee ea e	beef speed peach team refund medium	people magazine key niece receipt
cat	a	mango tram crash tax carry bank	
car	ar a	garden charge starter pass drama cast	heart
clock	o	lorry cost plot bossy off on	watch want sausage because
horse	(o)or al aw	score floor bald wall prawns draw	warm course thought caught audience board
bull	u oo	full put cook foot look good	could should would woman
boot	oo u* ew	moody food argue rude few flew	suitcase juice shoe move soup through queue
computer	Many different spellings. /ə/ is always unstressed. <u>o</u>ther <u>ner</u>vous <u>a</u>bout com<u>plain</u> infor<u>ma</u>tion <u>ca</u>mera		
bird	er ir ur	term prefer dirty circuit nursery turn	learn work world worse journey
egg	e	lemon lend text spend plenty cent	friendly already healthy jealous many said

	usual spelling		! but also
up	u	public subject ugly duck hurry rush	money tongue someone enough touch couple
train	a* ai ay	save gate fail train may say	break steak great weight they grey
phone	o* oa	broke stone frozen slope roast coach	owe elbow although aubergine shoulders
bike	i* y igh	bite retire shy cycle flight lights	buy eyes height
owl	ou ow	hour mouth proud ground town brown	
boy	oi oy	boiled noisy spoilt coin enjoy employer	
ear	eer ere ear	beer engineer here we're beard appearance	really idea serious
chair	air are	airport upstairs fair hair stare careful	their there wear pear area
tourist	A very unusual sound. euro furious sure plural		
/i/	A sound between /ɪ/ and /iː/. Consonant + *y* at the end of words is pronounced /i/. happy angry thirsty		
/u/	An unusual sound between /ʊ/ and /uː/. education usually situation		

* especially before consonant + *e*

short vowels   long vowels   diphthongs

Consonant sounds

	usual spelling		! but also
parrot	p pp	plate pupil transport trip shopping apply	
bag	b bb	beans bill probably crab stubborn dubbed	
key	c k ck	court script kind kick track lucky	chemist's school stomach squid account
girl	g gg	golf grilled colleague forget aggressive luggage	
flower	f ph ff	food roof pharmacy nephew traffic affectionate	enough laugh
vase	v	van vegetables travel invest private believe	of
tie	t tt	taste tidy stadium strict attractive cottage	worked passed
dog	d dd	director afford comedy graduate address middle	failed bored
snake	s ss ce/ci	steps likes boss assistant ceiling cinema	science scene cycle
zebra	z s	lazy freezing nose cosy loves toes	
shower	sh ti (+ vowel) ci (+ vowel)	show dishwasher selfish cash ambitious explanation spacious sociable	sugar sure machine chef
television	An unusual sound.	revision decision confusion usually courgette	

	usual spelling		! but also
thumb	th	throw thriller healthy path maths teeth	
mother	th	the that with further together	
chess	ch tch t (+ure)	change cheat pitch match picture future	
jazz	j g dge	jealous just generous manager fridge judge	
leg	l ll	limit salary until reliable sell rebellious	
right	r rr	result referee primary fried borrow carriage	written wrong
witch	w wh	war waste western motorway whistle which	one once
yacht	y before u	yet year yoghurt yourself university argue	
monkey	m mm	mean arm romantic charming summer swimming	lamb
nose	n nn	neck honest none chimney tennis thinner	knee knew
singer	ng before g / k	cooking going spring bring think tongue	
house	h	handsome helmet behave inherit unhappy perhaps	who whose whole

voiced unvoiced

English sounds

- short vowels
- long vowels
- diphthongs

1 fish /fɪʃ/
2 tree /triː/
3 cat /kæt/
4 car /kɑː/
5 clock /klɒk/
6 horse /hɔːs/
7 bull /bʊl/
8 boot /buːt/
9 computer /kəmp'juːtə/
10 bird /bɜːd/
11 egg /eg/
12 up /ʌp/
13 train /treɪn/
14 phone /fəʊn/
15 bike /baɪk/
16 owl /aʊl/
17 boy /bɔɪ/
18 ear /ɪə/
19 chair /tʃeə/
20 tourist /'tʊərɪst/

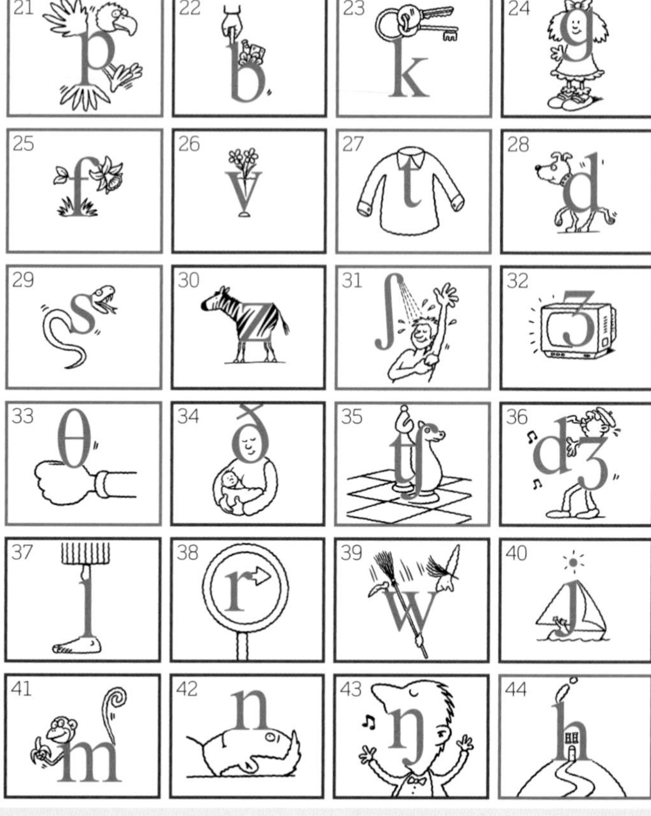

- voiced
- unvoiced

21 parrot /'pærət/
22 bag /bæg/
23 key /kiː/
24 girl /gɜːl/
25 flower /'flaʊə/
26 vase /vɑːz/
27 tie /taɪ/
28 dog /dɒg/
29 snake /sneɪk/
30 zebra /'zebrə/
31 shower /'ʃaʊə/
32 television /'telɪvɪʒn/
33 thumb /θʌm/
34 mother /'mʌðə/
35 chess /tʃes/
36 jazz /dʒæz/
37 leg /leg/
38 right /raɪt/
39 witch /wɪtʃ/
40 yacht /jɒt/
41 monkey /'mʌŋki/
42 nose /nəʊz/
43 singer /'sɪŋə/
44 house /haʊs/

Christina Latham-Koenig
Clive Oxenden

with Jane Hudson

ENGLISH FILE

Intermediate Workbook A with key

Paul Seligson and Clive Oxenden are the original co-authors of
English File 1 and *English File 2*

Practise listening out of class

For Workbook audio, go to
www.oup.com/elt/english file

Select your level.

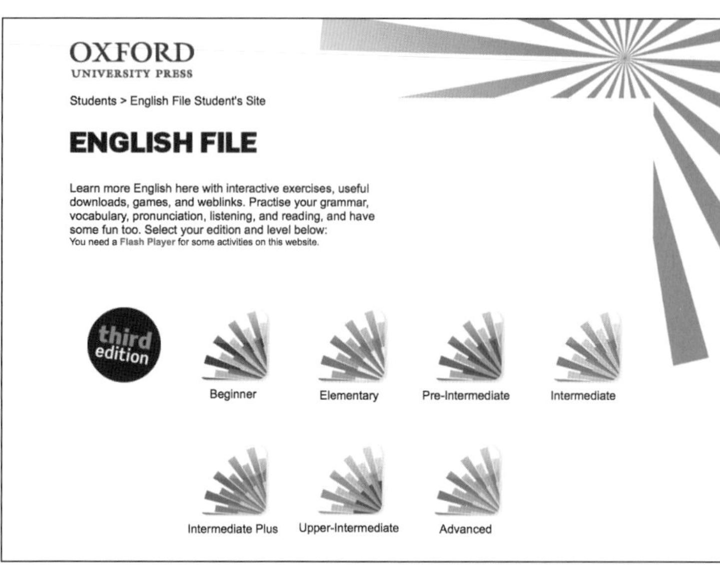

Select **Downloads**.

Select **Audio**: **Workbook**.

Contents

The two biggest best-sellers in any bookshops are the cookbooks and the diet books. The cookbooks tell you how to prepare the food and the diet books tell you how not to eat any of it.

Andy Rooney, US humourist

1A Mood food

1 VOCABULARY food and cooking

a Circle the word that is different. Explain why.

1 (beans) grapes peach raspberry
The others are all *fruit*.
2 chicken duck lamb salmon
The others are all ________.
3 beetroot cabbage pear pepper
The others are all ________.
4 aubergine lemon mango melon
The others are all ________.
5 crab mussels beef prawns
The others are all ________.
6 cabbage cherry courgette cucumber
The others are all ________.

b Complete the crossword.

c Complete the sentences with the words in the box.

fresh frozen low-fat raw spicy takeaway ~~tinned~~

1 *Tinned* tomatoes usually last for about two years.
2 I don't feel like cooking. Let's get a ________ for dinner.
3 Are there any ________ peas in the freezer?
4 I'm not very keen on ________ fish, so I never eat sushi.
5 Hannah's on a diet, so she's bought some ________ yoghurt to have for dessert.
6 They eat a lot of ________ food in Mexico.
7 We buy ________ bread from the baker's every morning.

2 PRONUNCIATION short and long vowel sounds

a Write the words in the chart.

beef carton chicken chocolate cook crab cucumber jar mango peach fork prawns sausage squid sugar tuna

1 ɪ fish	2 iː tree	3 æ cat	4 ɑː car
______ ______	*beef* ______	______ ______	______ ______
5 ɒ clock	6 ɔː horse	7 ʊ bull	8 uː boot
______ ______	______ ______	______ ______	______ ______

b 1.1 Listen and check. Then listen again and repeat the words.

Pronouncing difficult words

c Write the words.

1 /ˈbɔɪld/ *boiled*
2 /ˈkæbɪdʒ/ ______
3 /ˈspaɪsi/ ______
4 /rəʊst/ ______
5 /greɪps/ ______
6 /fruːt/ ______
7 /beɪkt/ ______
8 /ˈmelən/ ______
9 /ˈəʊbəʒiːn/ ______

d 1.2 Listen and check. Then listen again and repeat the words.

3 GRAMMAR present simple / continuous, action and non-action verbs

a Are the highlighted phrases right (✓) or wrong (✗)? Correct the wrong phrases.

1 Does your girlfriend like seafood? ✓
______
2 Lucy's in the kitchen. She makes a cup of tea. ✗
She's making
3 Are you eating out every weekend? ☐
______
4 I don't know what to cook for dinner. ☐
______
5 Are you thinking the fish is cooked now? ☐
______
6 We're having lunch with my parents every Sunday. ☐
______
7 My mother's in the garden. She's cutting the grass. ☐
______
8 I'm not wanting any potatoes with my fish, thanks. ☐
______
9 Do you prefer steamed rice to fried rice? ☐
______
10 Jack's on the phone. He orders some pizzas. ☐
______

b Complete the sentences with the present simple or continuous form of the verbs in brackets.

1 Our neighbours *grow* all of their own vegetables. (grow)
2 My mother ______ usually ______ at the weekend. (not cook)
3 Do you want to come for lunch on Sunday? We ______ roast lamb. (have)
4 We ______ tonight because there's a football match on TV. (not go out)
5 ______ you usually ______ your birthday with your family? (spend)
6 That restaurant ______ delicious mussels at lunchtime. (serve)
7 How often ______ you ______ in a typical week? (eat out)
8 I ______ a starter because I'm not hungry. (not have)
9 We ______ often ______ steak. (not buy)
10 My boyfriend's on a diet so he ______ on fried food. (cut down)

4 READING

a Read the article once and put the headings in the correct place.

A Can I eat apples?
B How can I prevent serious illnesses?
~~C How should I start the day?~~
D Do I really need to eat five a day?

The truth about healthy eating

Food experts are always telling us what we should and shouldn't eat, but they often give us different advice. Our food writer, Teresa Gold, has had a look at all the information to work out what is fact and what is fiction.

1 *C*
A full-English breakfast will certainly stop you feeling hungry, but it's high in calories which means that you'll put on weight if you have it regularly. A healthier option is to have just the egg. Boil it instead of frying it, and eat it with a piece of toast made with brown bread. Breakfast cereals are very high in sugar, so if you feel like cereal, have muesli – with no added sugar. You can also get your first vitamins of the day by drinking a glass of freshly-squeezed orange juice.

2 ______
Fruit and vegetables contain the vitamins and minerals we need to stay healthy. But five is actually a fictional number thought up by an American nutritionist. She looked at what the average person ate and doubled it. According to more recent research, the right number is actually eight. The research shows that people who have eight pieces of fruit and vegetables a day are much less likely to suffer from heart disease than those who eat three.

3 ______
This particular fruit has had some bad publicity because dentists say it can harm our teeth. While it's true that apples do contain a little sugar, they are also a source of fibre. Nutritionists say that we need about 18g of fibre a day, and a medium apple – peel included – contains about 3g. Some varieties contain more fibre than others, so you should choose carefully.

4 ______
The key to good health is a balanced diet which contains fats and carbohydrates as well as proteins, vitamins, and minerals. Fats may be high in calories, but they also contain vitamins. According to the World Cancer Research Fund, you should only have about 500g of red meat per week – a steak is about 100g. One type of food on its own won't kill or cure you, but eating the right amount of the right food will stop you getting ill.

b Read the article again. Mark the sentences T (true) or F (false).

1 A full-English breakfast every morning isn't good for you. *T*
2 The best breakfast is any type of cereal. ___
3 An American nutritionist carefully calculated the amount of fruit and vegetables we should eat. ___
4 We should eat more than five pieces of fruit and vegetables per day. ___
5 Apples contain a lot of sugar. ___
6 All apples have the same amount of fibre. ___
7 Fats can be good for us. ___
8 You can eat as much red meat as you want to. ___

c Look at the highlighted words and phrases. What do you think they mean? Use your dictionary to look up their meaning and pronunciation.

5 LISTENING

a 1.3 Listen to a radio phone-in programme about the article in exercise **4**. Tick (✓) the caller(s) who completely agree with it.

A William ☐ C Harry ☐
B Kate ☐ D Rosie ☐

b Listen again and answer the questions.

Which caller...?

1 thinks that some fruit and vegetables are unhealthy ___
2 says that most children prefer fast food ___
3 eats very little fruit ___
4 is very healthy because he/she eats a lot of fruit and vegetables ___

c Listen again with the audioscript on p.69.

USEFUL WORDS AND PHRASES

Learn these words and phrases.

carbohydrates /kɑːbəʊˈhaɪdreɪts/
protein /ˈprəʊtiːn/
awake /əˈweɪk/
oily /ˈɔɪli/
powerful /ˈpaʊəfl/
relaxed /rɪˈlækst/
sleepy /ˈsliːpi/
stressful /ˈstresfʊl/
violent /ˈvaɪələnt/
ready-made food /redi meɪd ˈfuːd/

Happy families are all alike; every unhappy family is unhappy in its own way.

First line of 'Anna Karenina' by Leo Tolstoy, Russian writer

1B Family life

1 GRAMMAR future forms

a Complete the sentences with the correct form of the verbs or phrases on the right.

1 My brother hates his job. *He's going to look for* a new one. — **he / look for** (an intention)
2 Don't worry about the drinks. ______ for them. — **I / pay** (an offer)
3 ______ some more coffee? — **I / make** (an offer)
4 Do you think ______ before you're 30? — **you / get married** (a prediction)
5 ______ to my cousin's wedding. We'll be on holiday. — **we / not go** (an arrangement)
6 **A** Are you ready to order?
B Yes, ______ the steak. — **I / have** (an instant decision)
7 ______ 21 on my next birthday. — **I / be** (a fact)
8 ______ your parents for a meal this weekend? — **we / invite** (a suggestion)
9 I'm going to the shops. ______ long. — **I / not be** (a promise)
10 ______ a party for my grandmother's 80th birthday tomorrow. — **we / have** (an arrangement)

b Complete the dialogues with the correct future form of the verbs in brackets.

1

1 **A** *Are* you *going away* this weekend? (go away)
B No, we ______ here. Why? (stay)
A We ______ a barbecue. Would you like to come? (have)

2

2 **A** I'm too tired to cook. ______ we ______ a Chinese takeaway? (order)
B Good idea. I ______ the restaurant. What do you want for your starter? (call)
A I ______ spring rolls, please. (have)

3

3 **A** What time ______ you ______ in the morning? (leave)
B I ______ the six o'clock train. (get)
A I ______ you a lift to the station, then. (give)

4

4 **A** What ______ you ______ tonight? (do)
B I ______ the new James Bond film. Do you want to come? (see)
A No, thanks. I've seen it. You ______ it! (love)

5

5 **A** ______ I ______ you do the washing up? (help)
B OK. I ______ and you can dry. But please be careful with the glasses. (wash)
A Don't worry. I ______ anything! (not break)

2 each other

Rewrite the sentences with *each other*.

1 My brother's shouting at my sister and she's shouting at him.
My brother and sister *are shouting at each other*.
2 Rob doesn't know Alex and Alex doesn't know Rob.
Rob and Alex ______________________.
3 I'm not speaking to my sister and she isn't speaking to me.
My sister and I ______________________.
4 I don't understand you and you don't understand me.
We ______________________.
5 The coach respects the players and they respect him.
The coach and the players ______________________.

3 PRONUNCIATION sentence stress

a 1.4 Listen and complete the sentences.

1 *When* are you going to *book* your *holiday*?
2 I'm ______ going to ______ the ______ yet.
3 I'm going to ______ ______.
4 ______ are you ______ ______?
5 I'm ______ some ______.
6 I'm ______ ______ my ______.
7 ______ will you ______ your exam ______?
8 I ______ get them ______ ______.
9 I'll ______ them on ______.

b Listen again and repeat. Copy the rhythm.

4 VOCABULARY family, adjectives of personality

a Complete the sentences with a family word.

1 Your mother and father are your p*arents*.
2 Your grandfather's father is your gr______-gr______.
3 A child who has no brothers or sisters is an on______ ch______.
4 Your brother's daughter is your n______.
5 Your father's sister is your a______.
6 Your partner, your children, your parents, and your brothers and sisters are your im______ f______.
7 Your father's new wife is your s______.
8 Your wife's or husband's father is your f______-i___-l______.
9 Your aunts and uncles and your cousins are your ex______ f______.
10 Your brother's or sister's son is your n______.

b Match the comments with the personality adjectives in the box.

aggressive ambitious independent jealous reliable self-confident selfish sensible ~~spoilt~~ stubborn

1 'When I want something, my parents always give it to me.'
spoilt
2 'I don't like my boyfriend talking to other women.'
______
3 'I'm always there when my friends need my help.'
______
4 'Those are my pens and you can't borrow them.'
______
5 'I'm going to go to bed early so I can sleep well before my exam tomorrow.'
______
6 'I'll hit you if you do that again!'
______
7 'I feel quite comfortable when I'm speaking in public.'
______
8 'I'd like to be the manager of a big multi-national company.'
______
9 'That's what I think and I'm not going to change my mind.'
______
10 'I'd prefer to do this on my own, thanks.'
______

c Write the opposite adjectives. Use a negative prefix if necessary.

1 generous *mean*
2 kind ______
3 lazy ______
4 mature ______
5 organized ______
6 sensitive ______
7 talkative ______
8 tidy ______

5 READING

a Read the article once. Why do the Bedouins prefer to live together in a big family group?

Extreme family ties

Family can be an important part of a person's life, and for some nationalities being close to your family is more important than it is to others. For example, families in Southern Europe are generally quite close, although in the past they spent even more time together. This is also true of families in the Middle East. But it is the Bedouin people who have the closest ties of all.

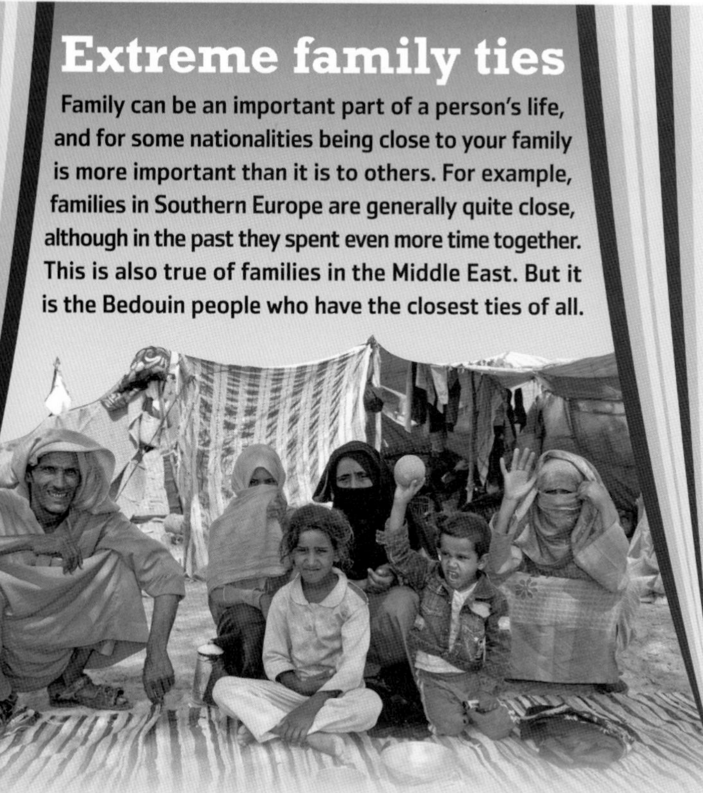

Traditional Bedouin families live in large tents about half the size of a basketball court. The tents are divided into two sections: the first is for receiving guests in true Bedouin style – they have the reputation of being the world's most generous hosts. Visitors are always served a big meal as soon as they arrive. The second part of the tent is the family's shared kitchen, living room, dining room, and bedroom. They don't have tables and chairs, as the whole family sits on the floor to eat. And instead of beds, everybody sleeps on mattresses, which are piled into a corner of the room during the day.

Several generations usually share the tent. The head of the family is the mother, and she is the one who gives the orders. Her husband and her children live with her, even when the children are married and have their own children. The sons and sons-in-law look after the animals, while the daughters and daughters-in-law clean the tent, cook the meals, and look after the younger grandchildren. The older ones are left to run around outside. There may often be as many as 30 people under the same roof.

The few young people who have left the family to live in the city visit their mothers nearly every day. It can be quite a surprise to see a shiny new Mercedes pull up outside one of the tents and watch a smart young man get out to greet his relatives.

Bedouin people do not like to be separated from their families and there is a very good reason why. If they are poor, sick, old, or unemployed, it is the family that supports them. Elderly people are never left alone, and problems are always shared. Children who work in the city are often responsible for their families financially. In this way, Bedouin families aren't just close; they are a lifeline.

b Read the article again. Choose the correct answers according to the information given.

1 In the past, most families in Southern Europe and the Middle East were…
   a smaller. (b) closer. c richer.
2 There isn't much … in a Bedouin tent.
   a furniture b light c space
3 Bedouin … spend most of the day inside.
   a men b women c children
4 Young Bedouins who live in the city…
   a hardly ever go home.
   b don't earn much money.
   c don't lose touch with their families.
5 Members of a Bedouin family help each other to…
   a survive. b get a job. c choose clothes.

c Look at the highlighted words and phrases. What do you think they mean? Use your dictionary to look up their meaning and pronunciation.

6 LISTENING

a 1.5 Listen to a couple, Terry and Jane, talking about going to live with the in-laws. What do they decide at the end of the conversation?

b Listen again and mark the sentences T (true) or F (false).

1 Terry and Jane are both very tired. *T*
2 Terry is more optimistic about the future than Jane. ___
3 Terry's parents have suggested the family move in with them. ___
4 Terry says that if they all lived together, his parents would babysit. ___
5 Jane thinks that the new plan would mean less housework for her. ___
6 Jane worries that the grandparents would spoil the children. ___

c Listen again with the audioscript on p.69.

USEFUL WORDS AND PHRASES

Learn these words and phrases.

boarding school /'bɔːdɪŋ skuːl/
childhood /'tʃaɪldhʊd/
gang /gæŋ/
gathering /'gæðərɪŋ/
rivalry /'raɪvlri/
sick /sɪk/
value /'væljuː/
fight /faɪt/
aware of /ə'weə əv/
no wonder /nəʊ 'wʌndə/

Practical English Meeting the parents

1 REACTING TO WHAT PEOPLE SAY

Complete the dialogues.

1 **Ben** Oh [1] n*o*__! I don't [2] b________ it!
Charlotte What's wrong!
Ben I didn't tell my mum that you don't eat meat.
Charlotte You're [3] k________!
Ben No, I'm not. Never [4] m________. I'll tell her now.
Mum! Charlotte's a vegetarian.
Mum [5] R________?
Charlotte Yes, but it isn't a problem.
Mum What a [6] p________! I've made a meat lasagne. But there's plenty of salad.
Charlotte That's fine. Thanks, Mrs Lord.

2 **Steve** We have something to tell you. We've found a house that we like.
Jill [7] H________ fantastic!
Steve And it isn't too expensive.
Jill That's great [8] n________! Could I see it some time?
Steve [9] W________ a great idea! I'll call and make an appointment.

2 SOCIAL ENGLISH

Complete the dialogues with the phrases in the box.

~~a really nice guy~~ Go ahead How do you see I mean
How incredible Not really That's because things like that

1 **A** What did you think of my dad?
B He's *a really nice guy*.
2 **A** ________ your future?
B I think we'll be very happy together.
3 **A** I hear you speak Spanish. Are you bilingual?
B ________. But I can speak it quite well.
4 **A** I'm sorry. I'm not feeling hungry.
B ________ you ate too much for lunch!
5 **A** You know, I think we went to the same school.
B ________!
6 **A** Can I have another piece of chicken, please?
B ________. There's more in the kitchen.
7 **A** What sort of books do you read?
B Biographies, history books, ________.
8 **A** You won't want to go to the concert with us.
B But I will! ________, I love classical music.

3 READING

a Read the text and answer the questions.

In which place...?
1 can you see a celebrity *Café Carlyle*
2 do musicians come to hear other musicians perform ________
3 can you hear international styles of jazz ________
4 can you see what's happening online ________
5 should you buy a ticket before you go ________
6 does the music finish very late ________

Jazz in New York

New York is famous for its jazz, and for music fans no trip to the city is complete without a visit to one of the many jazz venues. Here are four of the many places you can go to hear jazz being performed.

Barbès

Barbès is a bar and performance venue in the South Slope part of Brooklyn. Come here to listen to musical styles from all over the world, such as Mexican, Lebanese, Romanian, and Venezuelan along with traditional American styles. Usually $10 to get in.

55 Bar

Located in Greenwich Village, this small club, which started in 1919, has a very interesting history. Come to hear jazz guitarists play, and expect to see lots of serious jazz fans and music students from the local universities and music schools. Usually $10–20.

Smalls

This club was created in 1994, but has already become very famous in New York as it saw well-known players such as Norah Jones begin their career here. The club closed in 2002, but opened again in 2004, with a more comfortable room and a website that features live streaming video of all performances. It opens from 4 p.m. to 4 a.m. $20 to get in.

Café Carlyle

Come to the ground floor of the famous Carlyle Hotel to visit the Café Carlyle. It's particularly worth going on Monday nights – not only will you hear jazz from the Eddy Davis New Orleans Jazz Band, but you will also hear the famous film director Woody Allen play with them. As well as being a director, Woody Allen is also a jazz musician. Sets at 9:30. The venue holds only 90 and is often sold out, so it's a good idea to book ahead. But it isn't cheap – tickets start at $90.

b Underline five words or phrases you don't know. Use your dictionary to look up their meaning and pronunciation.

When a man tells you he got rich through hard work, ask him 'Whose?'

Don Marquis, US Writer

2A Spend or save?

1 VOCABULARY money

a Complete the sentences with the correct verb in brackets.

1 My sister *wastes* a lot of money on clothes she never wears. (wastes / saves)
2 I can't ______________ to buy a flat of my own. (pay / afford)
3 You'll have to ______________ a lot of money if you want to travel around the world next year. (cost / save)
4 Kevin ______________ about €1,000 a month in his new job. (wins / earns)
5 That painting ______________ a lot of money. (charges / is worth)
6 My uncle is doing a bike ride to ______________ money for charity. (raise / save)
7 We still ______________ the bank a lot of money. (owe / earn)
8 Mary ______________ £5,000 from her grandfather when he died. (inherited / invested)
9 The plumber ______________ me €100 for mending my shower. (cost / charged)
10 Can you ______________ me $200 until I get paid? (borrow / lend)

b Complete the sentences with the correct preposition.

1 I'll pay *for* the meal if you get the drinks.
2 They charged us €5 __________ a bottle of water.
3 They got __________ debt when they bought their new house.
4 We've borrowed some money __________ my parents.
5 My grandparents always pay __________ cash.
6 I don't mind lending money __________ family.
7 They spent a lot of money __________ their son's education.
8 Can I pay __________ credit card?
9 If I lend you the money, when can you pay me __________?
10 Phil invested all his money __________ his own company.

c Complete the advertisement with the words in the box.

~~bank account~~ bills cash machine loan mortgage note salary tax

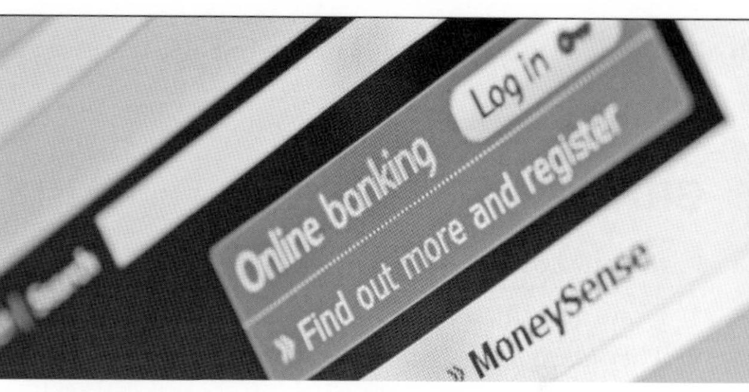

What's so good about CASH Internet Banking plc

OUR ACCOUNT SERVICES

Open a [1] *bank account* with us and we'll give you a free gift – you'll get a tablet computer if you earn over €3,000 a month. Consult our online service 24/7 and use your card in the [2] __________ of any bank to take out as much or as little money as you want – coins aren't available, but you can take out a €5-[3] __________ if you wish. Does your company pay your [4] __________ directly into the bank? Then we won't charge you anything for your card. We'll even pay all your [5] __________ for you, free of charge.

OUR FINANCING SERVICES

Do you need to borrow money for a car, a holiday, or a new laptop? We'll give you a [6] __________ of up to €10,000 for whatever you want to buy.

And how about a new house? We can give you a [7] __________ at one of the lowest interest rates on the market.

OUR EXTRA SERVICES

How much [8] __________ do you pay? Talk to our specialists to make sure you're paying the right amount – they can help you pay less.

Come to CASH Internet for the best accounts, the best services, and the best savings.

2 PRONUNCIATION the letter *o*

a Circle the word with a different sound.

1 ʌ up	2 ɒ clock	3 əʊ phone	4 ɔː horse	5 ɜː bird
money nothing (sorry) worry	cost shopping dollar clothes	done owe note loan	afford worse store mortgage	work world short worth

b 2.1 Listen and check. Then listen again and repeat the words.

3 GRAMMAR present perfect and past simple

a Circle the correct answer.

1 I (*have never owed*) | *never owed* any money to the bank in my life.
2 They *have charged* | *charged* us too much for our meal last night.
3 Rachel wants to buy a flat, but she *hasn't saved* | *didn't save* enough money yet.
4 Paul *hasn't inherited* | *didn't inherit* anything from his grandmother when she died.
5 I can't pay you back. I *haven't been* | *didn't go* to the cash machine yet.
6 How much *has your TV cost* | *did your TV cost*?
7 *Have you paid* | *Did you pay* your father back yet?
8 I *haven't had* | *didn't have* any coins, so I couldn't put any money in the parking meter.
9 *Have you ever invested* | *Did you ever invest* any money in a company?
10 My girlfriend has a really well-paid job. She *has earned* | *earned* €45,000 last year.

b Complete the dialogues with the correct form of the verbs in brackets.

1 **A** When _did_ your son _buy_ his car? (buy)
B When he ________ his driving test last month. (pass)

2 **A** How much money ________ you ________ from your sister yesterday? (borrow)
B About €100, but I ________ already ________ it all. (spend)

3 **A** ________ you ________ a new flat yet? (find)
B Yes, and the bank ________________ to give me a mortgage. (just agree)

4 **A** ________ you ever ________ any money to a friend? (lend)
B Only to my boyfriend when he ________ a new phone. (need)

5 **A** ________ your mother ________ an appointment with the doctor yet? (make)
B Yes, she ________ him yesterday and she's seeing him tomorrow. (call)

4 READING

a Read the first chapter of a book about Daniel Suelo once. Where did he decide to live?

1 With friends. ☐
2 With family. ☐
3 In the countryside. ☐
4 In a city. ☐

The man who quit money

In the first year of the twenty-first century, a man standing by a busy road in the middle of the United States took his life savings out of his pocket – $30 – laid it inside a phone booth, and walked away. He was 39 years old, came from a good family, and had been to college. He was not mentally ill, nor did he have any problems with drugs or alcohol. The decision was made by a man who knew exactly what he was doing.

In the twelve years since then, as the **stock market** has risen and fallen, Daniel Suelo has not earned, received, or spent a single dollar. In an **era** when anyone who could sign his name could get a mortgage, Suelo did not apply for loans. As public debt rose to eight, ten, and finally thirteen trillion dollars, he did not pay taxes, or accept any type of help from the government.

Instead he went to live in a cave in Utah, where he picks fruit and wild onions, collects animals that have been killed on the roads, takes old food that has gone past its **sell-by date** out of bins, and is often fed by friends and strangers. 'My philosophy is to use only what is freely given or **discarded**,' he writes. While the rest of us try to deal with taxes, mortgages, **retirement plans**, and bank accounts, Suelo no longer even has an identity card.

Daniel is not a typical tramp. He often works – but refuses to be paid. Although he lives in a cave, he is extremely social, remains close to friends and family, and has discussions with strangers on his website which he checks at the local library. He has cycled far, travelled on freight trains, hitch-hiked through nearly every state in the United States, worked on a fishing boat, collected mussels from Pacific beaches, caught salmon in **streams** in Alaska, and spent three months living in a tree after a storm.

'I know it's possible to live with zero money,' Suelo declares. And he says you can live well.

b Read the chapter again and choose the correct answers.

1 What do we learn about the man in the first paragraph?
   a He had just left school.
   (b) He had thought about his actions carefully.
   c He had had a difficult childhood.
2 What has Daniel Suelo done since he changed his life?
   a He has got into debt.
   b He has bought a house.
   c He hasn't used any money.
3 How does he get enough to eat?
   a He finds food.
   b His family cook for him.
   c He buys food.
4 What's Daniel Suelo like?
   a He's shy.
   b He's lazy.
   c He's outgoing.
5 How does he get from one place to another?
   a He cycles everywhere.
   b He uses different methods of transport.
   c He always uses trains.

c Look at the highlighted words and phrases. What do you think they mean? Use your dictionary to look up their meaning and pronunciation.

d Complete the sentences with one of the highlighted words or phrases.

1 Clean fresh water often comes from mountain *streams*.
2 It's important to have a ________ ________ for when you get old.
3 The giant fish sculptures in Rio were made using ________ plastic bottles.
4 The early nineteenth century was an important ________ for opera.
5 He has shares in some companies, so he's interested in what happens on the ________ ________.
6 You might get ill if you eat food after its ________-________ ________.

5 LISTENING

a 2.2 Listen to four speakers talking about how they manage on their incomes. Match the speakers with their situation.

Speaker 1 *d*   a a single parent
Speaker 2 __   b a family with children
Speaker 3 __   c a single retired person on a pension
Speaker 4 __   d a young person who lives with his / her parents

b Listen again and mark the sentences T (true) or F (false).

Speaker 1
1 He doesn't earn much money. *F*
2 He saves most of his salary. __
Speaker 2
3 She doesn't own the flat where she lives. __
4 She thinks money is more important than family. __
Speaker 3
5 He can't live on his income. __
6 He isn't in debt. __
Speaker 4
7 She only works in a shop at weekends. __
8 She spends most of her money on her children. __

c Listen again with the audioscript on p.69.

USEFUL WORDS AND PHRASES

Learn these words and phrases.

cheques /tʃeks/
contracts /'kɒntrækts/
figures /'fɪgəz/
recession /rɪ'seʃn/
salesman /'seɪlzmən/
broke /brəʊk/
a gamble /ə 'gæmbl/
a millionaire /ə mɪljə'neə/
go on sale /gəʊ ɒn 'seɪl/
set up a business /set ʌp ə 'bɪznəs/

Only I can change my life. No one else can do it for me.
Carol Burnett, US actress & comedienne

2B Changing lives

1 GRAMMAR present perfect simple + *for* / *since*; present perfect continuous

a Write the words and phrases in the box in the correct column.

~~2005~~ ages a fortnight Christmas six months I was little the last two days Tuesday years and years you last called

for	since
________	*2005*
________	________
________	________
________	________
________	________

b Complete the sentences with the present perfect simple form of the verb in brackets and *for* or *since*.

1 I*'ve had* my car *for* about a month. (have)
2 My mum ________ ill ________ last Friday. (be)
3 We ________ each other ________ we were at school. (know)
4 He ________ for the same company ________ five years. (work)
5 They ________ in Scotland ________ they got married. (live)
6 My parents ________ away ________ the weekend. (go)
7 I ________ to go to Australia ________ a long time. (want)
8 She ________ to me ________ last year. (not speak)

c Complete the dialogues with the present perfect continuous form of the verbs.

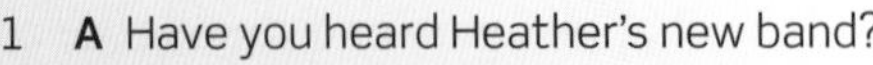
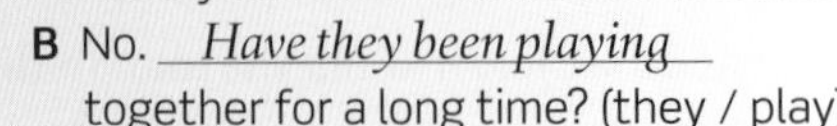

1 **A** Have you heard Heather's new band?
B No. *Have they been playing* together for a long time? (they / play)

2 **A** How long was your flight?
B Twelve hours. ________ all day. (we / travel)

3 **A** My brother has a very good job in New York.
B Really? How long ________ ________ there? (he / work)

4 **A** Diana's found a new flat, at last.
B Oh good! ________ one for ages. (she / look for)

5 **A** Why does Liam's teacher want to see you?
B ________ his homework lately. (he / not do)

6 **A** You're late.
B Yes, I know. Sorry. ________ ________ long? (you / wait)

7 **A** You look exhausted.
B ________ the children all day! (I / look after)

d Circle the correct form. If both forms are possible, tick (✓) the sentence.

1 How long *have you lived* | *have you been living* abroad? ✓
2 *I've studied* | *I've been studying* (circled) Chinese for two years.
3 Hannah *has had* | *has been having* the same boyfriend since she was at school.
4 How long *has Mark played* | *has Mark been playing* the bass guitar?
5 *He's worked* | *He's been working* in this school since he started teaching.
6 *I've known* | *I've been knowing* you for years.
7 *We've gone* | *We've been going* to the same dentist since we were children.
8 *You've worn* | *You've been wearing* that coat for years!

2 PRONUNCIATION sentence stress

a 2.3 Listen and complete the sentences.

1 I've been _travelling_ all _day_.

2 How ________ have they been going ________ together?

3 She's been ________ ill since ________.

4 They ________ been ________ here for long.

5 We've been ________ the house all ________.

6 I ________ been ________ well lately.

b Listen again and repeat the sentences. Copy the rhythm.

3 READING

a Read the article once and match the photos 1–3 with the paragraphs A–C.

b Read the article again. Answer the questions with the letters A, B, or C.

Which organization…?

1 takes people for a fortnight or a month _B_
2 encourages sightseeing ___
3 offers accommodation in tents ___
4 says what volunteers should bring ___
5 gives volunteers free afternoons ___
6 lets volunteers stay with others in a hut ___
7 arranges accommodation with local people ___
8 only needs volunteers in the summer ___

c Look at the highlighted words and phrases. What do you think they mean? Check with your dictionary.

d Complete the sentences with one of the highlighted words or phrases.

1 My little niece only wants to play on the _swing_ when we go to the park.

2 If you all ________ ________ ________, we'll be able to buy our colleague a nice leaving present.

3 I'd rather see animals in ________ than in a zoo.

4 The school is organizing an after-school club for ________ children in the area.

5 The people waiting for the buses were standing underneath the ________ because it was raining.

6 We're moving house at the weekend. Can you come and ________ ________ ________ with the packing?

Do *you* want to be a volunteer?

A The Book Bus

Do you enjoy reading? Do you like children? Then why not volunteer for our mobile library service in Zambia? We work with disadvantaged children in state primary schools, and it's a lot of fun. We read stories, do art projects, and organize activities to help the children learn English. After breakfast at 7 a.m., we head to our first school in time for the beginning of the school day. Every morning we visit at least four schools, and we spend about an hour in each one. We get back to camp at around 2 p.m. for lunch, and after that you have the afternoon free to relax, or prepare activities. The project takes place from May to September, and it's open to everyone. Volunteers have to pay for their own flight and make a contribution to the project.

B The Great Orang-utan Project

Are you an animal lover? If you are, then you should come to Kubah National Park in Borneo. We need people to help us look after our orang-utans. Unfortunately, you won't be able to touch the animals, as they are being prepared to be released into the wild, but you'll work very near them. You'll spend your time in the Wildlife Centre repairing the shelters where the orang-utans live, or building new ones. You might have to make a swing, or install some ropes where the animals can play. You'll have your own room in a wooden hut which looks out onto the rainforest. The programme lasts for two or four weeks and it costs £1,280 or £1,865 respectively, excluding flights.

C Construction in Peru

Are you good at making things? If you are, and you'd like to take part in a construction project, how about coming to Peru to lend a hand? You'll be based in Cuzco in south-eastern Peru, and you'll be involved in the construction of a small school, and a community centre or an orphanage. You may have to paint and do repairs to existing buildings, or build new ones in and around the city. You'll live with a Peruvian family, and you'll eat all your meals together in their house. All of the houses have electricity and running water, but you'll have to go to an internet café in Cuzco if you want to go online. You are expected to work from Monday to Friday, and at the weekend you can explore some of the fantastic sights in the region. Please bring your own work clothes.

4 VOCABULARY strong adjectives

a Complete the adjective for each picture.

1 She's absolutely fr*eezing*.

2 It's d__________!

3 They're really d__________.

4 He's h__________.

5 It's absolutely en__________.

6 They're f__________.

b Complete the sentences with a strong adjective.

1 **A** Are you **sure** the meeting is today?
B Yes, I'm absolutely *positive*.

2 **A** Is your boyfriend's flat **small**?
B Yes, it's really __________.

3 **A** Were your parents **angry** about your exam results?
B Yes, they were __________.

4 **A** Is your sister **frightened** of insects?
B Yes, she's absolutely __________ of them.

5 **A** Were you **surprised** when you passed your driving test?
B Yes, I was really __________.

6 **A** Were the children **hungry** when they arrived?
B Yes, they were absolutely __________.

5 LISTENING

a 2.4 Listen to a news story about an American family who are travelling around the world doing voluntary work. Tick (✓) the places they have already visited.

1 Australia	✓	7 Paraguay	☐
2 Antarctica	☐	8 Peru	☐
3 China	☐	9 Russia	☐
4 Haiti	☐	10 Rwanda	☐
5 India	☐	11 Thailand	☐
6 Kenya	☐	12 Zanzibar	☐

b Listen again and answer the questions.

1 What did J.D. Lewis use to do?
He used to be an actor.

2 How old are the children?
__________.

3 How much is the trip going to cost?
__________.

4 What's the name of his organization?
__________.

5 What did they do in Thailand?
__________.

6 How did they help the children in Rwanda?
__________.

7 Who did they help in Kenya?
__________.

8 What does J. D. Lewis hope his organization will do in the future?
__________.

c Listen again with the audioscript on p.70.

USEFUL WORDS AND PHRASES

Learn these words and phrases.

blisters /ˈblɪstəz/
charity /ˈtʃærəti/
kayak /ˈkaɪæk/
lorry /ˈlɒri/
target /ˈtɑːgɪt/
melt /melt/
paddle /ˈpædl/
risky /ˈrɪski/
go forward(s) /gəʊ ˈfɔːwəd/
sponsor projects /spɒnsə ˈprɒdʒekts/

A good traveller has no fixed plans.
Lao Tzu, Taoist Philosopher

3A Race across London

1 VOCABULARY transport

a Complete the crossword.

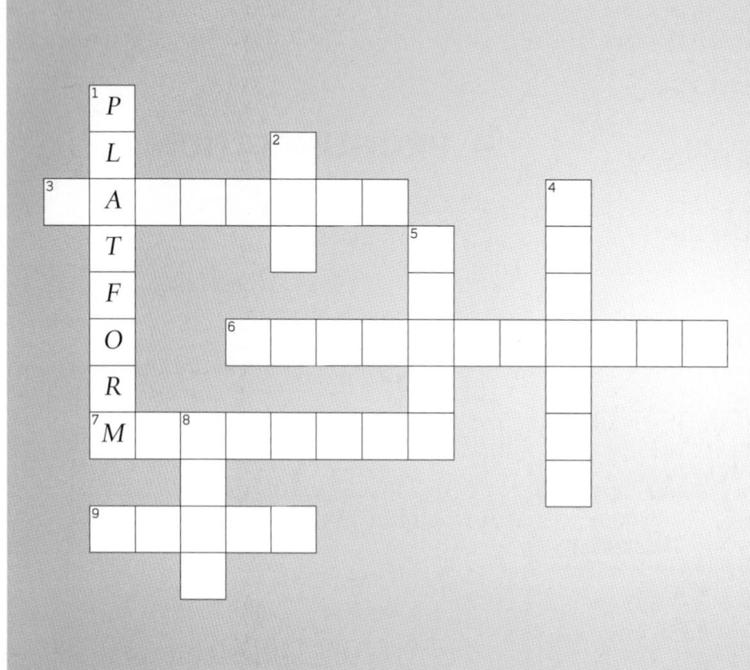

Clues down ↓

1 It's where you wait for a train in the station.
2 It's bigger than a car but smaller than a lorry.
4 It's like a motorbike but less powerful.
5 It's used for transporting large quantities of things by road.
8 It's a type of bus that moves by electricity along special rails in the road.

Clues across →

3 It's one section of a train.
6 It's a type of railway system, called the Tube in London or Metro in other cities.
7 It's a fast road where traffic can travel long distances between large towns.
9 It's a comfortable bus that's used for long journeys.

b Complete the compound nouns with one word.

1 Don't forget to put your *seat* belt on.
2 You'll get a __________ fine if you leave your car there.
3 Sorry we're late. We were stuck in a __________ jam in the city centre.
4 We got held up by the __________ works on the motorway.
5 I wish cyclists would use the __________ lane instead of the pavement.
6 We need to fill up at the __________ station before we set off.
7 The traffic is always worse during the __________ hour.
8 There aren't any cabs waiting at the __________ rank.
9 Slow down! There are __________ cameras on this road.
10 We stopped at the __________ lights and waited for them to turn green.

2 PRONUNCIATION /ʃ/, /dʒ/, and /tʃ/

a Circle the word with a different sound.

1 dʒ jazz	2 ʃ shower	3 dʒ jazz	4 tʃ chess
carria**ge** **j**ourney (ru**sh**)	cra**sh** **s**eat belt sta**t**ion	**ch**eck-in passen**g**er traffic **j**am	**ch**emist's coa**ch** depar**t**ure

b 3.1 Listen and check. Then listen again and repeat the words.

3 GRAMMAR comparatives and superlatives

a Complete the sentences with one word.

1 Petrol isn't as expensive in the USA *as* it is in the UK.
2 My father drives more slowly ________ my mother.
3 They said that today was ________ hottest day of the year.
4 Let's go by train. It's ________ comfortable than the coach.
5 This is the ________ flight I've ever been on. I'll never fly with this airline again.
6 I think trains are ________ dangerous than cars. There are fewer accidents.
7 It's ________ to go by tube than by bus. Buses are much slower.
8 The M25 is ________ busiest motorway in the UK.
9 You're at the Sheraton? We're staying at the same hotel ________ you.
10 Why don't we go hitchhiking? It's the ________ expensive way to travel.

b Write sentences with the information from the survey. Use the comparative or the superlative.

Where to go?
We reveal the results from our reader survey of three popular holiday destinations.

	Cancun (Mexico)	Copenhagen (Denmark)	Sydney (Australia)
It's cheap	★★★	★	★★
It's crowded	★★★	★	★★
It's easy to get to	★★	★★★	★
It's exciting	★★★	★★	★★
It's hot	★★★	★	★★★
It's relaxing	★	★★★	★★

1 Cancun / cheap / Copenhagen
Cancun is cheaper than Copenhagen.
2 Cancun / crowded / of the three destinations
________________.
3 Copenhagen / easy to get to / Sydney
________________.
4 Sydney / exciting / Cancun
________________.
5 Sydney / hot / Copenhagen
________________.
6 Copenhagen / relaxing / of the three destinations
________________.

c Rewrite the comparative sentences in **b** using *(not) as ... as.*

1 **expensive** (sentence 1)
Cancun isn't as expensive as Copenhagen.
2 **difficult** (sentence 3)
____
3 **exciting** (sentence 4)
____
4 **cold** (sentence 5)
____

4 PRONUNCIATION linking

a 3.2 Listen and complete the sentences.

1 The *most* *relaxing* way to travel is by train.
2 The seven hours in the airport was the ________ ________ part of the holiday.
3 The ________ ________ place to visit is the museum.
4 Flying is a lot ________ ________ than going by coach.
5 They should have the party at their house. It's much ________ than ours.
6 Scooters aren't ________ ________ ________ motorbikes.

b Listen again and repeat the sentences. Listen carefully to the linked words. Copy the rhythm.

5 READING

a Read the article once. Which is the oldest form of transport?

Unusual ways of getting around

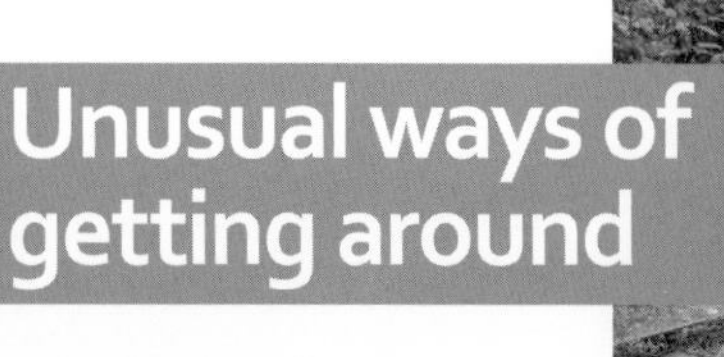

Bamboo trains

This is the best way to see rural Cambodia. A bamboo train, or *nori* as the locals call it, is a bamboo platform on wheels which travels along tracks. It's powered by an engine, and it can reach a speed of 40 kilometres per hour. Passengers sit on a grass mat on the nori. Noris may not be as comfortable as conventional trains, but they're certainly a lot cheaper. Pick up a nori from Battambang Station, but remember to agree on a price before you get on.

Totora reed boats

These boats have been around for centuries. They are made from the reeds that grow on the banks of Lake Titicaca, one of the largest lakes in South America. As well as making boats from totora reeds, the local people use them to make their houses, which they build on floating islands. Totora reed boats are still used for hunting and fishing, but today some of the local people transport people across the lake in them. Travelling on a reed boat among the floating islands of the lake is a must for visitors to Peru.

Jeepney

A jeepney is the most common form of public transport in the Philippines. They are made out of the jeeps left on the islands by the American army at the end of the Second World War. The people gave the jeeps a roof, put in two long seats on either side and painted them, turning them into small buses. Jeepneys have open windows instead of air conditioning. They're often packed with passengers and there are no bus stops – the driver just slows down to let the passengers jump on and off.

Dog sleds

Dog sledding is a unique experience as it's something you can't do in many other parts of the world. It was once the only way to get around in the snow of Alaska in the US, but now its use is limited to winter sports and tourism. The best time to try it is from January to March – in the summer there isn't enough snow so the dogs pull sleds on wheels. The ride can be a bit bumpy as the sled sometimes goes over stones and the dogs bark a lot. All the same, it's an opportunity not to be missed.

b Read the article again. Mark the sentences T (true) or F (false).

1 Noris are a good way of seeing Cambodian cities. *F*
2 The train fare is not always the same. __
3 Totora reed boats are made from special plants. __
4 Today the boats are only used to carry tourists. __
5 Jeepneys have been used in the Philippines for about twenty years. __
6 There are usually a lot of people in jeepneys. __
7 Most people in Alaska don't travel by dog sled any more. __
8 Dog sleds are a very relaxing way to travel. __

c Look at the highlighted words and phrases. What do you think they mean? Use your dictionary to look up their meaning and pronunciation.

6 LISTENING

a 3.3 Listen to the experiences of five speakers who were doing dangerous things while they were driving. Match the speakers with the things they were doing.

Speaker 1 *E* — A Putting on make-up
Speaker 2 __ — B Listening to his/her favourite music
Speaker 3 __ — C Writing a text message
Speaker 4 __ — D Setting or adjusting a satnav
Speaker 5 __ — E Talking on a mobile

b Listen again and answer the questions.

1 What did Speaker 1's car crash into? *A van*
2 How far had Speaker 2 driven past Exeter before she realized her mistake? ______
3 Where did Speaker 3 end up? ______
4 Who did Speaker 4 nearly hit? ______
5 What colour were the traffic lights when the accident happened to Speaker 5? ______

c Listen again with the audioscript on p.70.

USEFUL WORDS AND PHRASES

Learn these words and phrases.

adjust (satnav) /ə'dʒʌst/
reach /riːtʃ/
be ahead of /biː ə'hed əv/
crash (into) /kræʃ/
get stuck (in a traffic jam) /get 'stʌk/
get worse /get 'wɜːs/
turn red /tɜːn 'red/
turn round /tɜːn raʊnd/
do your hair /duː jɔː 'heə/
put on make-up /pʊt ɒn 'meɪk ʌp/

Men want to be a woman's first love. Women like to be a man's last romance.
Oscar Wilde, Irish writer

3B Stereotypes – or are they?

1 GRAMMAR articles: *a / an, the*, no article

a Circle the correct answers.

1 I think *girls* | *the girls* are better at learning *languages* | *the languages* than *boys* | *the boys*.
2 Did you lock *door* | *the door* when you left *house* | *the house* this morning?
3 My sister is married to *German* | *a German*. He's *engineer* | *an engineer*.
4 I don't usually like *fish* | *the fish*, but *salmon* | *the salmon* we had last night was delicious.
5 We go to *cinema* | *the cinema* once *a week* | *the week*.
6 Don't worry! It's not *the end* | *end* of the *world* | *world*.
7 Do you think *women* | *the women* are more sensitive than *men* | *the men*?
8 What *beautiful* | *a beautiful* day! Let's have *lunch* | *a lunch* in the garden.

b Are the highlighted phrases right (✓) or wrong (✗)? Correct the wrong phrases.

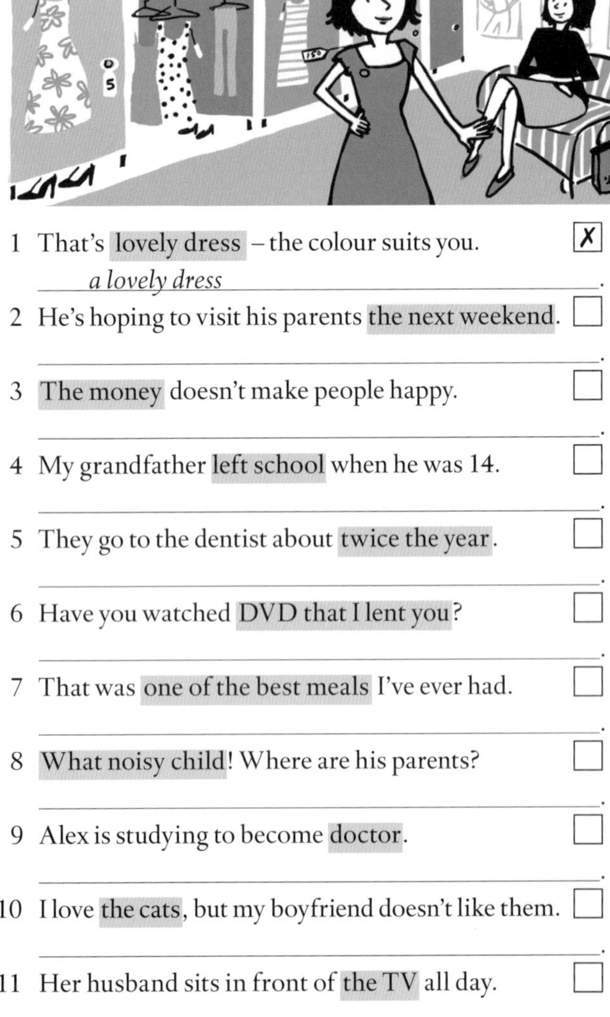

1 That's lovely dress – the colour suits you. ✗
a lovely dress
2 He's hoping to visit his parents the next weekend. ☐
____
3 The money doesn't make people happy. ☐
____
4 My grandfather left school when he was 14. ☐
____
5 They go to the dentist about twice the year. ☐
____
6 Have you watched DVD that I lent you? ☐
____
7 That was one of the best meals I've ever had. ☐
____
8 What noisy child! Where are his parents? ☐
____
9 Alex is studying to become doctor. ☐
____
10 I love the cats, but my boyfriend doesn't like them. ☐
____
11 Her husband sits in front of the TV all day. ☐
____
12 She always gets to the work at half past five. ☐
____

2 PRONUNCIATION /ə/, sentence stress, /ðə/ or /ðiː/?

a 3.4 Listen and complete the sentences.

1 I'd like to *speak* to the *manager*.
2 I've put the _______ on the _______.
3 _______ are we going to _______ tonight?
4 Could you _______ the _______ for a moment?
5 She needs to see a _______ about her _______.
6 We want to _______ for a _______ tomorrow.

b Listen again and repeat. Copy the rhythm.

c 3.5 Listen and repeat the phrases. Pay attention to the pronunciation of *the*.

1 The conversation was about the woman next door.
2 The university invited a guest to speak at the meeting.
3 I sometimes go to the theatre in the evening.
4 We took the lift instead of walking up the stairs.
5 The office gave me all the information I needed.
6 The grey skirt is nice, but I prefer the black one.

3 READING

a Read the article once and put the headings in the correct place.

A Men are better navigators than women
B Women talk more than men
C Men don't see colours as well as women

Stereotypes supported by science

1 ____________

Men have a reputation for wearing clothes that don't look good together – if men do look good, it's because their girlfriends or wives have helped them get dressed. Why's that?

Science says: Let's take a look at chromosomes – the parts of our DNA that control many things about us. The colour red is carried only by the X chromosome. Women have two X chromosomes, and so they are more likely to be able to see red. Men only have one X chromosome. How we see colour depends on the ability to see red, blue, and green, so women are more likely to see colours better. Being able to see colours well was important in prehistoric times when women looked for fruit for food. They had to be able to tell the difference between the types of fruit on the trees so that they didn't choose a type that was poisonous. For them, seeing different colours meant they could survive.

2 ____________

Most men have a natural ability to read maps while women usually need to turn them round. How come?

Science says: Men are able to see the size and position of things much quicker than women. This ability is called 'spatial awareness'. Researchers discovered in a study of four-year-old children that only one girl has this ability for every four boys. Once again, the explanation can be found in the past. Do you remember those prehistoric women? Well, while they were looking for fruit, the men travelled long distances to hunt animals. When they had caught enough, they had to find their way home again. And this is where they learnt 'spatial awareness'. The women didn't need it because they hardly ever went out of sight of their homes, but for the men, it was vital.

3 ____________

Humans are social animals, so why is it that men don't like sharing their problems while women tell their best friends everything?

Science says: The answer is in the brain. The parts responsible for language are 17% larger in a woman's brain than in a man's brain. Also, women use both the left and the right side of the brain to use language, while men use only one side – their strongest side. And there's more. The part of the brain that connects the two parts together – the corpus callosum – is larger in women too, which means that they can move information from one part to the other part more quickly. Nobody is sure why these differences exist, but it's clear that women have a definite advantage over men when it comes to communication.

b Read the article again. Choose the right answers.

1 Men can find it difficult to perceive…
 a three colours.
 (b) one colour.
 c any colours.

2 Seeing colours well helped prehistoric women…
 a find interesting things to eat.
 b cook food correctly.
 c choose the right fruit.

3 The results of the study showed that…
 a four-year-olds don't have spatial awareness.
 b boys learn spatial awareness before girls.
 c girls don't have spatial awareness.

4 Women didn't need spatial awareness in prehistoric times because…
 a the men were always with them.
 b they never left home.
 c they didn't travel far from home.

5 Men are worse at communicating because…
 a part of their brains are smaller.
 b their brains are 17% smaller.
 c their brains are larger.

6 The function of the corpus callosum in the brain is…
 a to communicate between both sides.
 b to store different languages.
 c to control the language process.

c Look at the highlighted words and phrases. What do you think they mean? Use your dictionary to look up their meaning and pronunciation.

d Complete the sentences with one of the highlighted words or phrases.

1 It's a *definite* *advantage* to have good exam results if you want to go to university.
2 Don't eat those mushrooms you found outside! They could be ____________.
3 Who's ____________ ____________ making this mess?
4 She's ____________ ____________ to accept if you invite her partner as well.
5 Italian people ____________ ____________ ____________ for being great cooks.
6 It's ____________ I finish the report before the end of the day.

4 VOCABULARY collocation: verbs / adjectives + prepositions

a Circle the correct prepositions.

1. They're arriving *at* / *on* / *in* London on Friday.
2. That suitcase belongs *for* / *from* / *to* me.
3. Shall we ask someone *at* / *for* / *of* directions?
4. We might go camping, but it depends *in* / *of* / *on* the weather.
5. Everybody laughed *about* / *at* / *to* me when I fell off the chair.
6. Who's going to pay *for* / *of* / *with* the meal?
7. I dreamt *about* / *from* / *with* my old school friends last night.
8. That girl reminds me *about* / *of* / *to* my cousin.

b Complete the sentences with the correct prepositions.

1. Tony used to be married *to* Teresa.
2. My boyfriend isn't very keen __________ vegetables.
3. They're worried __________ their teenage son.
4. We're not very interested __________ abstract art.
5. I'm very different __________ my sister.
6. Adam's very good __________ maths.
7. I'm fed up __________ this weather.
8. He's famous __________ his role in *Sherlock Holmes*.

5 WHEN ARE PREPOSITIONS STRESSED?

a 3.6 Listen and complete the dialogues.

1 **A** Who did you *argue* *with*?
B I __________ with my __________.

2 **A** Who are you __________ __________?
B I'm __________ at __________!

3 **A** What are you so __________ __________?
B I'm __________ about my __________.

4 **A** What are you __________ __________?
B I'm __________ to the __________.

b Listen again and repeat. Copy the rhythm.

6 LISTENING

a 3.7 Listen to a radio phone-in programme. Which speaker has the most traditional view about men doing the cooking?

1 Nick ☐ 2 Eve ☐ 3 Frank ☐ 4 Martina ☐

b Listen again and mark the sentences T (true) or F (false).

1. Nick is unemployed. *T*
2. He wouldn't like to be a chef. ___
3. Eve cooks all the meals in her house. ___
4. She spends a lot of time cleaning the kitchen. ___
5. Frank thinks that girls work harder than they used to. ___
6. Frank thinks that girls nowadays can cook. ___
7. Martina's partner does all the cooking. ___
8. Martina respects men that can cook. ___

c Listen again with the audioscript on p.71.

USEFUL WORDS AND PHRASES

Learn these words and phrases.

claim (vb) /kleɪm/
reduce /rɪ'djuːs/
almost /'ɔːlməʊst/
slightly /'slaɪtli/
whereas /weər'æz/
according to /ə'kɔːdɪŋ tuː/
in fact /ɪn 'fækt/
range from /'reɪndʒ frəm/
tend to /'tend tə/
be sceptical of / biː 'skeptɪkl əv/

Practical English A difficult celebrity

1 GIVING OPINIONS

Complete the dialogue.

John I love this song. Can you turn it up?
Anna Do I have to? It's really old.
John It may be old, but it's one of my favourites. [1] P*ersonally*, I think pop music was better in the past than it is now. What do you [2] th________?
Anna No, I don't think that's [3] r________. In my [4] op________, there is some great music around. And some of today's singers have fantastic voices.
John I [5] ag________. But very few of them write their own music. If you [6] as________ me, the real musicians are the ones who write the songs and then perform them live on stage. Don't you [7] ag________?
Anna To be [8] h________, I don't know a lot about it. I just put the radio on and listen to what they're playing!

2 SOCIAL ENGLISH

Complete the dialogues. Use a phrase containing the word in brackets.

1 **A** Hello! *I'm* *back*! (back)
B Hi! Did you have a good day?
2 **A** I'm going out for a walk now. Do you want to come?
B ________ ________ ________ ________. I'll get my coat. (minute)
3 **A** I've brought you some flowers.
B Thank you. That's ________ ________ ________. (kind)
4 **A** ________ ________ ________ what you said about moving abroad? (mean)
B Yes. I think it'll be a great opportunity for us.
5 **A** You look upset. What's the matter.
B Nothing really. ________ ________ ________ my boyfriend's away and I really miss him. (just)

3 READING

a Read the text. Mark the sentences T (true) or F (false).

1 New York taxis are all the same model of car. *F*
2 A medallion number has four numbers and one letter. ___
3 An off-duty cab won't pick you up. ___
4 You should stand in the street until a taxi stops for you. ___
5 When you get in a taxi, the price starts at 40 cents. ___
6 You pay per minute if there are problems with traffic. ___
7 Taxi drivers like to be paid in cash. ___

NEW YORK TAXIS

New York taxis provide an essential service to New Yorkers and tourists for getting around the city. There are over 12,000 yellow medallion taxicabs so it doesn't take long to see one.

What does a New York taxi look like?

New York taxis come in many different shapes and sizes, but to be official taxis they must be yellow. They must also have a special code called a medallion number: one number, then one letter, and two more numbers. A bronze badge with the same code should also be displayed on the hood.

Only taxis with the above are legally licensed to pick you up!

How will I know when a New York taxi is available?

It's all in the lights! When just the centre light illuminates the medallion number, the taxi is available to be hailed. When the centre light is off and both sidelights are on (illuminating the words 'Off Duty'), the taxi is off duty and won't stop for you.

How to hail a New York taxi.

First, try to hail a taxi in the direction you are already going; it saves time and money. When you see an available taxi, make sure it's safe and step off the pavement whilst holding your hand up high. If for any reason you don't get the driver's attention, step back onto the pavement and wait for the next available taxi and repeat the process. It's as simple as that.

New York taxi fares.

Once you step into the cab the meter will be turned on. This is called the 'flag-drop fare' and is $2.50. After that it will cost you 40 cents for every 400 metres, or 40 cents per minute if you are stuck in traffic. There is a flat-rate charge of $45 from Manhattan to JFK Airport.

If you're happy with the journey, you should tip your driver between 15% and 20% of the total fare. Paying by cash is preferred, however all taxis now accept credit cards.

b Underline five words or phrases you don't know. Use your dictionary to look up their meaning and pronunciation.

Failure is not falling down. Failure is falling down and not getting up again.
Richard Nixon, former US President

4A Failure and success

1 GRAMMAR *can, could, be able to*

a Circle the correct form. Tick (✓) if both are correct.

1 She *can* / *is able to* swim really well because she used to live by the sea. ✓

2 You need to *can* / *be able to* drive to live in the country.

3 Luke *could* / *was able to* read when he was only three years old.

4 If it doesn't rain tomorrow, *we can* / *we'll be able to* go for a long walk.

5 Sorry, I've been so busy that I *haven't could* / *haven't been able to* call until now.

6 If Millie had a less demanding job, she *could* / *would be able to* enjoy life more.

7 I've never *could* / *been able to* dance well, but I'd love to learn.

8 We're really sorry we *couldn't* / *weren't able to* come to your wedding.

9 I *used to can* / *used to be able to* speak a bit of Polish, but I've forgotten most of it now.

10 *Can you* / *Will you be able to* make the dinner tonight?

11 To work for this company, you *must can* / *must be able to* speak at least three languages.

12 I hate *not can* / *not being able to* communicate with the local people when I'm travelling.

b Read Matthew Banks' CV. Then complete the sentences with the correct form of *can*, *could* or *be able to*.

1 Matthew *can* sail.
2 He __________ speak a little Chinese when he started working in Hong Kong.
3 He __________ speak German.
4 He __________ design websites since 1999.
5 He'd like __________ speak Russian.
6 He __________ finish his PhD before he left the USA.
7 He __________ speak a little Russian soon.

Name: Matthew Banks
Date of Birth: 22/09/1980

Qualifications
Degree in French with Marketing (2003)
Master's in Business Administration (2006)
Started Ph.D in Business (2009) – incomplete

Work Experience
1998–2000: Trainer and Operator with Texas Instruments, London
2003–2009: Assistant then Marketing Manager, Texas Instruments, Dallas, USA
2009–present: Managing Director, AHH Marketing Services Ltd, Hong Kong

Other Skills
IT skills – advanced. Course in web design 1999.
Full driving licence

Languages
French (fluent)   Chinese (basic) certificate 2008
I hope to start Russian classes next January.

Hobbies and Interests
Watersports, especially sailing and windsurfing

2 PRONUNCIATION sentence stress

4.1 Listen and repeat the sentences. Copy the rhythm.

1 She can **sing** very **well**.
2 I've **never** been **able** to **ski**.
3 Can you **read** a **map**?
4 You won't **be able** to **go out** tomorrow.
5 He hasn't **been able** to **walk very fast** since he **hurt** his **leg**.
6 They aren't **able** to **come** tonight.

3 READING

a Read the article once and match the paragraphs A–D with the photos 1–4.

Failure: the first step towards success

Many people who have found success started out by failing. Below are four of the most famous.

A Some people consider this man to be the greatest scientist that has ever lived. However, his early life was nothing special. He was very small as a child and he was a very poor student. When he was twelve, his mother took him out of school so that he could learn how to run the family farm. Unfortunately, he wasn't very good at that either, so in the end he was sent back to school. After eventually passing his exams, he went to Cambridge University where he became a brilliant scholar. Later, he developed his law of gravity.

B This man is one of the most famous inventors of all time, which is incredible when you think he only went to school for three months. After his teacher lost patience with him, his mother taught him from home and he learnt many important lessons from reading books. His working life started as badly as his schooling had, and he was fired from his first two jobs. However, this gave him more time to experiment – by the end of his life he had invented over a thousand devices. His most famous invention was a certain type of light bulb.

C Ask anyone to name the most famous film director in Hollywood and many of them will say this man's name. However, his career in cinema started badly, as he was rejected three times from film school. He eventually started his studies at a different school, but he dropped out to become a director before he had finished. Since then he has won the Oscar for Best Director twice and three of his films have broken box office records. He went back to school in 2002 to finish his studies and earn his BA degree.

D Although he is one of the most successful businessmen and computer programmers of all time, this man didn't actually finish university. He was very bright at school and went to Harvard University, but he spent most of his time using the university's computers for his own projects and didn't do much studying. After dropping out, he decided to start his own company with a friend. This company failed, but he persisted and won a contract with IBM which eventually resulted in his company becoming one of the most powerful and recognized brands in the world today.

b Read the article again. Mark the sentences T (true) or F (false).

1 Isaac Newton nearly became a farmer. *T*
2 He was never a very good student. ___
3 Thomas Edison missed three months of school when he was a child. ___
4 He didn't make a good impression on his bosses at the start of his working life. ___
5 Steven Spielberg couldn't go to the film school he wanted to. ___
6 He has never finished his university course. ___
7 Bill Gates failed university. ___
8 His first company wasn't successful. ___

c Look at the highlighted words and phrases. What do you think they mean? Use your dictionary to look up their meaning and pronunciation.

d Complete the sentences with one of the highlighted words or phrases.

1 The child's parents *lost* *patience* with her and sent her to her room.
2 He wasn't enjoying university, so he ______ ______ after the first year.
3 After several months, she ______ managed to persuade her boyfriend to see an opera.
4 My colleague ______ ______ for sending personal emails from work.
5 My husband refuses to buy expensive ______ of clothing.
6 There was an enormous queue at the ______ ______ because it was the opening night of the film.

4 VOCABULARY *-ed / -ing* adjectives

a Right (✓) or wrong (✗)? Correct the wrong adjectives.

1 My sister can't swim. She's frightening of the water. ✗
frightened
2 Looking after small children can be very tired. ☐
______
3 His exam results were very disappointing. ☐
______
4 I was very embarrassed when my phone rang in the meeting. ☐
______
5 Clare was very surprising because she didn't know they were coming. ☐
______
6 We took lots of photos because the view was so amazing. ☐
______
7 Are you interested in motor racing? ☐
______
8 She felt frustrating because she couldn't get on the surf board. ☐
______

b Complete the sentences with the correct form of the adjectives in brackets.

1 I enjoyed the book, but the film was a bit *boring*. (bored / boring)
2 I felt very ______ when I realized my mistake. (embarrassed / embarrassing)
3 He's ______ of dogs. He can't go anywhere near them. (frightened / frightening)
4 The final quarter of the match was really ______. (excited / exciting)
5 We haven't heard from her since she arrived in Bangkok – it's very ______. (worried / worrying)
6 Your trip sounds really ______ – tell me more! (interested / interesting)
7 I'm fed up with this terrible weather – it's so ______. (depressed / depressing)
8 Max was very ______ when he wasn't chosen for the job. (disappointed / disappointing)

c Circle the *-ed* adjectives in exercise **b** where *-ed* is pronounced /ɪd/.

Reflexive pronouns

d Complete the sentences with the correct word.

1 The best way to get healthy is to make *yourself* do exercise every day.
2 Jon and Harry help ______ to food whenever they come to my house.
3 Helena painted the bathroom ______.
4 The computer turns ______ off if nobody uses it for a while.
5 I always sing to ______ when I'm in the shower.
6 We found the flat ______, without any help from a company.

5 LISTENING

a 4.2 You are going to hear five speakers talking about mistakes they have made in a foreign language. Listen and complete the sentences.

Speaker 1 was speaking *French* to ______.
Speaker 2 was speaking ______ to ______.
Speaker 3 was speaking ______ to ______.
Speaker 4 was speaking ______ to ______.
Speaker 5 was speaking ______ to ______.

b Listen again and complete the table.

	What they wanted to say	What they actually said
Speaker 1	*inhaler*	
Speaker 2		
Speaker 3		
Speaker 4		
Speaker 5		

c Listen again with the audioscript on p.71.

USEFUL WORDS AND PHRASES

Learn these words and phrases.

link /lɪŋk/
scuba-dive /'skuːbə daɪv/
skills /skɪlz/
(dance) steps /steps/
multilingual /mʌlti'lɪŋgwəl/
fluently /'fluːəntli/
basic phrases /beɪsɪk 'freɪzɪz/
language barrier /'læŋgwɪdʒ bæriə/
teach-yourself books /'tiːtʃ jə'self bʊks/
more exceptions than rules /mɔːr ɪk'sepʃnz ðən ruːlz/

When a man opens the car door for his wife it's either a new car or a new wife.

Duke of Edinburgh, husband of Queen Elizabeth II

4B Modern manners?

1 VOCABULARY phone language

Complete the sentences.

1 You mustn't use your phone in a qu*iet* z*one*.
2 When you finish a phone call, you h__________ u__________.
3 If someone doesn't answer their phone, you can leave a m__________ on their v__________.
4 If you're in a meeting, you can put your phone on s__________ or v__________ mode.
5 If someone's phone is off, you can c__________ b__________ later.
6 The sound your mobile makes when someone calls you is a r__________.
7 If you want to text your friends more cheaply, you can use in__________ m__________.
8 When you call someone, you have to d__________ their number by pressing some keys.
9 If someone is already talking on their mobile when you call, the line is b__________ or en__________.
10 You can protect the display of your mobile or computer with a sc__________.

2 GRAMMAR modals of obligation: *must, have to, should*

a Circle the correct form. Tick (✓) if both are possible.

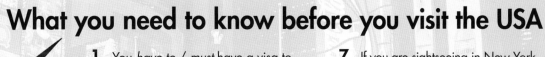

What you need to know before you visit the USA

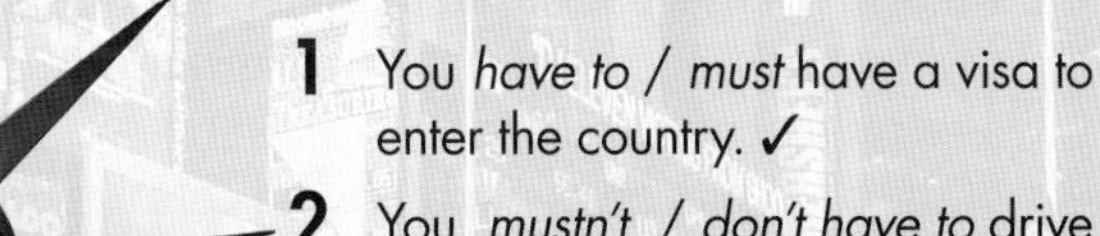

1 You *have to* / *must* have a visa to enter the country. ✓
2 You *mustn't* / *don't have to* drive on the left! Here we drive on the right!
3 You *mustn't* / *don't have to* pay to visit most museums and art galleries. Entrance is usually free.
4 You *have to* / *should* go on a ferry to visit the Statue of Liberty. You can't go by bus.
5 You *have to* / *must* wear a seat belt at all times in a car.
6 You *must* / *should* always try to arrive on time for an appointment or meeting. Americans are very punctual!
7 If you are sightseeing in New York, you *must* / *should* buy a MetroCard which gives you cheaper travel on the subway and buses.
8 You *mustn't* / *don't have to* smoke in any public building. It is prohibited by law.
9 When talking to American people, you *shouldn't* / *don't have to* ask them about their salary. Some people might think this is rude.
10 You *must* / *have to* answer some questions when you go through immigration.

b Correct any mistakes in use or form in the highlighted phrases. Tick (✓) the correct sentences.

1 **People mustn't use** their mobile phones when they're talking to you.
People shouldn't use
2 **I must** go to work by bus yesterday. My car was being repaired.
____
3 **Do you have to** wear a suit and tie at work?
____
4 **You don't have to play** football here. It says 'no ball games'.
____
5 My father is a taxi driver and **he should work** nights.
____
6 **I didn't have to cook** last night because we went out for dinner.
____
7 In the future, perhaps **everyone must speak** English and Chinese.
____
8 You don't look well. **You should to go home**.
____

3 PRONUNCIATION silent consonants, linking

a ~~Cross out~~ the silent consonant in the words.

1 ~~w~~rite
2 receipt
3 hour
4 shouldn't
5 exhausted
6 walk
7 could
8 debt

b 4.3 Listen and check. Then listen again and repeat the words.

c Listen and repeat the sentences. Try to link the words.

1 You shouldn't speak on the phone when you're driving.
2 You must always wear your seat belt in the car.
3 You don't have to wear a uniform.
4 You mustn't ask for money.
5 You have to watch out for pickpockets.
6 You should take a present for them.

d 4.4 Listen and check. Then listen again and repeat the sentences.

4 READING

a Read the article once and tick (✓) the best summary.

1 How men should behave towards women in the 21st century. ☐
2 How men behaved towards women in the past. ☐
3 The difference between men's and women's manners. ☐

Ladies first?

Nobody knows how long people have been using the words 'Ladies First', nor is anyone sure where the concept came from. However, neither of these facts matter today. The important question is whether the tradition is still relevant, and if men should continue respecting it.

In the past, there was a strict set of rules concerning men's behaviour towards women – or rather 'ladies' as they were called then. Men wearing hats used to take them off in the presence of women. They used to stand up whenever a woman entered or left a room, and they did the same at a dining table. Men used to hold a door for a woman to allow her to go through first. They always used to pay for meals – but we'll come back to that one later. All of these customs were considered good manners, and people looked down on men who did not conform.

In fact, this set of rules actually made things easier for men. If they broke a rule, they knew perfectly well that they were going to offend somebody. Today, it is much easier to cause offence without meaning to. For example, if a man opens a door to let a woman through first, and she does so without saying thank you, the man may feel offended. And if a man invites a woman to a restaurant of his choice on their first date, and then asks her to pay her half of the bill, it may be the woman who gets upset. Women no longer want to be treated as the weaker sex, which leaves men in a dilemma. On the one hand, men are conscious of the 'Ladies First' tradition, but on the other, they do not want to offend. Often, they don't know what to do.

The best advice is this: if in doubt, men should follow the rules of 'Ladies First'. Even if the woman considers the behaviour inappropriate, she will still realize that the man has good manners. This is particularly relevant on that first date we were talking about. If the man has invited the woman out, then he should pay the bill. Actually, it's the invitation to dinner itself that is important here, not the amount of money spent. In general, women appreciate a picnic or a home-made dinner just as much as an expensive meal.

So the answer to our original question is: yes. 'Ladies First' is still relevant today, but not in the same way as it was in the past. Most women appreciate a kind gesture made by a man, but he should never accompany it with the words 'Ladies First' – it spoils the effect completely!

b Read the article again and choose the right answer.

1 According to the article…
   a the idea of 'Ladies first' started in the Middle Ages.
   b the idea of 'Ladies first' is a new idea.
   ⓒ it's not known when the idea of 'Ladies first' started.
2 In the past…
   a men didn't know how to behave towards women.
   b 'Ladies first' was very polite.
   c it didn't matter if men broke the rules.
3 Nowadays, men…
   a aren't sure how to behave towards women.
   b behave in the same way towards women.
   c have new rules to follow.
4 According to the article, men should…
   a not think about what women want.
   b follow the rules of 'Ladies first'.
   c not follow the rules of 'Ladies first'.
5 According to the article, women…
   a always want expensive things.
   b don't like it when men cook.
   c like a meal at home or in a restaurant.

c Look at the highlighted words and phrases. What do you think they mean? Use your dictionary to look up their meaning and pronunciation.

d Find the highlighted words or phrases in the text to match the definitions.

1 not right for a particular situation *inappropriate*
2 an action that shows other people how you feel ______
3 understand the value of something ______
4 an idea ______
5 upset somebody ______
6 thought they were better than ______

5 LISTENING

a 4.5 Listen to a radio programme about good manners in different countries. What kind of advice do the four people ask about? Tick (✓) the correct answers. There is one piece of advice you do not need to use.

1 Advice about how to behave in business situations. ☐
2 Advice about body language. ☐
3 Advice about meeting new people. ☑
4 Advice about queuing. ☐
5 Advice about visiting someone's house. ☐

b Listen again and choose the right answers.

1 According to the expert, in Thailand you should not give a 'wai' to…
   a people who are older than you.
   b anyone.
   ⓒ people who are younger than you.
2 How many flowers are OK to give someone in Austria?
   a an odd number
   b an even number
   c it doesn't matter
3 Which gesture, often made by policemen, is an insult in Greece?
   a 'Come here.'
   b 'Stop.'
   c 'Go away.'
4 A foreign person in South Korea…
   a mustn't bow to anyone.
   b must bow to everyone.
   c can bow to show politeness.
5 According to the expert, if a Korean person is happy, they bow very…
   a quickly.
   b slowly.
   c deeply.

c Listen again with the audioscript on p.72.

USEFUL WORDS AND PHRASES

Learn these words and phrases.

etiquette /'etɪkət/
manners /'mænəz/
host / hostess /həʊst/ /'həʊstəs/
behave /bɪ'heɪv/
deserve /dɪ'zɜːv/
disturb /dɪ'stɜːb/
inappropriate /ɪnə'prəʊpriət/
insulting /ɪn'sʌltɪŋ/
allergic to /ə'lɜːdʒɪk tə/
should have (written) /ʃʊd əv/

It's not whether you win or lose that matters,
but whether I win or lose.

Sandy Lyle, Scottish golfer

5A Sporting superstitions

1 GRAMMAR past tenses

Complete the sentences with the correct form of the verbs in brackets. Use the past simple, past continuous, or past perfect.

1 We were late. When we *arrived* (arrive), everyone else *had finished* (finish) their lunch and they *were sitting* (sit) in the garden having coffee.
2 They ________ (drive) to the airport when they suddenly ________ (remember) that they ________ (not turn off) the lights.
3 The match ________ (already / start) when we ________ (turn on) the TV. England ________ (lose) and they ________ (play) very badly.
4 I ________ (not recognize) many people at my old school reunion because everyone ________ (change) a lot in twenty years.
5 My sister ________ (wait) to go out for dinner yesterday when her boyfriend ________ (call) her to say that he ________ (not can) come because his car ________ (break down).
6 Manchester City ________ (beat) Manchester United yesterday. United ________ (win) 1–0 in the first half, but City ________ (score) two goals in the second half.
7 He ________ (run) to the station, but the nine o'clock train ________ (already / leave). The station was empty except for two people who ________ (wait) for the next train.
8 It ________ (start) raining when I ________ (walk) to work. I ________ (call) a taxi because I ________ (not wear) a coat and I ________ (not have) an umbrella.

2 PRONUNCIATION /ɔː/, /ɜː/

a Circle the word with a different sound.

1 ɔː horse	2 ɜː bird	3 ɔː horse	4 ɜː bird
ball caught warm up (work out)	first hurt sport world	draw fought score slope	court serve circuit worse

b 5.1 Listen and check. Then listen again and repeat the words.

3 READING

a Read the article on p.31 once. Complete the sentences.

1 The boy was playing ________.
2 He cheated by taking ________.

b Read the article again. Mark the sentences T (true) or F (false).

1 According to the article, people usually learn not to cheat when they are young children. *F*
2 Blank tiles can be used when players haven't got the right letter. __
3 It was the first time that the boy had played in the tournament. __
4 The previous day, the boy had beaten Arthur Moore. __
5 Moore caught the boy while he was making a word. __
6 He saw the boy take a blank tile out of his pocket. __
7 The boy answered the tournament director's questions truthfully. __
8 He wasn't allowed to continue playing. __

c Look at the highlighted words and phrases. What do you think they mean? Use your dictionary to look up their meaning and pronunciation.

d Complete the sentences with one of the highlighted words or phrases.

1 James *discreetly* bought the present when his wife wasn't looking.
2 Sam ________ telling lies about her colleagues.
3 The athlete was ________ after he made three false starts.
4 My computer is broken, so I'm going to ________ it with a new one.
5 She became ________ when she found the train tickets in his pocket .
6 He couldn't ________ the man of lying because there was no proof he had done anything bad.
7 Jack beat his ________ 6–1, 6–3.
8 They ________ to stealing after they lost their jobs.

CHEATS NEVER PROSPER

It's fairly normal for young children to cheat when they're playing board games. As they grow older, they realize that the fun is actually in taking part in the game, not necessarily in winning it. By the time they reach their teens, they have usually learnt not to cheat. Sadly, this was not the case of a player in a national board game championship held annually in the USA. The player wanted to win so much that he resorted to cheating.

The board game was Scrabble. This is a word game that was created in 1938 by an American architect called Alfred Mosher Butts. In the game, players have to make words from individual letters on small squares called 'tiles', and then put the words on a board. Two of the most useful tiles in the game are the blanks, which are tiles without any letters on them. A blank isn't worth any points, but a player can use it to replace any letter of the alphabet.

The cheat in this particular tournament was a 15-year-old boy from Orlando, in the USA. He had surprised organizers in the early stages of the competition by beating some of the best players, despite the fact that he had never played in competitions before. This made some of the other players suspicious, including the man who caught him, 43-year-old Arthur Moore. Moore had already played the boy the day before, and Moore had won the match, although the boy had had both of the blank tiles. In Scrabble, before a new game starts the players put the tiles from the previous game back into a small bag. This time, Moore had a good look at the tiles on the table before he and his opponent put them in the bag to start the game. He was not surprised to see that the two blanks were together on the table in front of the boy. As the two players were putting the tiles into the bag, Moore discreetly watched the boy's left hand. He saw the boy pick up the two blanks, and put his hand under the table. This was the signal for Moore to call one of the organizers and accuse the boy of cheating.

When the boy was taken away for questioning, he admitted taking the two blanks during the game and hiding them under the table. As a result of his cheating, the tournament director disqualified him and banned him from playing in the competition again.

4 VOCABULARY sport

a Read the definitions and write the words.

1 an area of water that swimmers use
swimming pool

2 the person who controls a football match
r________

3 a track where Formula 1 cars race
c________

4 to hit something with your foot
k________

5 somebody who is very enthusiastic about sport
f________

6 an area where golf is played
c________

7 do exercise to become healthy and strong
g________ f________

8 an area of ground where people play football
p________

9 a person who trains people to compete in certain sports
c________

10 a large structure, usually with no roof, where people can sit and watch sports
st________

b Complete the sentences with the past simple of the verbs in the box.

beat draw get injured lose ~~play~~ score throw train warm up win

1 The USA *played* Russia in the final of the basketball last night.

2 The team ________ hard every day before the tournament.

3 The French runner ________ the race. He got the gold medal.

4 The players ________ ________ by jogging and doing short exercises just before the game started.

5 England and Spain ________ their match 2–2.

6 I didn't play well in the semi-final. I ________ 2–6, 1–6.

7 Marc ________ the ball to his brother, but his brother dropped it.

8 Brazil ________ Sweden. They had a much better team.

9 The Argentinian striker ________ four goals in the last match.

10 Our best player ________ ________ in the second half, and was taken off the pitch to see the team's doctor.

5 LISTENING

a 5.2 Listen to a radio programme about a sporting scandal. Which country won the competition in the end?

____

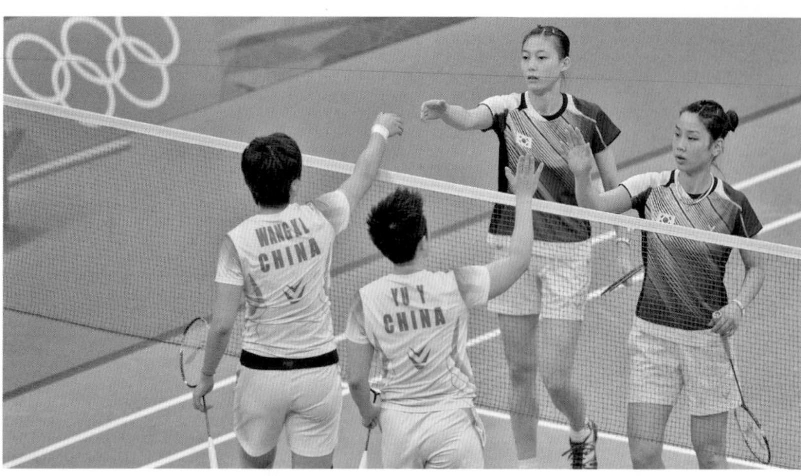

b Listen again and mark the sentences T (true) or F (false).

1 The scandal happened during the tennis tournament of the 2012 Olympics. *F*

2 South Korea and India were involved in the scandal. ___

3 It happened during the first stage. ___

4 One way they cheated was by hitting the shuttlecock into the net. ___

5 The same thing happened in another match. ___

6 The teams cheated because they had been offered money. ___

7 The crowd didn't enjoy the matches. ___

8 South Korea won the silver medal. ___

c Listen again with the audioscript on p.72.

USEFUL WORDS AND PHRASES

Learn these words and phrases.

fate /feɪt/
rituals /ˈrɪtʃuəlz/
superstition /suːpəˈstɪʃn/
bounce /baʊns/
cheat /tʃiːt/
reveal /rɪˈviːl/
sweat /swet/
a luck charm /ə ˈlʌk tʃɑːm/
result in /rɪˈzʌlt ɪn/
tie your shoelaces /taɪ jə ˈʃuːleɪsɪz/

Love is like war – easy to begin, but hard to end.
Anonymous

5B Love at Exit 19

1 GRAMMAR *usually* and *used to*

a Correct any mistakes in the highlighted phrases. Tick (✓) the correct sentences.

1 Where did you used to live before you moved here?
did you use to live?
2 Jerry used to have a beard, but now he's shaved it off.
✓
3 I usually go to the gym when I leave work.
____
4 My wife doesn't use to wear make-up. She doesn't like it.
____
5 Did you use to have long hair?
____
6 I use to walk to work. My office is only ten minutes from my house.
____
7 Carol didn't used to talk to me, but now she always says hello.
____
8 Do you use to get up late on Sundays?
____
9 Did you used to watch cartoons when you were little?
____
10 We don't usually stay in expensive hotels, but this weekend is special.
____

b Complete the sentences with *usually* or the correct form of *used to*, and the verbs in brackets.

1 She *used to wear* glasses, but now she has contact lenses. (wear)
2 He ______________ animals, but now he has a dog. (not like)
3 I ______________ my parents on Sunday. It's good to talk to them. (call)
4 I ______________ to French classes, but I stopped because I don't have time now. (go)
5 We never ______________, but now we go to restaurants twice a week. (eat out)
6 I ______________ late, but today I have a lot to do. (not work)
7 My sister ______________ very shy, but now she's quite confident. (be)
8 They ______________ me a present on my birthday, but this year they forgot! (give)

2 PRONUNCIATION sentence stress; the letter *s*

a 5.3 Listen and repeat. Copy the rhythm.

1 **Where** did you **use** to **live**?
2 Did you **use** to **wear glasses**?
3 They **used** to **have** a lot of **money**.
4 He **used** to **go** to my **school**.
5 We **used** to **work together**.
6 You **used** to **have long hair**.
7 We **didn't use** to **get on**.
8 I **didn't use** to **like** it.

b Circle the word with a different sound.

1 snake	2 zebra	3 shower	4 television
see (friends) most social	eyes easy especially nowadays	tissue please sure sugar	usually pleasure decision music

c 5.4 Listen and check. Then listen again and repeat the words.

3 VOCABULARY relationships

a Complete the sentences with the people in the box.

classmates close friend colleague couple ex fiancé flatmate ~~wife~~

1 We're married.	She's my *wife*.
2 I share a flat with her.	She's my ______.
3 I work with him.	He's my ______.
4 We used to go to school together.	We were ______.
5 I'm going to marry him.	He's my ______.
6 I used to go out with her.	She's my ______.
7 We've known each other for a long time. I tell her everything.	She's a ______.
8 We've been going out together for three years.	We're a ______.

b Complete the text with the past simple of the verbs in the box.

be together become friends break up
get to know get in touch get on get married
go out together have (sth) in common
lose touch ~~meet~~ propose

Anna [1] *met* Luke when she started work. They [2] __________ each other quickly because they sat next to each other in the office. They soon [3] __________ and they discovered that they [4] __________ a lot __________ because they were both sports fans. They [5] __________ a few times after work and they fell in love. They [6] __________ for a year, but they argued a lot and in the end they [7] __________. After that, Anna got a new job in a different town and so they [8] __________. Ten years later, they [9] __________ again on *Facebook*. They were both still single and Mark had changed jobs, too. They decided to try again, and this time they [10] __________ better than before, maybe because they weren't working together. After six months, Luke [11] __________ and Anna accepted. They [12] __________ last spring. A lot of their old colleagues from work came to the wedding!

4 READING

a Read the article once. How many friends does the average American have?

__________.

Your friends in numbers

HOW MANY FRIENDS does the average person have? A researcher at Cornell University in the USA has recently done a study into this question, by finding out the number of friends a typical American has. He has just published the results. The researcher interviewed more than 2,000 adults aged 18 and over in his study. He asked them to list the names of the people they had discussed serious matters with in the last six months. About 48% of the people taking part gave the researcher one name, 18% gave him two, and about 29% gave him more than two.

These results contrast dramatically with the news published by social networking site Facebook recently. They said that the average user on the site has 130 friends. The Cornell University study found the average number of friends to be a lot lower – 2.03 to be exact. The researcher from Cornell has explained that the difference lies in the definition of the word *friend*. A friend on Facebook may be a person that the user has met by chance or someone that they will never meet in real life. However, the friends in his study are close friends, who participants feel comfortable discussing their problems with.

In a similar study conducted 25 years ago, participants had a higher number of close friends. Then, the average number was three. Despite the lower number, the researcher does not believe that people are getting more isolated. Instead he thinks it's a sign that they are becoming better at choosing who they can trust with their secrets.

This is supported by the number of people in the study who could not think of any names of close friends they would discuss their personal problems with. The percentage of these participants is the same this time as it was 25 years ago. In both studies, just over 4% of the participants gave researchers no names. Apparently, the people who fall into this category are more likely to be men, or people with less education.

In general, the researcher from Cornell regards these findings as positive. In his opinion, they suggest that, at least in the case of Americans, people are not becoming less sociable.

b Read the article again and choose the best answer.

1 Most people in the Cornell University study had spoken about something important with…
   ⓐ one person.
   b two people.
   c more than two people.
2 The news published by *Facebook* is different from the results in the Cornell study because…
   a the people are different ages.
   b the studies are from different years.
   c the relationships aren't the same.
3 According to a previous study, people had __________ close friends in the past.
   a more
   b the same number of
   c fewer
4 The number of people with no close friends is __________ it was in the past.
   a higher than
   b the same as
   c lower than
5 The results of the Cornell study show that Americans today are __________ they used to be.
   a more sociable than
   b as sociable as
   c less sociable than

c Look at the highlighted words and phrases. What do you think they mean? Use your dictionary to look up their meaning and pronunciation.

d Complete the sentences with one of the highlighted words or phrases.

1 I found an old painting *by* *chance* while I was cleaning the attic.
2 I wouldn't __________ my son with my phone. He'll probably break it.
3 How much money does __________ __________ __________ earn per year?
4 They talked about __________ __________ first, and then moved on to the less important things.
5 The richer parts of town __________ __________ with the poorer outskirts.
6 Some teenagers are __________ __________ __________ because they spend so much time on their computers.

5 LISTENING

a 5.5 You are going to hear a radio programme about research on love and attraction. Number the topics in the order you hear them.

a How to use your eyes at a first meeting. __
b Body language at a first meeting. __
c How to use your voice at a first meeting. *1*
d How much to smile at a first meeting. __

b Listen again and mark the sentences T (true) or F (false).

1 It's very important to say the right thing the first time you talk to someone you like. *F*
2 A person is often attracted to someone else because of their body language. __
3 Looking into someone's eyes can make them feel more attracted to you. __
4 There were two weddings after an experiment in New York. __
5 Standing up straight is a good way to keep someone's attention. __
6 A person will copy your body language if they think you are interesting. __
7 It is impossible to know if someone is smiling when you're talking to them on the phone. __
8 Often when one person smiles, other people smile too. __

c Listen again with the audioscript on p.73.

USEFUL WORDS AND PHRASES

Learn these words and phrases.

candle /'kændl/
commuter /kə'mjuːtə/
cute /kjuːt/
likely /'laɪkli/
raise the barrier /reɪz ðə 'bæriə/
addicted to (sth) /ə'dɪktɪd tə/
night shifts /'naɪt ʃɪfts/
turn out (to be) /tɜːn 'aʊt/
exchange a few words /ɪks'tʃeɪndʒ ə fjuː wɜːdz/
find the courage (to do sth) /faɪnd ðə 'kʌrɪdʒ/

Practical English Old friends

1 PERMISSION AND REQUESTS

a Complete the requests with the correct form of the verbs in the box.

~~do~~ join pass meet take visit

1 Could you *do* me a big favour? [*d*]
2 Do you mind if I ______ you? [ ]
3 Would you mind ______ me at the airport? [ ]
4 Is it OK if we ______ my parents this weekend? [ ]
5 Can you ______ the salt? [ ]
6 Do you think you could ______ me to the station? [ ]

b Match the requests from **a** with the responses a–f.

a Of course not. Take a seat.
b Sure. Here it is.
c Yes, of course. What time's your train?
~~d It depends what it is!~~
e Not at all. When do you land?
f Sure. Which day would be best?

2 SOCIAL ENGLISH

Complete the dialogue.

Jay Dan! It's great to [1] s*ee* you.
Dan You too, Jay. It's been years.
Jay How [2] c______ you're so late?
Dan My flight was delayed and then I had to wait ages for a taxi.
Jay Well, you're here now. Do you want something to eat?
Dan No [3] w______, man! I want to go out and see the city!
Jay Don't you want to unpack first?
Dan No, I can do that later. But I'll take a shower, if you don't [4] m______.
Jay Sure. Go ahead.
Dan This is great. You and me getting ready to go out.
Jay Yeah. It's just like the old [5] d______.
Dan Right, I'm ready. Let's go. We have a lot to [6] t______ about.

3 READING

Getting around the USA

America is huge, so flying is the quickest way to get around the country. It can be expensive though, so here are some other ways of getting around.

If you aren't in a hurry, the best alternative is to go by car. You have to be at least 25 years old to rent a car in the States, and you need a valid driver's license and a major credit card to do so. There are a lot of rental car companies, and their prices vary a lot. Compare companies before you decide which one to use, and remember it can be cheaper to book for a week than for a day.

If you prefer to be driven rather than driving yourself, the next best way to travel is by bus. Greyhound is the major long-distance bus company, and it has routes through the USA and Canada. Tickets are much cheaper if you buy them seven days in advance, and there are often other offers. If you're travelling with a friend, your companion gets 50% off if you buy the tickets three days before you travel, and children aged between two and 11 get a 40% discount.

An alternative to using the bus is to take the train. Amtrak is the American rail company, and it has long-distance lines connecting all of America's biggest cities. It also runs buses from major stations to smaller towns and national parks. Fares vary depending on the type of train and the seat, but you need to reserve at least three days ahead to get a discount. Students with an International Student Card get 15% off the standard fare. Bring your own food, as the dining car is quite expensive.

a Read the text and answer the questions.

1 What do you need to hire a car in America
You need a valid driver's license and a major credit card.
2 What is the difference between all the car rental companies?
______
3 Where does the Greyhound bus company operate?
______
4 How can you save money if you're travelling alone by bus?
______
5 How much do students pay on Amtrak trains?
______
6 What should long-distance rail passengers take with them?
______

b Underline five words or phrases you don't know. Use your dictionary to look up their meaning and pronunciation.

Listening

1.3

Presenter Welcome back to the show. Today, we've been discussing Teresa Gold's article *The truth about healthy eating*. And now it's time for you, the listeners, to tell us what you think. The lines are open, so all you have to do is call 091 344 5792 and talk to one of our operators. That's 091 344 5792. And it looks like we have our first caller. William from Manchester, tell us what you think about the article.

William Well, I'd like to say that I don't agree with the article at all. I don't eat much fruit or vegetables and I'm perfectly healthy. I haven't been off sick from work for years – I can't remember the last time I had to stay in bed. This five-a-day thing is a load of rubbish, really, isn't it?

Presenter Um…thank you, William. I think we have another caller on line two. Kate from Newcastle, are you there?

Kate Yes, I am. Well, I'm sure the writer knows what she's talking about, but it isn't that easy, is it? I mean, it's hard enough to get kids to eat vegetables at the best of times, but with all these burger bars and pizza places around, it's nearly impossible. Once they get the taste for junk food, you can forget the five-a-day, I can tell you!

Presenter Thanks, Kate. And who's our next caller?

Harry Um, my name's Harry and I'm from Southampton.

Presenter And what do you think, Harry?

Harry Well, I'd like to say that I think that the article is right. I mean, the writer talks about eating a lot of fruit and vegetables, which is something that we've always done in my family. My mum's a great cook, and she's always used completely natural ingredients in her cooking and we're hardly ever ill…

Presenter Thank you, Harry. Let's go back to line two again, where we've got Rosie from Cardiff. Rosie, what's your opinion?

Rosie Well, the writer seems to think that ALL fruit and vegetables are good for you, and I don't think that's quite right. I mean, what about potatoes? They contain a lot of carbohydrates, which can make you put on weight, if you aren't careful – it's even worse if you fry them. And then some fruit, like melon for example, has a lot of sugar. Personally, I think you should eat a bit of everything and not too much of one thing.

Presenter Thanks for that, Rosie. And that's all we've got time for today. We'll be speaking to the writer of the article after the break.

1.5

Terry I'm exhausted!

Jane Me too. I haven't stopped all day.

Terry Neither have I.

Jane Oh well. I suppose it'll get easier when the children grow up.

Terry Do you think so?

Jane Of course. When they're older, they'll be more independent. We won't have to do everything for them any more.

Terry And how long will that take? Five, six years? Or maybe never!

Jane Look, what's the problem, Terry?

Terry Nothing. It's just that we never have time for each other these days. We're always with the children!

Jane But that's what happens when you have children. It'll get better!

Terry I don't know…My parents were talking about us going to live with them. Do you think it would be easier for us if we lived with my parents?

Jane Well, I suppose it'd have its advantages.

Terry Yes, I mean for one thing there'd always be someone to look after the children.

Jane That sounds good.

Terry And we could go out in the evening without the children. Just imagine that!

Jane Hmm. That doesn't really matter to me.

Terry And there would be more people to share the housework, too. It wouldn't always be the same person who does the shopping, cleans the house, and cooks the meals.

Jane Yes, but there would be more people in the house, so there would be more work to do. Shopping and cooking for six isn't the same as doing it for four.

Terry I suppose so.

Jane And another disadvantage is that we wouldn't have any privacy.

Terry True

Jane And you know what your parents are like. They let the children do everything they want to do.

Terry Hmm. I guess you don't want to move in with my parents, then.

Jane Not really, no. Would you like to move in with mine?

Terry No, definitely not…Actually, things aren't so bad right now.

Jane I agree.

Terry And the children will be older soon.

Jane Yes, they will.

Terry That's settled then. We're staying here.

Jane Fine.

2.2

Speaker 1 Can I live on my salary? Well, I don't have many problems really, because I'm still living with Mum and Dad. Don't get me wrong, I give my mum some rent, but it's definitely much cheaper than living on your own. I've got quite a good salary actually – I'm a graphic designer. I don't really spend much – I buy some new clothes every now and then, and I have to put petrol in my car, of course, but apart from that, it's just going out at the weekend really. Most of my money goes into a savings account so that I can buy my own house one day.

Speaker 2 I find it really hard to live on my income, because I've only got a part-time job. Being on my own with my daughter means that my mom has to look after her when I'm at work. At least I don't have to pay for childcare! The flat we live in is rented, so that's where most of the money goes. I don't think I'll ever be able to afford our own place, because the bank won't give me a mortgage. Apart from the rent, my money goes on food and clothes for my daughter. Still, I mustn't complain. I've got a lovely daughter, and that's all that matters really.

Speaker 3 I think I'm quite lucky really. I'm fairly healthy for my age, I've got enough money to live on, and I've got my children and grandchildren! When I say I've got enough money, I don't have any fancy holidays or anything like that. But I'm comfortable. I've paid the mortgage, so that's one less expense, and I haven't got any bank loans to pay either. My one little luxury is going out for lunch a few times a week with some friends. I suppose that's where most of my money goes really – on food!

Speaker 4 Can we live on our salaries? Well, I'm not very sure, actually! My husband is a teacher, so he doesn't earn that much – certainly not enough to bring up two children! That means I have to go out to work as well – I've got a full-time job at the local supermarket. And that's our biggest problem really, because we need someone to look after the children. Our child-minder costs a fortune –we spend more on childcare than we do on our mortgage! Then there's food and new clothes for the children, too. Honestly, it isn't cheap having kids these days!

2.4

Presenter And now to end the programme with an inspirational story, we have John to tell us about an incredible journey.

John Yes, thank you, Helen. Have you ever thought about travelling around the world and trying to help people as you go? Well that's what an American father and his two adopted sons are currently doing. J.D. Lewis is a single parent and a former actor. He's taken his sons, Jackson, 14 and Buck, 9, out of school for a year to make the trip with him. And their plan is to help people along the way by doing voluntary charity work.

Presenter That sounds wonderful, but it must be an expensive trip. How much will it all cost?

John It's going to cost them $300,000 in total.

Presenter That's a lot of money – how did they afford it?

John Well, J.D. Lewis didn't have all the money, so he set up an organization called Twelve In Twelve to help raise money, and with the help of individuals and some companies, they managed to raise the money.

Presenter Twelve In Twelve, that's an unusual name. Why did he call it that?

John For a very good reason. Not only is their trip going to last twelve months, but their plan is to visit twelve countries. This month, they're in Australia, where they're working with the most important ethnic group in the region – the Aborigines. J.D. and his family are helping to get medical supplies to these people, who often live a long way from the major cities.

Presenter And is that the first place they've visited?

John Oh no, so far they have visited seven countries. Their first stop was Russia, where they looked after babies in an orphanage in the city of Tomsk. From there, they travelled to China, where they worked with children with physical disabilities in Beijing. Then, they flew to Thailand where they helped look after the animals at the Elephant Nature Park.

Presenter What a variety of places. Where did they go next?

John Their next stop was India, where they worked with children in the poorest district of the city of Hubli. Then they left Asia and flew to Africa. In Rwanda, they taught English to children who had lost their parents in the civil war. From there, they went to Zanzibar, an island off the coast of Tanzania.

Presenter That sounds very exotic! What did they do there?

John They helped families prepare an art fair, where they could sell things that they had made. Next, they went to Kenya, where they wrote and acted in a play with children who have HIV.

Presenter Wow, I bet that was very rewarding. Did they go anywhere else in Africa?

John No, that was the end of Africa. From Kenya, they flew to Australia, which is where they are right now.

Presenter All that sounds amazing, but their journey isn't over, is it?

John No, J.D. and his family still have four places to go: Antarctica, Paraguay, Peru, and Haiti. Not only are they trying to do things to help other people, but they are hoping to learn a lot of new things themselves. And J.D. Lewis hopes that the Twelve In Twelve organization will encourage other families to do what he has done with his sons.

Presenter Well, good luck to J.D. Lewis and family on the rest of their incredible journey. And that's all we've got time for tonight. Join us again tomorrow when we'll be bringing you more real-life stories.

3.3

Speaker 1 One morning last winter, I was driving to work late when my mobile rang. I knew it was my boss so I answered it. Suddenly, the van in front of me stopped because there was someone crossing the road. I was talking to my boss, so I reacted too late and my car went into the back of the van. Fortunately, I was driving really slowly at the time, so I didn't do much damage to the van, but the front of my car was a real mess. Since then, I never use my phone when I'm driving.

Speaker 2 I was driving down to Devon one summer to visit my parents, who live in Exeter. It's quite a long journey, so I had taken my MP3 player with me to connect to the car radio. Surprisingly, there wasn't much traffic on the motorway, so I arrived in Devon quite quickly. However, I was having such a good time listening to my music, that I completely missed the exit for Exeter. I didn't realize until I had gone another 30 kilometres and so I had to turn round and drive all the way back again! It just goes to show what can happen when you aren't concentrating.

Speaker 3 We were on holiday last year, when we had a little accident. We were going somewhere we'd never been before, so we were following the instructions on my satnav. We heard on the radio that there'd been a big crash on one of the roads we needed to travel on, so I started adjusting my satnav to find a different road to take. I took my eyes off the road and suddenly we came to a corner. I saw the corner too late, so I went straight on and drove into the middle of a field. We were really lucky, though, because no one was hurt.

Speaker 4 I don't usually get up early enough to put my make-up on, so I normally put it on in my car. Well, I used to put it on in the car – now I wait until I get to my office. You see, I had a bit of a shock the other week, when I nearly didn't stop at a zebra crossing. I was looking in the mirror instead of at the road, so I didn't see this little boy run out – to tell you the truth, I hadn't even seen that there was a zebra crossing there. I just had time to put on the brakes and I missed the little boy by about a millimetre. I was quite shocked afterwards, though.

Speaker 5 I was driving into town to meet my girlfriend for dinner, when she sent me a text message. I decided to read it, in case it was important. Anyway, the message said that my girlfriend was already at the restaurant, and I wanted her to know that I was going to be a bit late, so when I stopped at a red light, I started to write a reply. But I didn't notice when the traffic lights turned green, and the car behind crashed into the back of me. The driver of the car said he thought I was going to drive off and so he moved forward and hit me. Of course I didn't tell him I was texting.

3.7

Presenter Traditionally in the UK, women have cooked more than men, but it looks as though things might be changing. According to a recent survey by a frozen foods company, nearly half of all men in this country now prepare the family meals. And they aren't just doing it because they have to – it's because they enjoy it. The survey showed that 44% of men who were questioned do all of the cooking, and surprisingly, 15% of women questioned said that they didn't know how to cook. So, it seems as if men are moving into the kitchen and perhaps women are moving out. Is this good news? What do you think? Call us on 061 532 3364 and tell us your opinion. I'll give you that number again – it's 061 532 3364.

And here's our first caller, Nick from Maidstone, in Kent. Nick, what do you think about this new trend?

Nick I'm really pleased to see more men in the kitchen. In fact, I'm one of them! I lost my job a few months ago, and now I do all the cooking at home. I make a different dish every day, and sometimes I meet up with my friends to exchange recipes. My girlfriend says she really likes my food, and she even thinks that I should train to be a professional chef. I'm seriously thinking about doing that.

Presenter Well, the very best of luck to you, Nick. Who's our next caller? Ah, yes… It's Eve from Bradford. Do you cook, Eve?

Eve No, I don't. But my husband does. He's a much better cook than me, so we decided from the very start that he would do all the cooking. And he makes some great meals – mostly curries. But there's one problem.

Presenter What's that, Eve?

Eve He makes a terrible mess of the kitchen, and I have to clean up after him. I don't know what's worse, actually, cooking myself or cleaning the kitchen!

Presenter Oh, come on Eve – it can't be that bad! Now I think we've got someone on line two. Yes, it's Frank from Aberdeen. What do you think about men taking over the kitchen, Frank?

Frank Well, I'm not surprised, to be honest with you. It seems to me that girls are getting lazier and lazier these days – it's only the older mums and grandmothers that know how to cook. I mean, how can a woman possibly get married if she can't cook? I think it's a disgrace!

Presenter Thank you, Frank. So, not all of our listeners think it's a good thing. How about our next caller, Martina, from Dublin? Is it good news or bad news for you, Martina?

Martina Good news. Definitely. In my house, I do all the cooking. My boyfriend doesn't cook at all – he can't even fry an egg! I mean, we both go out to work, so why can't we share the cooking? I'm really fed up with it, I really am. But I'm really happy for all those women out there who have found a real man. I know how you feel when you have to do everything yourself.

Presenter Let's hope Martina's boyfriend is listening in, so that he knows how she feels. We'll take some more calls after the break.

4.2

Speaker 1 I suffer from asthma and I usually carry an inhaler around with me just in case I get an attack. Anyway, I was on a work trip – I was in Paris – I had forgotten my inhaler and I was having problems breathing. So I went to a chemist's and asked for 'un aspirateur', which I thought was the French word for 'inhaler'. I realized it wasn't when the girls behind the counter looked very confused. It turned out that I had asked for a vacuum cleaner, 'aspirateur', instead of an inhaler, 'inhalateur'.

Speaker 2 I was in Istanbul with a Turkish friend of mine and we decided that we wanted to buy some bread. I wanted to try out the Turkish I knew so I said that I would ask for it. So we found this tiny little shop and we went in. I said to the shop assistant in my best voice 'taze erkek' which I thought meant 'fresh bread'. Unfortunately, I got the word for bread 'ekmek' confused with the word for man 'erkek', so what I had actually asked for was 'a fresh young man'. Luckily, my friend came to my rescue and asked for the bread correctly, but I felt a bit embarrassed!

Speaker 3 I was 14, and I was on an exchange visit with my school in Madrid. It was the first night and I was at home with my Spanish host family, the Garcías, having dinner. We'd finished the main course and it was time for dessert, so the wife, Maria, asked me if I'd like some fruit. I saw some bananas in the fruit bowl, so I asked for a 'platón', at which point the whole family looked at me strangely. They then explained to me that I'd actually asked for a large plate. 'Platón' means 'large plate' whereas 'banana' is 'plátano'.

Speaker 4 I was in Verona in Italy with my husband, and it was a very hot day, so we decided to get something to drink. So we sat down at this café in the square and we looked at the menu. I decided that I would have peach juice, so when the waiter came to our table, I asked him for some 'succo di pesce'. As soon as I'd finished speaking, he burst out laughing. He quickly apologized and explained in English that I'd asked him for fish juice and not peach juice. Fish is 'pesce' in Italian, and peaches are 'pesca'.

Speaker 5 I went to Corfu on holiday when I was about 15 and there were lots of beautiful Greek girls around, so I wanted to make a good impression by speaking Greek to them. So every morning when I saw them I said good morning to them: 'kalamári'. They always used to look at me as if I was completely mad and I never understood why. Later in the holiday someone told me that good morning is in fact 'kalimera', not 'kalamári'. I'd been saying 'squid' to them every morning not 'good morning' so I'm not surprised they thought I was mad!

4.5

Presenter Hello and welcome to *The Traveller's Guide*. Now, last week we asked our British listeners who are going to go abroad to send us their questions about good manners in other countries, and we've invited our resident expert Ruth Dempsey to the show to answer them. Welcome to the programme, Ruth.

Ruth Thank you.

Presenter So the first question, Ruth. This comes from Katy in Glasgow, who is going to travel around Thailand next summer. Katy wants to know what she should do when she first meets people in Thailand.

Ruth Well, Katy, most of the time, a simple handshake will be fine. But if someone gives you a 'wai', that is a small bow with the hands held together close to the body, you must do the same. But, if the person is of lower social status than you, so if they are younger than you, or they are a waiter, for example, you shouldn't return the 'wai'.

Presenter Very useful advice, Ruth. The next question is from Mark in Liverpool, who is going to Austria with his girlfriend, to meet her family for the first time. He asks: 'Is there anything I should or shouldn't do?'

Ruth Austrian culture is similar to British culture in a lot of ways, but there are a few differences to remember. Don't be late. If you say you are going to arrive at a particular time, make sure you arrive at that time. Take a gift to give to her parents and some flowers for her mother, but only in odd numbers, so for example nine flowers are OK, but ten would be considered bad luck.

Presenter That sounds like good advice for you, Mark. Right, our next caller is Julie in Lincoln. She is going to Greece on holiday, but doesn't speak the language. She asks: 'As I don't speak any Greek I will be communicating mostly with my hands. Are there any gestures I shouldn't use?'

Ruth Absolutely, Julie. The most important one to remember is the 'thumbs up', which in the UK means 'good' or 'OK'. But it is very insulting to a Greek person. Another one is the UK hand gesture for 'stop', where you show someone your hand with your fingers straight together, like a policeman. But again this is an insult in Greece.

Presenter Good luck, Julie. And we've got time for one more, and this question is from Claire in Swansea. She's going to South Korea for her job, and she would like some tips on business behaviour over there.

Ruth The most important thing to remember is that South Koreans like to bow a lot. As a foreigner, you won't be expected to, but it is a good way of showing respect, and the deeper you bow, the happier you are.

Presenter Very interesting. Ruth Dempsey, thank you for joining us.

Ruth My pleasure.

5.2

Speaker 1 Welcome back to the show. We've been talking about famous sports cheats in today's programme, and now we're going to hear about another scandal. The sport was badminton, and the venue was the 2012 Olympic Games in London. Tom is here to tell us about it. Hi, Tom.

Tom Hello, everybody.

Presenter So who was involved in the scandal, Tom?

Tom Well, the scandal involved four of the teams in the women's doubles competition. In total, eight players were disqualified for cheating: two pairs from South Korea, a pair from China, and a pair from Indonesia.

Presenter And what exactly happened?

Tom Well, basically the teams played badly on purpose to make sure they lost their matches.

Presenter Why would they do that?

Tom Well, to explain that I'll very quickly tell you about how the competition works. The matches are divided into different stages. Teams play against other teams in their group in the first stage, and if they win, they play in the next stage. So sometimes, a team might get a good opponent very early in the competition, which means they might not get through to the next stage.

Presenter Got it. So when did the cheating happen?

Tom Well, the problem started on the last day of the first stage. In the morning, the first Chinese team won their match, finishing second in their group. The second Chinese team were going to play against a South Korean team that evening, and whoever won that match would be likely to play against the first Chinese team in the next stage.

Presenter Why was this a problem?

Tom Neither team wanted to play against the first Chinese team because the South Korean team were sure they would lose, and the second Chinese team didn't want to play against a team from the same country yet, because that would mean that only one Chinese team was left to try to win a medal. So both teams both tried to lose against each other instead.

Presenter How did they do that?

Tom Well, both the South Koreans and the second Chinese team started missing shots. When they served, they either hit the shuttlecock into the net or they hit it so hard that it went outside the lines on the court. In the end, they looked like amateurs whereas they were in fact some of the best players in the world.

Presenter So who lost the match?

Tom The second Chinese team. South

Korea beat them in both sets.

Presenter What about the other two teams?

Tom Well, they tried to do exactly the same thing in the next match.

Presenter Which teams were these, again?

Tom Indonesia and another South Korean pair.

Presenter So in both matches, the teams tried to lose instead of trying to win so they'd have a better chance of winning a medal. Is that right?

Tom Yes. That's exactly what happened. And it was really obvious, too – all the spectators started booing, it was so bad. After the second match there was an investigation and all eight players were disqualified.

Presenter And what about the competition? Did it stop there?

Tom No, it carried on without the disqualified players.

Presenter And who won the gold medal in the end?

Tom The first Chinese team. They beat the Japanese team in both sets. It was quite a good match, actually!

Presenter Tom, thanks for joining us.

Tom My pleasure.

5.5

Presenter Hello and welcome to the show. Now, a lot of research has been done recently into love, what causes it, and what we do to attract someone. Mary is in the studio with us today, and she's going to explain the results of some of these studies to us. Mary, welcome to the show.

Mary Hello.

Presenter Let's start with how to meet new people. Some people like to start a conversation with a person they like by saying something clever or funny. But how useful is this?

Mary Not very useful at all I'm afraid, Jeremy. Research shows that only 7% of attraction has anything to do with what you say. It's the tone and the speed of your voice that makes a difference. This makes up 38% of attraction. But the most important thing of all is body language. This contributes to a massive 55% of attraction.

Presenter So what can we do to improve our body language?

Mary Well, it seems that the best way to make the person you're talking to feel attracted to you is to look into their eyes. An American psychologist did an experiment about this in New York. He got complete strangers to stare into each other's eyes for two minutes without talking. Afterwards many of the couples said that they had strong feelings of attraction to each other, and one of the couples even got married!

Presenter Really? Staring must be the thing to do then! Is there any more advice on body language?

Mary Well it's important to have a relaxed body position. You need to show the other person that you are comfortable being with them. Also, try not to be far away from them. Of course there is a comfortable distance, but try leaning a little closer to them than usual, it will show you're interested, and hold their attention better. Don't forget to watch their body language, too. If they position their body in a similar way to you, it means they find you interesting too. This is called 'mirroring'.

Presenter Is there anything that seems to work well when you're talking to someone you're attracted to?

Mary Not surprisingly, it seems that you're in with a good chance if you smile. Anyone who's ever spoken to someone on the phone will tell you that it's easy to tell when the other person is smiling, because you can hear it in their voice. When talking to a potential partner, a smile will not only affect your tone of voice, keeping it light and fun, but it will also show the other person that you are happy to be with them. And don't forget that a smile is extremely contagious, and before long the other person will be smiling back at you. This will make them feel happier, a feeling which they will quickly connect with you.

Presenter How interesting, and very true! Unfortunately, that's all we've got time for now, Mary, but thank you so much for joining us.

Mary You're welcome.

Answer key

1A

1 VOCABULARY

a 2 salmon <u>meat</u>
3 pear <u>vegetables</u>
4 aubergine <u>fruit</u>
5 beef <u>seafood</u>
6 cherry <u>vegetables</u>

b Down: 2 baked 4 roast
Across: 2 boiled 3 fried 5 steamed

c 2 takeaway
3 frozen
4 raw
5 low-fat
6 spicy
7 fresh

2 PRONUNCIATION

a 1 chicken, squid
2 beef, peach
3 crab, mango
4 carton, jar
5 chocolate, sausage
6 fork, prawns
7 cook, sugar
8 cucumber, tuna

c 2 cabbage
3 spicy
4 roast
5 grapes
6 fruit
7 baked
8 melon
9 aubergine

3 GRAMMAR

a 3 Do you eat out
4 ✓
5 Do you think
6 We have
7 ✓
8 I don't want
9 ✓
10 He's ordering

b 2 doesn't, cook
3 are / 're having
4 aren't going out
5 Do, spend
6 serves
7 do, eat out
8 am / 'm not having
9 don't, buy
10 is / 's cutting down

4 READING

a 2 D
3 A
4 B

b 2 F
3 F
4 T
5 F
6 F
7 T
8 F

5 LISTENING

a C

b 1 D
2 B
3 A
4 C

1B

1 GRAMMAR

a 2 I'll pay
3 Shall I make
4 you'll get married
5 We aren't going
6 I'll have
7 I'll be
8 Shall we invite
9 I won't be
10 We're having / We're going to have

b 1 are / 're staying / are / 're going to stay, are / 're having / are / 're going to have
2 Shall ... order, 'll call, 'll have
3 are ... leaving / are ... going to leave, 'm getting / 'm going to get, 'll give
4 are ... doing / are ... going to do, am / 'm going to see, 'll love it
5 Shall ... help, 'll wash, won't break

2 *each other*

2 don't know each other
3 aren't speaking to each other
4 don't understand each other
5 respect each other

3 PRONUNCIATION

a 2 not, book, flight
3 look, online
4 Who, meeting, tonight
5 meeting, friends
6 not, meeting, girlfriend
7 When, get, results
8 won't, this, week
9 get, Monday

4 VOCABULARY

a 2 great-grandfather
3 only child
4 niece
5 aunt
6 immediate family
7 stepmother
8 father-in-law
9 extended family
10 nephew

b 2 jealous
3 reliable
4 selfish
5 sensible
6 aggressive
7 self-confident
8 ambitious
9 stubborn
10 independent

c 2 unkind
3 hard-working
4 immature
5 disorganized
6 insensitive
7 quiet
8 untidy

5 READING

a They can help each other when they have a problem.

b 2 a
3 b
4 c
5 a

6 LISTENING

a They decide not to move in with Terry's parents.

b 2 F
3 T
4 T
5 F
6 T

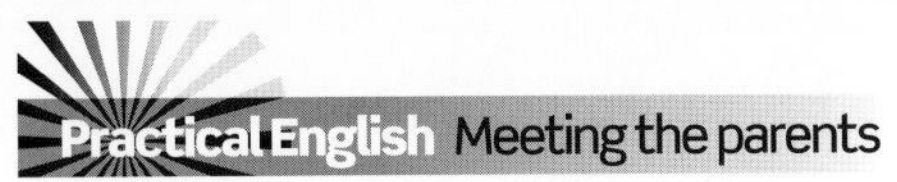

Practical English Meeting the parents

1 REACTING TO WHAT PEOPLE SAY

2 believe
3 kidding
4 mind
5 Really
6 pity
7 How
8 news
9 What

2 SOCIAL ENGLISH

2 How do you see
3 Not really
4 That's because
5 How incredible
6 Go ahead
7 things like that
8 I mean

3 READING

a 2 55 Bar
3 Barbès
4 Smalls
5 Café Carlyle
6 Smalls

2A

1 VOCABULARY

a 2 afford
3 save
4 earns
5 is worth
6 raise
7 owe
8 inherited
9 charged
10 lend

b 2 for
3 into
4 from
5 in / by
6 to
7 on
8 by
9 back
10 in

c 2 cash machine
3 note
4 salary
5 bills
6 loan
7 mortgage
8 tax

2 PRONUNCIATION

a 2 clothes
3 done
4 worse
5 short

3 GRAMMAR

a 2 charged
3 hasn't saved
4 didn't inherit
5 haven't been
6 did your TV cost
7 Have you paid
8 didn't have
9 Have you ever invested
10 earned

b 1 passed
2 did ... borrow, have / 've ... spent
3 Have ... found, has just agreed
4 Have ... lent, needed
5 Has ... made, called

4 READING

a 3

b 2 c
3 a
4 c
5 b

d 2 retirement plan
3 discarded
4 era
5 stock market
6 sell-by date

5 LISTENING

a 2 a
3 c
4 b

b 2 T
3 T
4 F
5 F
6 T
7 F
8 T

2B

1 GRAMMAR

a **for:** ages, a fortnight, six months, the last two days, years and years
since: Christmas, I was little, Tuesday, you last called

b 2 has/'s been, since
3 have/'ve known, since
4 has /'s worked, for
5 have/'ve lived, since
6 have gone, for
7 have/'ve wanted, for
8 hasn't spoken, since

c 2 we've been travelling
3 has he been working
4 She's been looking for
5 He hasn't been doing
6 Have you been waiting
7 I've been looking after

d 3 has had
4 ✓
5 ✓
6 I've known
7 We've been going
8 You've been wearing

2 PRONUNCIATION

a 2 long, out
3 feeling, yesterday
4 haven't, living
5 cleaning, morning
6 haven't, sleeping

3 READING

a 2 A
3 C

b 2 C
3 A
4 C
5 A
6 B
7 C
8 A

d 2 make a contribution
3 the wild
4 disadvantaged
5 shelters
6 lend a hand

4 VOCABULARY

a 2 freezing
3 delighted
4 hilarious
5 enormous
6 filthy

b 2 tiny
3 furious
4 terrified
5 amazed
6 starving

5 LISTENING

a 3, 5, 6, 9, 10, 11, 12

b 2 14 and nine.
3 $300,000.
4 Twelve in Twelve.
5 They looked after elephants.
6 They taught them English.
7 Children who have HIV.
8 Encourage other families to do the same.

3A

1 VOCABULARY

a Down: 2 van 4 scooter 5 lorry 8 tram
Across: 3 carriage 6 underground
7 motorway 9 coach

b 2 parking
3 traffic
4 road
5 cycle
6 petrol
7 rush
8 taxi
9 speed
10 traffic

2 PRONUNCIATION

a 2 seat belt
3 check-in
4 chemist's

3 GRAMMAR

a 2 than
3 the
4 more
5 worst
6 less
7 better / quicker
8 most
9 as
10 least

b 2 Cancun is the most crowded of the three destinations.
3 Copenhagen is easier to get to than Sydney.
4 Sydney is less exciting than Cancun.
5 Sydney is hotter than Copenhagen.
6 Copenhagen is the most relaxing of the three destinations.

c 2 Copenhagen isn't as difficult to get to as Sydney.
3 Cancun is more exciting than Sydney.
4 Sydney isn't as cold as Copenhagen.

4 PRONUNCIATION

2 least enjoyable
3 most interesting
4 more expensive
5 bigger
6 as expensive as

5 READING

a Totora reed boats.

b 2 T
3 T
4 F
5 F
6 T
7 T
8 F

6 LISTENING

a 2 B
3 D
4 A
5 C

b 2 30 kilometres / kms.
3 In the middle of a field.
4 A little boy.
5 Green.

3B

1 GRAMMAR

a 2 the door, the house
3 a German, an engineer
4 fish, the salmon
5 the cinema, a week
6 the end, the world
7 women, men
8 a beautiful, lunch

b 2 next weekend
3 Money
4 ✓
5 twice a year
6 the DVD that I lent you
7 ✓
8 What a noisy child
9 a doctor
10 cats
11 ✓
12 gets to work

2 PRONUNCIATION

a 2 flowers, table
3 What, do
4 open, window
5 doctor, headaches
6 go, walk

3 READING

a 1 C
2 A
3 B

b 2 c
3 b
4 c
5 a
6 a

d 2 poisonous
3 responsible for
4 likely
5 have a reputation
6 vital

4 VOCABULARY

a 2 to
3 for
4 on
5 at
6 for
7 about
8 of

b 2 on
3 about
4 in
5 from
6 at
7 with
8 for

5 WHEN ARE PREPOSITIONS STRESSED?

a 1 argued, dad
2 laughing, at; laughing, you
3 excited, about; excited, holiday
4 listening, to; listening, radio

6 LISTENING

a 3

b 2 F
3 F
4 T
5 F
6 F
7 F
8 T

Practical English A difficult celebrity

1 GIVING OPINIONS

2 think
3 right
4 opinion
5 agree
6 ask
7 agree
8 honest

2 SOCIAL ENGLISH

2 Hang on a minute
3 kind of you
4 Did you mean
5 It's just that

3 READING

a 2 F
3 T
4 F
5 F
6 T
7 T

c 2 dropped out
3 eventually
4 was fired
5 brands
6 box office

4 VOCABULARY

a 2 tiring
3 ✓
4 ✓
5 surprised
6 ✓
7 ✓
8 frustrated

b 2 embarrassed
3 frightened
4 exciting
5 worrying
6 interesting
7 depressing
8 disappointed

c excited, interested, disappointed

d 2 themselves
3 herself
4 itself
5 myself
6 ourselves

5 LISTENING

a 1 chemist's
2 Turkish, shopkeeper
3 Spanish, host family
4 Italian, waiter
5 Greek, some girls

b 1 vacuum cleaner
2 fresh bread, fresh young man
3 banana, large plate
4 peach juice, fish juice
5 good morning, squid

4A

1 GRAMMAR

a 3 ✓
4 ✓
5 haven't been able to
6 ✓
7 been able to
8 ✓
9 used to be able to
10 ✓
11 must be able to
12 not being able to

b 2 could / was able to
3 can't / isn't able to
4 has been able to
5 to be able to
6 couldn't / wasn't able to
7 'll / will be able to

3 READING

a 1 C
2 A
3 D
4 B

b 2 F
3 F
4 T
5 T
6 F
7 F
8 T

4B

1 VOCABULARY

a 2 hang up
3 message, voicemail
4 silent, vibrate
5 call back
6 ringtone
7 instant messaging
8 dial
9 busy, engaged
10 screensaver

2 GRAMMAR

a 2 mustn't
3 don't have to
4 have to
5 ✓
6 should
7 should
8 mustn't
9 shouldn't
10 ✓

b 2 I had to
3 ✓
4 You mustn't play
5 he has to work
6 ✓
7 everyone will have to speak
8 You should go home.

3 PRONUNCIATION

a 2 receipt
3 hour
4 shouldn't
5 exhausted
6 walk
7 could
8 debt

4 READING

a 1

b 1 C
2 E
3 B
4 F
5 A

d 1 inappropriate
2 gesture
3 appreciate
4 concept
5 offend
6 looked down on

5 LISTENING

a 1, 2, 5

b 2 a
3 b
4 b
5 c

5A

1 GRAMMAR

2 were driving, remembered, hadn't turned off
3 had already started, turned on, were losing, were playing
4 didn't recognize, had changed
5 was waiting, called, couldn't, had broken down
6 beat, were winning, scored
7 ran, had already left, were waiting
8 started, was walking, called, wasn't wearing, didn't have

2 PRONUNCIATION

a 2 sport
3 slope
4 court

3 READING

a 1 Scrabble
2 the blank tiles

b 2 T
3 T
4 F
5 F
6 F
7 T
8 T

d 2 admitted
3 disqualified
4 replace
5 suspicious
6 accuse
7 opponent
8 resorted

4 VOCABULARY

a 2 referee
3 circuit
4 kick
5 fan
6 course
7 get fit
8 pitch
9 coach
10 stadium

b 2 trained
3 won
4 warmed up
5 drew
6 lost
7 threw
8 beat
9 scored
10 got injured

5 LISTENING

a China.

b 2 F
3 T
4 T
5 T
6 F
7 T
8 F

5B

1 GRAMMAR

a 3 ✓
4 doesn't usually wear
5 ✓
6 usually walk
7 didn't use to talk
8 Do you usually get up
9 Did you use to watch
10 ✓

b 2 didn't use to like
3 usually call
4 used to go
5 used to eat out
6 don't usually work
7 used to be
8 usually give

2 PRONUNCIATION

b 2 especially
3 please
4 music

3 VOCABULARY

a 2 flatmate
3 colleague
4 classmates
5 fiancé
6 ex
7 close friend
8 couple

b 2 got to know
3 became friends
4 had, in common
5 went out together
6 were together
7 broke up
8 lost touch
9 got in touch
10 got on
11 proposed
12 got married

4 READING

a 2.03

b 2 c
3 a
4 b
5 b

d 2 trust
3 the average person
4 serious matters
5 contrast dramatically
6 getting more isolated

5 LISTENING

a a 2
b 3
d 4

b 2 T
3 T
4 F
5 F
6 T
7 F
8 T

Practical English Old friends

1 PERMISSIONS AND REQUESTS

a 2 join
3 visit
4 meeting
5 pass
6 take

b 2 a
3 f
4 e
5 b
6 c

2 SOCIAL ENGLISH

2 come
3 way
4 mind
5 days
6 talk

3 READING

a 2 They all charge different prices.
3 It operates in the USA and Canada.
4 By buying your ticket seven days in advance.
5 Students get a 15% discount on the standard fare.
6 They should take their own food.

Great Clarendon Street, Oxford, OX2 6DP, United Kingdom

Oxford University Press is a department of the University of Oxford. It furthers the University's objective of excellence in research, scholarship, and education by publishing worldwide. Oxford is a registered trade mark of Oxford University Press in the UK and in certain other countries

First published in 2013
2021 2020 2019
10 9 8 7

ISBN: 978 0 19 452046 1 Student's Book / Workbook A

Printed in China

This book is printed on paper from certified and well-managed sources

ACKNOWLEDGEMENTS

The authors would like to thank all the teachers and students round the world whose feedback has helped us to shape English File.

The authors would also like to thank: all those at Oxford University Press (both in Oxford and around the world) and the design team who have contributed their skills and ideas to producing this course.

Finally very special thanks from Clive to Maria Angeles, Lucia, and Eric, and from Christina to Cristina, for all their support and encouragement. Christina would also like to thank her children Joaquin, Marco, and Krysia for their constant inspiration.

The publisher and authors would also like to thank the following for their invaluable feedback on the materials: Uğur Akpur, Robert Anderson, Kinga Belley, Brian Brennan, Isabel Gonzalez Bueno, Rachel Buttery-Graciani, Thelma Eloisa Félix de Oliveira, Maria Antonietta Di Palma, Maria Lorena Urquiza Droffa, Erika Feszl, Banu Ozer Griffin, Eamon Hamill, Gill Hamilton, Maria Belen Saez Hernaez, Jane Hudson, Deborah Keeping, Edit Liegner, Beatriz Martín, Sandy Millin, Magdalena Miszczak-Berbec, Magdalena Muszyńska, María Florencia Nuñez, Mónica Gómez Ruiz, Melis Senol, Rachel Smith, Emilie Řezníčková, Wayne Rimmer, Graham Rumbelow, Joanna Sosnowska, Ágnes Urbán, Pavlina Zoss.

STUDENT'S BOOK ACKNOWLEDGEMENTS

The Publisher and Authors are very grateful to the following who have provided information, personal stories, and/or photographs: Steve Anderson, p.6 (interview and photos); Rena Latham-Koenig, p.9 (photo); Jane Cadwallader, p.18 (interview and photos); Beatriz Martín, Sean Gibson, and Joaquin Cogollos, pp.34–35 (texts and photos); Juan Antonio Fernandez Marin, p.46 (interview). The authors would also like to thank Krysia Cogollos for invaluable research assistance, and to all the friends, colleagues, and family who have answered our endless questions.

The authors and publisher are grateful to those who have given permission to reproduce the following extracts and adaptations of copyright material:

p.10 Extract from 'He claims we used to play Cowboys and Indians. I recall him trying to suffocate me' by Tim Lott, The Times, 20 November 2010. Reproduced by permission of NI Syndication. p.10 Extract from 'The seven ages of an only child' by Joanna Moorhead, The Guardian, 4 March 2006. Copyright Guardian News & Media Ltd 2006. Reproduced by permission. p.17 Extract from 'The millionaire who couldn't write his name' by Karen Bartlett, The Times, 4 February 2011. Reproduced by permission of NI Syndication.

p.20 Extract from 'Blue Peter presenter Helen Skelton begins epic Amazon kayaking adventure' by Cassandra Jardine, Telegraph Online, 23 January 2010. © Telegraph Media Group Limited 2010. Reproduced by permission. p.20 Extract from 'Blue Peter presenter Helen Skelton's Amazon diaries: week one', Telegraph Online, 31 January 2010. © Telegraph Media Group Limited 2010. Reproduced by permission. p.21 Extract from '*Blue Peter* presenter Helen Skelton's Amazon diaries: week two', Telegraph Online, 8 February 2010. © Telegraph Media Group Limited 2010. Reproduced by permission. p.23 Extract from 'Not exactly life-changing, is it…' by Matt Rudd, The Sunday Times, 9 October 2011. Reproduced by permission of NI Syndication.pp.28–29 Extract from 'Gossip with the girls but men only have four subjects' by Peter Markham, The Daily Mail, 18 October 2001. Reproduced by permission of Solo Syndication. p.30 Extract from 'New baby? No problem for Commando Dad' by Neil Sinclair, The Times, 7 May 2012. Reproduced by permission of NI Syndication. p.36–37 Extract from 'Alex Rawlings most multi-lingual student in UK' by Hannah White-Steele, Cherwell.org, 24 February 2012. Reproduced by permission. p.38–39 Extract from 'Debrett's guide to mobile phone etiquette', Telegraph Online, 5 August 2011. © Telegraph Media Group Limited 2011. Reproduced by permission. p.40 Extract from 'Mother-in-law from hell sends harsh lesson in manners to "uncouth" bride-to-be in email that becomes worldwide sensation', The Daily Mail, 29 June 2011. Reproduced by permission of Solo Syndication. p.43 Extract from 'A Maestro Sets the Tone' by David Masello, The New York Times, 18 January 2012 © 2012 The New York Times. All rights reserved. Used by permission and protected by the Copyright Laws of the United States. The printing, copying, redistribution, or retransmission of this Content without express written permission is prohibited. p.45 Extract from 'Very superstitious: Andy Murray, Wimbledon and sport stars everywhere' by Matthew Syed, The Times, 1 July 2009. Reproduced by permission of NI Syndication. p.48 Extract from 'Sealed with a kiss and 35¢: how a singer and a toll booth operator set out on the road to love' by Will Pavia, The Times, 14 February 2012. Reproduced by permission of NI Syndication.

The publisher would like to thank the following for their kind permission to reproduce photographs: Adelante Africa pp.18, 19 (logo); Alamy Images pp.7 (Garlic prawns/Yiap Creative), (Dish of snails/Miscellaneoustock), (fancy food/Davide Piras), 10 (Girl in school uniform/Loop Images Ltd), 11 (girl in garden/ableimages), 14 (Ferrari/Oleksiy Maksymenko Photography), 15 (1 dollar bill/Steve Stock), 20 (Iguana/Martin Harvey), 21 (Mosquito/Redmond Durrell), 23 (Oxfam shop/Shangara Singh), 24 (Aerial view of Fulham Football Club/Andrew Holt), 24 (Eros Piccadilly/Neil Matthews), 25 (Plane landing/Robert Stainforth), 38 (old telephone/Ninette Maumus), 44 (helmet/Moe Kafer Cutouts), (skateboard/Urban Zone), (baseball mitt/Corbis Flint), (black belt/Richard Watkins), 115 (London Underground Station/Alex Segre), (Double decker bus/Steve Vidler), (Cyclist on Boris bike/format4), (London taxi/David R. Frazier Photolibrary, Inc), 152 (Cooking an egg/Gastromedia), (Boiled egg/studiomode), (Steamed sugar snap peas/Food and Drink Photos), 154 (1 euro coin/artpartner=images.com), (Close-up of coin/PjrStudio), (Ten Piece coin/incamerastock), 155 (Train station/David Cole), (Tour bus/Peter Titmuss), (M4 motorway/mkTransport), (Underground station/Greg Balfour Evans), (Post office van at Buckingham Palace/David Gee), (The American Orient Express train/Robert Harding Picture Library Ltd), (DHL lorry/Justin Kase ztwoz), (Couple on motor scooter/imagebroke), (Tram/Alex Segre), (Penalty charge notice on car/DBURKE), (Pedestrian area in inner city/Michael Runkel), (Petrol station/Ian Dagnall), (Gas main repairs/AKP Photos), (Buckling car seat belt/Tetra Images), (Speed camera/AKP Photo), (50mph speed limit sign/Jack Sullivan), (Yellow taxi cabs/Kumar Sriskandan), (Traffic jam/JTB Media Creation, Inc.), (Pedestrian crossing/Oote Boe 2), 157 (Football match/Jonathan Larsen/Diadem Images), (Football referee/imagebroker), (Emirates Stadium/Stadium Bank), (Soccer team/Corbis Super RF), (Brazilian soccer fans/Caro), (The Copper Box arena/Mark Davidson); BBC pp.20 (Helen Skelton), 21 (Helen in Canoe); Corbis pp.6 (food market/Alessandro Della Valle/Keystone), 11 (kids/Inti St.Clair, Inc./SuperStock), 21 (Dolphin/Kevin Schafer), 25 (2006 Mercedes-Benz ML500/David Freers/Transtock), (Cyclist in city/Image Source), (Speedboat/Rainbow/amanaimages), 37 (Young woman smiling/Westend61), (Woman wearing knitted hat/Brüderchen & Schwesterchen GmbH), 39 (Man using phone in theatre/John Lund/Paula Zacharias/Blend Images); Shannon DeCelle p.48 (toll booth); Stephen Lance Dennee p.48 (couple); Getty Images pp.7 (chicken casserole/Iain Bagwell/Photolibrary), 8 (family picnic/Gerard Fritz/Photographer's Choice), 14 (party girl/Luis Alvarez/Stockbyte), 20 (Butterfly/Stockbyte), (California condor/John Cancalosi), (Butterfly/Nation Wong), 24 (Business people rushing/Maciej Noskowski), (Trafalgar Square/Slow Images), 25 (Richard Hammond/Stuart Wilson), (Commuters on the London Underground/Dan Kitwood), (The Stig/Steve Haag/Gallo Images), (Jeremy Clarkson and James May/Mike Flokis), (London Tower Bridge/Medioimages/Photodisc), 29 (rooftop party/Tim Klein/Taxi), 36 (Theatre audience/Michael Cogliantry), 37 (Young woman smiling/Carlo A), (Casually dressed man/Lilly Roadstones), (Young man portrait/Tara Moore), (Smiling woman/Radius Images), 43 (music director Alan Gilbert/Charles Eshelman/FilmMagic), (London bicycle sharing scheme/Peter Macdiarmid), 44 (shuttlecock/Richard Drury/Digital Vision), (rugby ball/Thomas Northcut/Lifesize), (ice hockey stick/David Madison/Photographer's Choice RF), (skates/Kathy Quirk-Syvertsen/Photodisc), (rhythmic gymnastics equipment/Ray Moller/Dorling Kindersley), (table tennis/Sami Sarkis/Photographer's Choice RF), 45 (Serena Williams/Simon Bruty/Sports Illustrated), (Tiger Woods/Jamie Squire), (Fabien Barthez & Laurent Blanc/Patrick Hertzog/AFP), (Arsenal footballer Kolo Toure/Adrian Dennis/AFP), (Lines on tennis court/Marc Debnam), (Alexander Wurz/Rick Dole), 46 (Football referee/Graham Chadwick/Allsport), (Rosie Ruiz/David Madison), 47 (Diego Maradona/Bob Thomas), 106 (Tiger Woods/Jonathan

Madison), 47 (Diego Maradona/Bob Thomas), 106 (Tiger Woods/Jonathan Ferrey), (Kolo Toure/Hamish Blair), 110 (Laurent Blanc and goalkeeper Fabien Barthez/Philippe Huguen/AFP), (Alexander Wurz of Austria poses with his colour coded slippers/Mark Thompson/Allsport), 113 (Portrait of young woman/Westend61), 114 (Woman hugging children/moodboard), 115 (Regent Street, London/Alan Copson/JAIs), 152 (Jacket potato/Dave King), (Roast chicken/Jon Whitaker), (Grilled salmon/2011 Annabelle Breakey), 155 (Car crash/Chris Ryan), (Cycle lane/Tom and Steve), (Commuters on London Bridge/ Travelpix Ltd), (Traffic lights/Alan Schein), 157 (Coach Slaven Bilic/Dmitry Korotayev/Epsilon), (Tiger Woods/Kevin C. Cox), (Football captain armband/ Matthew Ashton/AMA), (Umpire at Wimbledon/VisitBritain/Andrew Orchard); iStockphoto p.30 (camouflage/CollinsChin); Kobal Collection p.117 (*The Godfather*/Paramount), Lostandtaken.com p.14 (Gold texture background); Nature Picture Library p.21 (Marbled hatchetfish/Reinhard/ARCO); Christina Latham-Koenig pp.6 (waiter), 7 (mussels), 9 (grandmother with child); Tim Lott p.10 (two brothers); Oxford University Press pp.45 (Tennis ball/Photodisc), 113 (Businesswoman/Blend Images); Jeff Pearce p.17; Piatkus p.11 (*Birth Order* book cover); Alex Rawlings p.37; Solo Syndication pp.40 (Heidi Withers), 105 (Heidi Withers wedding); South West News Service p.40 (Carolyn Bourne/ James Dadzitis/SWNS.com); Summersdale Publishers p.31; SuperStock pp.8 (couple arguing/PhotoAlto), 14 (celeb/Image Source), 28 (office gossip/ Westend61).

Pronunciation chart artwork by: Ellis Nadler

Commissioned photography by: Gareth Boden pp.26, 27, 30 (two dads in park), 38 (mobile phone); Ryder Haske: pp.12, 13, 32, 33, 52, 53; MM Studios p.152 (meat, fish and vegetable groups).

Illustrations by: Peter Bull: pp.20, 24; Olivier Latyk/Good Illustration Ltd: pp.34, 35, 138; Lyndon Hayes/Dutch Uncle: pp.16, 19; Astushi Hara/Dutch Uncle: pp.133, 134, 135, 137, 138, 156, 158; Sophie Joyce: p.47; Tim Marrs: pp.50–51; Joe McLaren: pp.4, 41; Matt Smith pp.30–31.

WORKBOOK ACKNOWLEDGEMENTS

The authors and publishers are grateful to the following who have given permission to reproduce the following extracts and adaptations of copyright material: p.12 Extract from THE MAN WHO QUIT MONEY by Mark Sundeen, copyright © 2012 by Mark Sundeen. Used by permission of Riverhead Books, an imprint of Penguin Group (USA) Inc.; p.19 Extract from http://www.roughguides.com/ article/10-unusual-types-of-transport/. Copyright © *2013 ROUGH GUIDES LTD.* Reproduced by permission of Rough Guides Ltd.; p.23 Extract from www. newyorktaxis.org. Reproduced by permission; p.36 Extract from 'USA: Getting there & around', www.lonelyplanet.com. Reproduced with permission from the Lonely Planet website www.lonelyplanet.com © 2012 Lonely Planet.

Sources: p.9 www.bbc.co.uk/news; p.15 www.ventureco-worldwide.com; p.15 www.thegreatprojects.com; p.26 www.bbc.co.uk; p.34 www.dailymail.co.uk; p.35 www.dailymail.co.uk.

The publishers would like to thank the following for their kind permission to reproduce photographs: Alamy Images pp.4 (Boiled egg/studiomode), (Cooking an egg/ Gastromedia), (Steamed sugar snap peas/Food and Drink Photos), 9 (Muzeina bedouin family/Stefano Ravera), 11 (Online banking/2020WEB), 15 (Kunda school children/Thomas Cockrem), 16 (Strawberry cake/LJSphotography), 16 (Muddy festival crowd/Everynight Images), 19 (Totora reed boat/Julia Rogers), (Dog sleds/Accent Alaska.com); Corbis pp.6 (Healthy and unhealthy food/Mike Kemp/Tetra Images), 7 (Couple watching television/Image Source), 15 (Woman hammering a nail/Ryan Smith/Somos Images), 16 (Blue whale/ Denis Scott), 18 (Cancun beach and hotels/Danny Lehman), (The Little Mermaid statue, Copenhagen/Richard Klune), (Sydney Opera House/John Gollings/Arcaid), 19 (Lory bamboo train/STRINGER/CAMBODIA/X80007/ Reuters), 19 (Jeepney truck/Christian Kober/Robert Harding World Imagery), 22 (Man preparing food/Ann Summa), 25 (Steven Spielberg/Luc Roux), 25 (Sir Isaac Newton/Sir Godfrey Kneller/The Gallery Collection), 25 (Bill Gates/Peer Grimm/dpa), 25 (Thomas Alva Edison/Corbis); Getty Images pp.4 (Grilled salmon/2011 Annabelle Breakey), (Jacket potato/Dave King), (Roast chicken/Jon Whitaker), 7 (Group on porch/Sean Justice), (Mechanic with customer/JGI), (Office colleagues/PhotoAlto/Eric Audras), (Couple washing dishes/Jose Luis Pelaez Inc), 10 (Woody Allen plays with band/Brian Hamill), 15 (Sepilok Orangutan Rehabilitation Centre/Andrew Watson), 16 (Lottery winners/Christopher Furlong), (Rowan Atkinson as Mr Bean/Joel Saget/AFP), 32 (Women's Doubles Badminton/Michael Regan), 36 (Car on highway/Car Culture); Shutterstock pp.16 (Dressed in winter clothes/Lobke Peers), 22 (Woman preparing meal/Flashon Studio), 23 (New York taxi cabs/ Bufflerump), 24 (Portrait of businessman/Andresr), 27 (Statue of Liberty/ Rubens Alarcon), (Times Square at night/Kobby Dagan), 34 (Young couple with dog/Monkey Business Images), 34 (Woman in conversation/Mik Lav).

Illustrations by: Satoshi Hashimoto/Dutch Uncle: p.14; Anna Hymas/New Division: p.20; Tim Marrs: p.13; Jerome Mireault/Colagene: p.28; Ellis Nadler: pronunciation symbols.

Commissioned photography: MMStudios: p.12.

Design by: Stephen Strong.